2018 Permit Technician Study Companion

2018 Permit Technician
Study Companion

ISBN: 978-1-60983-800-3

Manager of Development:	Doug Thornburg
Publications Manager:	Mary Lou Luif
Project Editor:	Sharon Gordy
Production Technician:	Emily Sargent
Cover Design:	Ricky Razo

COPYRIGHT © 2019
by
INTERNATIONAL CODE COUNCIL, INC.

ALL RIGHTS RESERVED. This publication is a copyrighted work owned by the International Code Council, Inc. ("ICC"). Without advance written permission from the ICC, no part of this book may be reproduced, distributed or transmitted in any form or by any means, including, without limitation, electronic, optical or mechanical means (by way of example, and not limitation, photocopying, or recording by or in an information storage retrieval system). For information on use rights and permissions, please contact: ICC Publications, 4051 Flossmoor Road, Country Club Hills, IL 60478. Phone 1-888-ICC-SAFE (422-7233).

The information contained in this document is believed to be accurate; however, it is being provided for informational purposes only and is intended for use only as a guide. Publication of this document by the ICC should not be construed as the ICC engaging in or rendering engineering, legal or other professional services. Use of the information contained in this workbook should not be considered by the user as a substitute for the advice of a registered professional engineer, attorney or other professional. If such advice is required, it should be sought through the services of a registered professional engineer, licensed attorney or other professional.

Trademarks: "International Code Council," the "International Code Council" logo, "ICC," the "ICC" logo and other names and trademarks appearing in this book are registered trademarks of the International Code Council, Inc., and/or its licensors (as applicable), and may not be used without permission.

Errata on various ICC publications may be available at www.iccsafe.org/errata.
First Printing: February 2019
PRINTED IN THE USA

TABLE OF CONTENTS

Study Session 1:

Basic Code Enforcement, Chapter 1—An Overview of Codes............................... 1
Quiz 20

Study Session 2:

Basic Code Enforcement, Chapters 2 through 4—
 Building Department Operations, Zoning Ordinances
 and Building Permits 27
Quiz 47

Study Session 3:

Basic Code Enforcement, Chapters 5 through 7—
 Reading Construction Documents, Performing a Plan Review and
 Conducting Inspections... 55
Quiz 80

Study Session 4:

2018 IBC Sections 101 through 104—
 Scope and Administration 87
Quiz 109

Study Session 5:

2018 IBC Sections 105 and 107—
 Scope and Administration 117
Quiz 134

Study Session 6:

2018 IBC Sections 108 through 116—
 Scope and Administration 141
Quiz 151

Study Session 7:

2018 IBC Chapter 3 and Sections 508 and 509—
 Occupancy Classification 157
Quiz 175

Study Session 8:
2018 IBC Chapters 6 and 12—
Types of Construction and Interior Environment 18
Quiz 20

Study Session 9:
2018 IZC Chapters 1 and 3 through 7—
Scope and Administration and Use Districts 20
Quiz 22

Study Session 10:
2018 IZC Chapters 8, 9, 11, 12 and 13
General Provisions, Special Regulations, Nonconforming Structures
and Uses, Conditional Uses and Planned Unit Developments 23
Quiz 24

Study Session 11:
2018 IZC Chapter 10—Signs 24
Quiz 26

Study Session 12:
Legal Aspects of Code Administration, Chapters 3 and 4—
Local Government Law and State Legislative Law..................................... 26
Quiz 27

Study Session 13:
Legal Aspects of Code Administration, Chapters 6 through 8—
Administration and Enforcement, Administrative Law and
Constitutional Law... 28
Quiz 30

Study Session 14:
Legal Aspects of Code Administration, Chapters 9 through 12—
Related Property Law Concepts, Liability for Intentional
Wrongdoing, Negligent Wrongdoing and Civil Rights Actions..................... 30
Quiz 32

Answer Keys 32

INTRODUCTION

This study companion provides practical learning assignments for independent study on subjects applicable to the responsibilities of a permit technician. It is based on the second edition of *Basic Code Enforcement*, the 2018 *International Building Code®* (IBC®) (Chapters 1, 2, 3, 6 and 12), the 2018 *International Zoning Code®* (IZC®) and the 2017 edition of *Legal Aspects of Code Administration*.

Independent study lets the student complete the program in an unregulated time period. Progressing through the workbook, the learner can measure his or her level of knowledge by using the exercises and quizzes provided for each study session.

The workbook is also valuable for instructor-led programs. In jurisdictional training sessions, community college classes, vocational training programs and other structured educational offerings, the study guide and the referenced publications can be the basis for classroom instruction.

All study sessions begin with a general learning objective specific to the session, the referenced sections or chapters under consideration and a list of questions summarizing the key points of study. Each session addresses selected topics from the referenced publications including excerpted text, related commentary, illustrations representing the topic under discussion and multiple choice questions that can be used to evaluate the student's knowledge. Before beginning the quizzes, the student should thoroughly review the referenced publications, focusing on the key points identified at the beginning of each study session. In addition, the definitions found in Chapter 2 of both the IBC and IZC, as well as the glossaries in the other two referenced publications, should be referred to often to understand the meanings of the terms and their application.

Although this study companion is primarily focused on those subjects of specific interest to the permit technician, it is also a valuable resource to other individuals who would like to learn more about code and zoning administration. The information presented is of importance to many building officials, plans examiners, field inspectors and property maintenance staff members.

This publication was initially developed by Steve Burger, CBO, formerly the building official for Folsom, California. Steve has been continuously involved in code administration since 1972 and has been involved in various activities related to the field of Permit Technician, including service on committees and the development of a comprehensive seminar, which he presents nationally to receptive audiences.

Subsequent to the 2009 edition, ICC Staff members Sandra Hyde and Steve Van Note have updated the content to the current referenced publications.

Questions or comments concerning this workbook are encouraged. Please direct your comments to ICC at studycompanion@iccsafe.org.

HISTORICAL PERSPECTIVE

Back in the early 1990s, the value of broader educational opportunities and appropriate recognition for permit technicians was becoming more and more apparent. This awareness spawned the formation of several Permit Technician organizations in California, Washington and several other states. These organizations sent requests to their legacy code organization asking that a certification program be developed similar to those offered for inspectors, plans examiners and building officials. After several years of defining goals and tasks, a voluntary certification category for Permit Technicians was created.

A Permit Technician Certification Exam Committee was selected, and the group had their first meeting in January, 1998. The committee comprised eight individuals, working in building departments in Washington, California, Texas, Colorado and Arizona, who were intimately familiar with the activities that occur at the front counter. Their ultimate task was to develop questions for a certification exam. However, prior to the development of exam questions, a job task survey was sent to 461 permit technicians asking what duties they performed and how often they performed these duties. Sixty-four percent responded to the survey. From this survey, four exam categories were created: General Administration, Legal Aspects, Plans and Documents, and Zoning and Site Development. Each category had a certain percentage of related questions, and all questions were required to have a reference to one or more specific applicable publications. The Permit Tech Certification Program's first examination was offered in 1998, and certification continues to be available through the International Code Council® (ICC®).

Since 1998, there have been numerous Permit Technician seminars, many of which have addressed the categories established by the Permit Technical Exam Committee and other critical areas related to working the front counter. Although many of these seminars have offered course handout materials valuable for use in future reference, there were many requests for a formal study guide for permit technicians.

In late 2004, I was approached by ICC to evaluate the potential for development of a *Permit Technician Study Companion*. The first edition of this new publication in 2006 was the result of the efforts of many people over several years. Special thanks go to Doug Thornburg, AIA, CBO, ICC Vice President and Technical Director of Products and Services for his expertise, guidance and extreme patience; Roxanne Michael, CBO, for her invaluable input and keen proofreading abilities; and various other staff members at ICC, all of whom helped make the *Permit Technician Study Companion* a long-awaited reality.

Steve Burger, CBO

About the International Code Council®

The International Code Council is a member-focused association. It is dedicated to developing model codes and standards used in the design, build and compliance process to construct safe, sustainable, affordable and resilient structures. Most US communities and many global markets choose the International Codes. ICC Evaluation Service (ICC-ES) is the industry leader in performing technical evaluations for code compliance fostering safe and sustainable design and construction.

Governmental Affairs Office: 500 New Jersey Avenue, NW, 6th Floor, Washington, DC 20001

Regional Offices: Eastern Regional Office (BIR), Central Regional Office (CH), Western Regional Office (LA)

888-ICC-SAFE (888-422-7233)

www.iccsafe.org

Study Session

1

Basic Code Enforcement, Chapter 1
An Overview of Codes

OBJECTIVE: To gain a better understanding of the development and role of building codes, standards and the International Code Council® (ICC®).

REFERENCE: *Basic Code Enforcement,* Chapter 1

KEY POINTS:
- What is a code? A model code? A building code?
- Who was Hammurabi?
- What is the purpose of codes?
- Who uses codes?
- What is the difference between a performance code and a prescriptive code?
- Who grants the authority to adopt codes?
- How are codes adopted?
- What kind of code adoption is invalid?
- What is the difference between a code and a standard?
- What is the purpose of a standard?
- Who is the International Code Council (ICC)?
- What services does the ICC provide?
- Why become certified?
- What are evaluation reports?

Topic: Definition
Reference: *Basic Code Enforcement*, 1.2
Category: An Overview of Codes
Subject: What is a Code?

Text: *A code is a collection of requirements that pertain to a specific subject and regulate specific practices.*

Discussion and Commentary: One definition of code is: "A set of rules, principles or laws (especially written ones)." There are codes of honor, traffic codes, codes of ethics, dress codes and, of course, building codes. Each establishes rules to be followed to achieve the desired result or goal.

Several definitions of *Code*

a collection of principles, laws, rules or regulations

a system of signals or symbols for communication

a set of instructions for a computer

a word, letter, number or other symbol used to mark or identify something

---

Although one definition of code means secrecy (as in a military code), the intent of building codes is to provide well-established and clear requirements to provide safety to buildings and their inhabitants.

Topic: What is a Model Code?	**Category:** An Overview of Codes
Reference: *Basic Code Enforcement,* 1.2.1	**Subject:** What is a Code?

Text: *A model code is a written set of regulations that provide the means for exercising reasonable control over construction, and is available for adoption by cities, counties, states or countries. Such codes are frequently amended by adopting jurisdictions with changes that are desirable for legal or local needs.*

Discussion and Commentary: One could think of a model code the same way one thinks of a model car. For example, a new model of a car comes out this year, with the latest technology incorporated into its design. Next year, the basic model may remain the same, but new technology is added based on safety and consumer needs. Every year, additions, deletions and revisions are provided so as to make the car more desirable, useable, safer and energy efficient.

A model code is similar to a car model in that every three years new elements of technology and updated safety requirements are added based on recent events and input from code, design, construction and industry representatives worldwide. The changes are compiled into the new code edition and published for adoption by a jurisdiction.

Study Session 1

Topic: What is a Building Code?	**Category:** An Overview of Codes
Reference: *Basic Code Enforcement,* 1.2.2	**Subject:** What is a Code?

Text: *A building code is a legal document that regulates the construction of structures and buildings. It also regulates the installation of fixtures, equipment and accessories.*

Discussion and Commentary: A building code is an organized, systematic presentation of a body of law that pertains to all facets of building construction, such as electrical, plumbing, heating, cooling, ventilation, exiting, structural, and fire and life safety issues. It is based on the intent of providing a minimum level of protection for the inhabitants and users of buildings and structures.

One Definition of a Building Code

A **building code** is a set of rules that specify the minimum acceptable level of safety for constructed objects such as buildings and nonbuilding structures. The main purpose of building codes is to protect public health, safety and general welfare as they relate to the construction and occupancy of buildings and structures. The building code becomes law of a particular jurisdiction when formally enacted by the appropriate authority.

Although building codes devote much of their contents to new buildings and structures, existing buildings are also covered when alterations or repairs are made, or when the use or occupancy changes.

Topic: Code of Hammurabi	**Category:** An Overview of Codes
Reference: *Basic Code Enforcement*, 1.3	**Subject:** History of Building Codes

Text: *The building code of Hammurabi, king of the Babylonian Empire, is the earliest known code of law, written in 2200 B.C. Note that exact requirements for construction are not given; rather, the code assesses penalties if the building is not properly constructed.*

Discussion and Commentary: Hammurabi's Code is considered a "performance" code rather than a "prescriptive" code. Rather than prescribe specifically how to construct a house, it merely delineates the results if the building does not perform properly. Today's modern codes are typically a combination of these two types of codes.

Translated Text from the Code of Hammurabi

A. If a builder builds a house for a man and does not make its construction firm and the house which he has built collapses and causes the death of the owner of the house—that builder shall be put to death.

B. If it causes the death of the son of the owner of the house, a son of the builder shall be put to death.

C. If it destroys property he shall restore whatever it destroyed and he shall rebuild the house which collapsed at his own expense.

In viewing the *International Building Code* (IBC), many prescriptive and performance regulations are used. Section 101.5 states that a permit will expire at the end of a specified time (180 days) but also allows the building official to grant an extension if "justifiable cause" is demonstrated. The term reasonable is also used in various sections of the code.

Topic: Protecting the Public **Category:** An Overview of Codes
Reference: *Basic Code Enforcement,* 1.4 **Subject:** Purpose of Codes

Text: *The purpose of the codes is to protect the public health, safety and welfare by regulating construction.*

Discussion and Commentary: Whether we are in our homes, offices, schools, stores, factories, restaurants or places of entertainment, we rely on the safety of structures that surround us every day. In the event of an emergency, first responders such as fire fighters and medical personnel also rely on the fact that the building they are entering was constructed so as to prevent collapse and minimize the spread of smoke and fire.

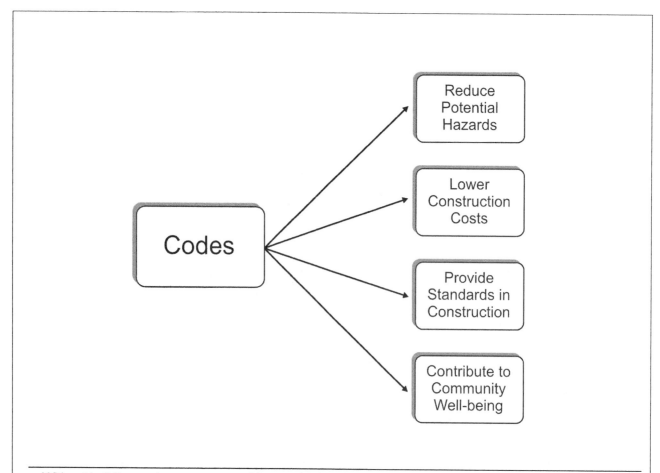

Without building codes, our communities would deteriorate along with property values. Insurance rates would rise as would the costs of maintaining the community. Building codes are a commitment to a jurisdiction's future.

Topic: Governments
Reference: *Basic Code Enforcement,* 1.5.1
Category: An Overview of Codes
Subject: Uses of Codes

Text: *Codes are adopted as laws or ordinances by governments such as states, counties, townships and cities. Once the code is adopted as law, structures in that jurisdiction must conform to that law.*

Discussion and Commentary: Until a code is officially and legally adopted, it is merely a book of suggestions or guidelines as to how buildings and structures may be constructed. However, once adopted, the code provides performance standards for the design, construction and maintenance of all buildings and structures in that jurisdiction and must be complied with. Penalties may be assessed to those who violate the provisions.

As established in Section 101.2.1 of the IBC, the "provisions in the appendices shall not apply unless specifically adopted." The building official must determine if some, all or none of the appendices become part of the code during the adoption process.

Topic: Performance vs. Prescriptive	**Category:** An Overview of Codes
Reference: *Basic Code Enforcement,* 1.6	**Subject:** Types of Regulations

Text: *A performance regulation states the purpose to be accomplished and allows design and engineering professionals to select alternate methods and materials, as long as they meet the minimum requirements for health, safety and welfare.*

A prescriptive regulation describes exactly what methods and materials are to be used as well as the size and location of components. As its name implies, this type of code is specific.

Discussion and Commentary: As discussed earlier, modern codes contain a mixture of performance and prescriptive regulations. Similarly, in a cookbook, specific requirements are established, such as "Heat grill to 350 degrees," "Place charcoal around edges of Hibachi," "Turn steak after 4 minutes."

Although many prescriptive requirements are necessary in the code, performance-based regulations permit designers and builders the latitude to construct buildings of any methods or materials that meet or exceed the intent of the code.

Topic: Authority to Adopt	**Category:** An Overview of Codes
Reference: *Basic Code Enforcement*, 1.7.1	**Subject:** Adoption of Codes

Text: *The authority to adopt codes is granted to the states by the federal government in Article 4 and Amendment 14 of the US Constitution. Political divisions in the state (e.g., townships, cities or counties) may be granted power to adopt laws regulating construction.*

Discussion and Commentary: Although many states allow individual jurisdictions to each adopt their own codes and local amendments, many states will adopt one state code that must be enforced by each jurisdiction in the state. As might be imagined, there are pros and cons to each system. State codes provide statewide uniformity, whereas local codes allow each jurisdiction to do what it believes is best for its citizens based on its economic situation, available staff, geographical conditions and future growth.

To facilitate adoption, several sections of this code contain blanks for fill-in information that needs to be supplied by the adopting jurisdiction as part of the adoption legislation. For this code, please see:

Section <u>101.1.</u> Insert: **[NAME OF JURISDICTION]**

Section <u>1612.3.</u> Insert: **[NAME OF JURISDICTION]**

Section <u>1612.3.</u> Insert: **[DATE OF ISSUANCE]**

A properly organized State Building Code Commission can benefit all affected parties. However, it can also be more susceptible to political forces that can affect the outcome of the code based on political influences rather than on what is considered beneficial to the citizens of that state.

Study Session 1

Topic: How are Codes Adopted?
Reference: *Basic Code Enforcement*, 1.7.4

Category: An Overview of Codes
Subject: Adoption of Codes

Text: *The I-Codes are adopted by reference in an ordinance in accordance with established procedures of the state or local jurisdiction. Enforcement may occur at the state or local levels.*

Some state laws permit local jurisdictions to adopt certain documents, such as building codes, by just referencing the model code.

Discussion and Commentary: Typically, jurisdictions wishing to adopt a building code must publish a public notice in the local newspaper informing the public of what regulations are going to be considered for adoption. If the jurisdiction is not permitted to adopt a regulation by "reference," then the entire document must be printed, word for word, in the newspaper. This can be both cumbersome and expensive. By merely referencing the document, such as the IBC, and enumerating the proposed amendments, the public can view the notice and seek additional information as they desire.

Adoption

The International Code Council maintains a copyright in all of its codes and standards. Maintaining copyright allows the ICC to fund its mission through sales of books, in both print and electronic formats. The ICC welcomes adoption of its codes by jurisdictions that recognize and acknowledge the ICC's copyright in the code, and further acknowledge the substantial shared value of the public/private partnership for code development between jurisdictions and the ICC.

The ICC also recognizes the need for jurisdictions to make laws available to the public. All I-Codes and I-Standards, along with the laws of many jurisdictions, are available for free in a nondownloadable form on the ICC's website. Jurisdictions should contact the ICC at adoptions@iccsafe.org to learn how to adopt and distribute laws based on the *International Building Code* in a manner that provides necessary access, while maintaining the ICC's copyright.

If documents are adopted by reference, the actual documents must be available for viewing by the public, typically in the Clerk's office, both before and after adoption. They must also be designated as public documents.

Topic: Invalid Adoptions
Reference: *Basic Code Enforcement*, 1.7.5
Category: An Overview of Codes
Subject: Adoption of Codes

Text: *Municipalities may attempt to adopt the code by reference without designating a particular edition or they may state, for example, "We hereby adopt the International Building Code, 2018 Edition, and all future editions when they are published." While this may seem like a wise shortcut to keep the code current, the courts have invalidated this practice on the grounds that the municipality is delegating law-making power to the code organization. Municipalities must determine if a particular edition of a code will be adopted and should not leave it up to the promulgating model code organization.*

Discussion and Commentary: Another practical reason for not adopting "all future editions" is that a jurisdiction may itself not be aware of when the next edition is actually published and, therefore, not be aware of when to start enforcing it. The building department may also not have received the proper training on the new edition and not be adequately equipped to begin conducting plan reviews or inspections. By adopting a specific edition, the municipality can prepare for the new adoption and allow it to become effective once the staff is prepared to begin enforcing it and affected parties have had their input considered.

The courts may also invalidate building regulations that prohibit devices, methods or materials that are equal to those permitted by the code.

Topic: Amendments to the Model Code
Reference: *Basic Code Enforcement,* 1.7.6
Category: An Overview of Codes
Subject: Adoption of Codes

Text: *Members of codes and standards organizations such as the ICC consist of state and local building code and fire officials, design and construction professionals, trade associations, and building material and equipment manufacturers and distributors. Their participation in the code development process brings a high level of expertise to the process and results in a consensus as to what is appropriate for inclusion in the model code.*

Discussion and Commentary: When adopting a model code, some jurisdictions amend the code to meet specific local needs. However, other than minor administrative amendments or those addressing special circumstances specific to the jurisdiction, numerous amendments are typically not recommended for several reasons.

Amendments to the Model Code:

- Increase construction costs, such as when very expensive building materials are substituted as requirements.
- Cause inconsistent application of the code from one jurisdiction to another.
- Compromise the uniformity of the entire code and the correlation among various sections of that code.
- Frequently have no technical basis and cannot be supported or defended by the jurisdiction or model code organization.

Whereas increasing the technical requirements of the code may be justified in rare instances, e.g., requiring fire sprinklers in buildings inaccessible to fire-fighting apparatus, relaxing code requirements, especially those pertaining to life safety, are discouraged. In the event a disaster occurs, the municipality may have a difficult time trying to explain the reasoning behind the omission of the pertinent code requirement, especially if it could have prevented the disaster.

Topic: What Are Standards?
Reference: *Basic Code Enforcement*, 1.8
Category: An Overview of Codes
Subject: Standards in Codes

Text: *A standard is a published technical document that represents an industry consensus on how a material or assembly is to be designed, manufactured, tested or installed so that a specific level of performance is obtained. A standard is not intended to be used as a primary law but as secondary authoritative references. While a model code becomes law when it is adopted by a jurisdiction, a standard only becomes law to the extent to which it is referenced in a model code.*

Discussion and Commentary: Because the code cannot be all-inclusive, it must reference other publications and standards. Codes typically specify *what* is required, whereas a standard typically indicates *how* full compliance is to be achieved. For example, the code may simply state that buildings of a certain size must provide an automatic fire sprinkler system. The appropriate standard provides the detail as to what type of system must be used and how it is to be installed (type and location of sprinkler heads, size of pipe, water flow, etc.)

IBC Section 102.4.1 generally states that when there are differences between the code and a referenced standard, the code shall apply.

Study Session 1

Topic: Standards Development
Reference: *Basic Code Enforcement,* 1.8.3

Category: An Overview of Codes
Subject: Standards in Codes

Text: *Most standards are developed on a voluntary basis by standards-writing organizations. In the United States, approximately 500 organizations follow procedures to achieve national consensus among groups affected by standards. Standards are developed in response to perceived needs. They are developed by the various interest groups that are most affected by them, with the advice and consensus of other interested parties.*

Discussion and Commentary: Standards pertaining to codes are wide and varied and establish such requirements as building ventilation, fire safety systems, accessibility, what type of concrete must be used, installation of construction materials and how the materials are to be tested, to name a few.

Standards Organizations Can Be Categorized into One of Four Groups

Type	Description	Standard	IBC Section Reference
Materials	Addresses product quality characteristics such as composition, dimensions and uniformity.	ASTM D312, Specification for Asphalt Used in Roofing	Table 1507.10.2
Design and engineering	Includes basic design procedures and engineering formulas. Describes methods of testing that determine the physical, functional or performance characteristics of specific materials or products.	AWC NDS, National Design Specification for Wood Construction	2306.1
Installation	Governs the installation of specific products or systems.	NFPA 13R, Installation of Sprinkler Systems in Residential Occupancies	903.3.1.2
Testing	Identifies methods and procedures for evaluating structural strength, fire resistance and other performance criteria.	ASTM E119, Test Methods for Fire Test of Building Construction and Materials	703.3

Standards come from many organizations, but their purpose is to provide either information on material quality or direction for design, installation or testing of systems.

Topic: International Code Council (ICC)
Reference: *Basic Code Enforcement*, 1.9
Category: An Overview of Codes
Subject: Development of the I-Codes

Text: *The International Code Council (ICC) is a non-profit organization dedicated to developing a single set of comprehensive and coordinated model construction codes.*

Discussion and Commentary: The I-Codes are revised and updated through an open process that invites participation by all stakeholders and affected parties. Codes are revised and rewritten in response to emerging technology and research. Any person may propose a change. A structured series of notice dates and public hearings ensures that each proposed change is made available for review by any interested party.

The International Codes are used throughout the United States and internationally.

Study Session 1

Topic: How are the I-Codes Developed? **Category:** An Overview of Codes
Reference: *Basic Code Enforcement,* 1.9.1 **Subject:** Development of the I-Codes

Text: *In order to ensure that the I-Codes reflect new developments in the construction industry, procedures have been established for reviewing proposed changes submitted for incorporation into the code.*

Discussion and Commentary: The International Codes are published every three years and contain a number of code changes that were developed during the three-year cycle. Changes in the content of the new codes can be easily noted as there will be a solid vertical line in the side page margins indicating where a change has occurred. In some instances only a word or two has been changed, while in other cases entire sections or even chapters have been revised.

The ICC Governmental Consensus Process for Code Development

- The process is based on the principles of openness, transparency, balance of interest and due process.
- Anyone may submit a proposed code change and participate in the hearings.
- There is one cycle of Committee Hearings and Public Comment Hearings between code editions.
- Only public safety officials representing the public interest are allowed to vote on code changes.
- New editions of the International Codes are published every 3 years.

The ICC codes are developed through what is known as a governmental consensus process. This means that, though all interested parties may participate, only code officials, and not private industry members, are permitted to cast the final vote as to what is placed in the code.

Topic: Summary	**Category:** An Overview of Codes
Reference: *Basic Code Enforcement,* 1.12	**Subject:** ICC Services

Text: *In addition to the promulgation of the codes, the International Code Council maintains various services to assist the code user.*

Discussion and Commentary: Besides publishing codes, the ICC also provides the following services: certification, training and professional development, code interpretation services, plan review, professional journals, national representation on standards-writing agencies and evaluation reports.

Provided by ICC

- **Certification**—Promotes professionalism, builds self-esteem, establishes professional credentials, demonstrates a solid commitment to a profession, demonstrates competence in the various code disciplines

- **Training and Professional Development**—Courses and reference books pertaining to all aspects of code administration, enforcement and technical aspects of the codes

- **Interpretation Services**—provides interpretations of all code sections. (However, final interpretation is left solely to the code official)

- **Evaluation Reports**—Detailed data of new technologies, materials and products that may not be specifically identified in the codes

These services can be viewed online at www.iccsafe.org. Available online training aids can be viewed at www.learn.iccsafe.org.

Topic: Certification

Reference: *Basic Code Enforcement*, 1.12.1

Category: An Overview of Codes

Subject: ICC Services

Text: *The foundation of an efficient and effective code enforcement department is a technically competent staff—no matter what size the jurisdiction, what code is enforced or what types of inspections are conducted. Certification can be achieved in various occupational categories by successful completion of one or more examinations. Additionally, the program has a maintenance provision to ensure that those who become certified maintain a reasonable level of knowledge as new methods and technology are developed.*

Discussion and Commentary: Although becoming certified does not automatically make one an expert in that particular field, it does demonstrate initiative, basic competence and a commitment to the code enforcement profession. Most certifications are obtained from having a basic knowledge in a particular field and through the studying, reading and hands-on application of the pertinent code books.

Many jurisdictions now require that new employees become certified in their particular field within a certain amount of time after being hired or before being promoted. Some also provide employees financial incentives to obtain additional certifications in related fields.

Topic: Evaluation Reports	Category: An Overview of Codes
Reference: *Basic Code Enforcement*, 1.12.7	Subject: ICC Services

Text: *Staying ahead of rapidly developing technology is difficult for design professionals and code officials. To aid in the review and acceptance of new products which are not specifically addressed in the codes, ICC offers voluntary product evaluation services. Manufacturers provide substantiation to the evaluation service staff who, in turn, publishes a report describing the product, its performance and limitations of acceptance. Evaluation reports are available online to all government agencies and the public. The use of evaluation reports is not mandatory, but does offer the code official a convenient means of staying abreast of new technologies and their application.*

Discussion and Commentary: A building official is not required to accept a product even if it has received a formal evaluation by ICC Evaluation Service (ICC-ES); however, most building officials use the information to allow the new product as long as its use and installation strictly comply with the evaluation report. These reports make it easier for a building official to accept, rather than reject, new products and technology.

A building official can accept new products without an evaluation report as long as he or she feels there is sufficient evidence that the product is safe and complies with the intent of the code. By relying on an ICC evaluation report, this function of the building official's job becomes much easier.

Study Session 1
Basic Code Enforcement, Chapter 1

1. What is a model code?
    a. Suggestions for constructing model homes
    b. A set of regulations that become law as soon as they are published
    c. Requirements for building common structures such as theaters and restaurants
    d. A written set of regulations available for adoption by local jurisdictions

    Reference_____

2. Hammurabi is best known for _____.
    a. establishing the first known building code
    b. establishing exact code requirements when constructing new buildings
    c. offering recommended practices for residential structures
    d. requiring that only certain building materials be used during construction

    Reference_____

3. According to Hammurabi, if a builder builds a house and it collapses and kills the owner, the _____.
    a. owner's family can sue the builder
    b. builder must pay the family twice the value of the home
    c. builder shall be put to death
    d. builder will forever be prohibited from constructing homes

    Reference_____

4. The main purpose of building codes is to _____.
   a. establish strict and inflexible construction regulations
   b. protect the public health, safety and welfare
   c. increase construction costs to ensure public safety
   d. provide revenue to the jurisdiction that adopts the code

   Reference_____

5. Which of the following is not a benefit of a state code?
   a. uniformity and compatibility
   b. elimination of unjustifiably restrictive requirements
   c. political influence over code regulations
   d. uniform, timely and appropriate acceptance of new products and technology

   Reference_____

6. Which of the following is not a characteristic of the ICC code development process?
   a. Anyone may submit a proposed code change.
   b. Code proposals are debated at public hearings.
   c. Participation is free and open to all interested parties.
   d. Final code changes are voted on by all interested parties.

   Reference_____

7. A performance type code _____.
   a. Allows flexibility, provided the final outcome meets the code's intent
   b. prohibits the use of materials not specifically covered in the code
   c. provides a specific list of rules to follow
   d. defers to the registered design professional for determining compliance

   Reference_____

8. Which of the following is not a service of ICC?
    a. certification of code professionals
    b. training and education materials
    c. setting permit and plan review fees
    d. publication of model codes

    Reference_____

9. What three model code organizations formed the ICC beginning in 1994?
    a. BOCA, CABO and ICBO   b. BOCA, ICBO and SBCCI
    c. CABO, ICBO and SBCCI   d. IAEI, BOCA and SBCCI

    Reference_____

10. A building code is adopted by a jurisdiction as _____.
    a. a referenced standard
    b. a guideline
    c. a resolution
    d. law

    Reference_____

11. A prescriptive code _____.
    a. describes exactly what methods and materials are to be used during construction
    b. allows flexibility during construction
    c. permits only licensed contractors or designers in the jurisdiction
    d. specifies the minimum qualifications of the building safety staff

    Reference_____

12. Standards are primarily developed _____.
    a. as general guidelines
    b. by industry organizations
    c. through the code development process
    d. as primary laws

    Reference_____

13. A building code _____.
    a. sets maximum standards for construction
    b. typically prohibits new methods and materials
    c. establishes minimum fees for permits and plan review
    d. is a legal document that regulates the construction of buildings and structures

    Reference_____

14. What are the two types of construction regulations?
    a. Prescriptive and specification
    b. Performance and prescriptive
    c. Performance and nonperformance
    d. Standards and specification

    Reference_____

15. A referenced standard _____.
    a. is an enforceable extension of the code
    b. supersedes the code requirement
    c. does not address installation methods
    d. only applies if specifically adopted

    Reference_____

16. The intent and purpose of an ICC model code is stated in _____ of that code.
    a. the preface
    b. Chapter 1
    c. Chapter 2
    d. the table of contents

    Reference_____

17. Who grants the authority to adopt codes?
    a. The governing body of the jurisdiction
    b. The county the jurisdiction is located in
    c. The federal government
    d. The building official

    Reference_____

18. The International Codes® can be adopted by _____.
    a. international organizations only
    b. reference
    c. publishing the entire code in the local newspaper
    d. maintaining three copies in the clerk's office available to the public

    Reference_____

19. A model code cannot be adopted without _____.
    a. referencing the specific edition
    b. amending portions of the technical requirements
    c. updating related permit and plan review fees
    d. establishing the minimum qualifications of the building official

    Reference_____

20. The maximum number of voting representatives for an ICC governmental member is _____.

    a. 4
    b. determined by the number of full-time employees
    c. determined by population
    d. 2

    Reference_____

21. Which of the following is not a benefit of becoming certified?

    a. Demonstrates a solid commitment to the profession.
    b. Establishes professional credentials.
    c. Improves career opportunities.
    d. Qualifies the certified individual as an expert.

    Reference_____

22. All of the following are found in an ICC Evaluation Service report except _____.

    a. a detailed description of the method or material being evaluated
    b. the manufacturer's name and address
    c. limitations of the method or material
    d. specific geographical cost data

    Reference_____

23. ICC's interpretation service _____.

    a. provides interpretations of misunderstood or confusing code requirements
    b. releases information only to licensed contractors and designers
    c. establishes the specific requirements when conducting the code adoption
    d. dictates the final meaning of complex code requirements

    Reference_____

24. An adopted code may become invalid if _____.
    a. it prohibits alternative methods or materials
    b. stricter administrative requirements are established
    c. permit and plan review fees are increased
    d. the code appendices are not adopted

    Reference_____

25. Which of the following is a key characteristic of the code development process?
    a. Only ICC members may submit a proposed code change.
    b. Persons with a vested interest in the results are not permitted to testify.
    c. Final voting is done by ICC governmental representatives.
    d. The code development committee must approve any successful code change.

    Reference_____

Study Session 2

Basic Code Enforcement, Chapters 2 through 4
Building Department Operations, Zoning Ordinances and Building Permits

OBJECTIVE: To become familiar with the administration of code enforcement, starting with a general view of the personnel and practices that make up a building department; focusing subsequently on the adoption and enforcement of zoning ordinances; and, finally, examining the building permit process as a means of securing code compliance.

REFERENCE: *Basic Code Enforcement,* Chapters 2 through 4

KEY POINTS:
- What is the function of a building safety department?
- Who are the key personnel of a building safety department?
- What is the administrative authority of a building official?
- When and why is a building permit required?
- How are operational costs offset?
- How are permit fees calculated? (See also Study Session 6.)
- What is the definition of zoning?
- What are the objectives and purpose of zoning?
- How is a zoning ordinance adopted and prepared?
- What are the two parts of a zoning ordinance?
- How does a zoning ordinance adjust for inequities?
- How is a zoning ordinance enforced?
- What does a zoning ordinance do?
- What is a building permit, and why is it required?
- Why is a permit application required?

Topic: Delegation of Police Powers **Category:** Building Department Operations
Reference: *Basic Code Enforcement*, 2.2 **Subject:** Function of a Building Department

Text: *A building department is a law enforcement agency within a local jurisdiction. Its main function is to verify that construction meets the building codes, which are laws, and gain compliance when there are deficiencies. Building codes take the form of ordinances adopted by local governments under the police power delegated to them by the states. The police power of the states to legislate for public health, safety and welfare is granted by the US Constitution. This police power is the source of all authority to enact building codes.*

Discussion and Commentary: Police power is the power of the state to legislate for the general welfare of its citizens. This power enables passage of such laws as building codes. It is from the police power delegated by the state legislature that local governments are able to enact building codes.

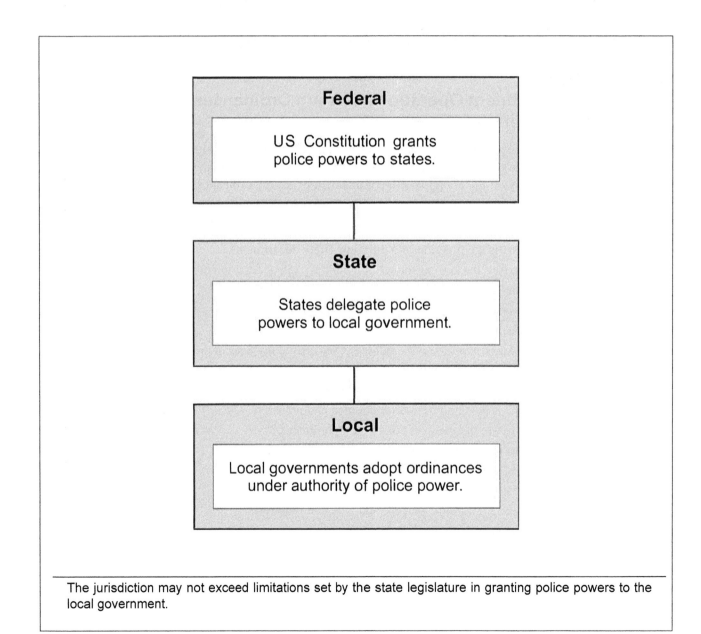

The jurisdiction may not exceed limitations set by the state legislature in granting police powers to the local government.

Topic: Administration
Reference: *Basic Code Enforcement*, 2.3
Category: Building Department Operations
Subject: Key Personnel

Text: *Although official titles and job descriptions vary, a building department typically has a department director and personnel to process applications, review plans and inspect construction to verify compliance with the code. In some small departments, one person may handle multiple duties. In some large departments, the duties of each employee may become very specialized.*

Discussion and Commentary: Although the building official is the primary administrator of the code, he or she is authorized by Section 103.3 of the IBC to appoint deputies who shall have such powers as delegated by the building official. There are many jurisdictions that may only have a one-person department where that person performs administrative, clerical, plan review and inspection duties while other larger jurisdictions may have single or multiple individuals to handle each of these primary functions.

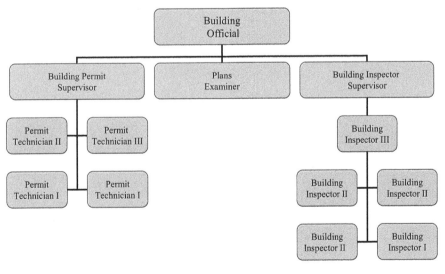

Section 103 of the IBC creates the Department of Building Safety, and Section 104 enumerates the duties and powers of the building official.

Study Session 2

Topic: Building Official **Category:** Building Department Operations
Reference: *Basic Code Enforcement,* 2.3.1 **Subject:** Key Personnel

Text: *The I-Codes use different terms for the person in charge of administering the codes. In the IBC and IRC, the term is building official, defined as the officer or other designated authority charged with the administration and enforcement of the code, or a duly authorized representative. The building official typically serves under the direction of a department head, municipal manager, city council or county board of supervisors.*

Discussion and Commentary: The building official's prime mission is to protect the public health, safety and welfare through the verification of compliance with the codes and prevention, correction or abatement of code deficiencies. The building official manages the building department and employs various individuals whose duties are to gain compliance with the code regulations. These individuals include plan examiners/reviewers; building, electrical, plumbing and mechanical inspectors; permit technicians; and support staff.

As defined in the IBC and IRC, the officer in charge of the building safety department is the building official. The IFC designates the fire code official as the person in charge. In the other ICC model codes, the designated authority is referred to as the "code official," whereas in the *National Electrical Code* he or she is referred to as the "authority having jurisdiction" (AHJ).

Topic: Plans Examiners/Reviewers **Category:** Building Department Operations
Reference: *Basic Code Enforcement,* 2.3.2 **Subject:** Key Personnel

Text: *The purpose of plan review is to verify that the proposed design of a building or structure complies with building codes and related ordinances. Methods used to review plans vary widely and generally depend on the size of the building department and the types of local construction projects. Some jurisdictions provide for no formal plan review, some perform extensive reviews, and others review only those plans for more complex structures or those signed by a licensed architect or engineer.*

Discussion and Commentary: A plans examiner's primary function is to verify that any plans submitted for a permit are in compliance with the jurisdiction's adopted ordinances. In order to accomplish this, submitted construction documents must be complete and accurate. Missing or incomplete documents slow down the plan review process and do not allow the plans examiner to conduct a full review. It is typically easier and less expensive to discover code noncompliance during plan review than during field inspection.

Some plan examiners perform multidisciplinary reviews while others perform only specialty reviews such as architectural, electrical, mechanical, plumbing, fire, structural or accessibility. Many jurisdictions also utilize the services of a plan review consultant to handle projects ranging from routine to complex, especially if the jurisdiction is understaffed or if they do not have reviewers to conduct specialty reviews.

Study Session 2

Topic: Building Inspectors   **Category:** Building Department Operations
Reference: *Basic Code Enforcement,* 2.3.3   **Subject:** Key Personnel

Text: *Building inspectors verify compliance with regulations related to the design, construction and use of buildings. They inspect methods and materials used in the construction of new as well as existing structures to ensure that building codes, health and safety regulations, construction standards and zoning ordinances are met. Building inspectors study construction documents for planned repairs of existing buildings, construction of new building projects and building sites being considered for development. Inspectors should keep detailed records and copies of reports pertaining to all of their inspections.*

Discussion and Commentary: Required inspections vary from jurisdiction to jurisdiction. Some only require inspections of the footings/foundation, rough framing and final, while others also verify insulation and other energy efficiency requirements, fire resistance and fire protection systems. It is imperative that detailed inspection records be kept in the event legal proceedings are required at a later date.

Section 110 of the IBC establishes minimum required inspections but also authorizes jurisdictions to require other inspections to verify compliance with the code. In addition, the building official may require special inspections as established in Chapter 17 of the IBC.

Topic: Permit Technicians **Category:** Building Department Operations
Reference: *Basic Code Enforcement*, 2.3.4 **Subject:** Key Personnel

Text: *Permit technicians perform a multitude of building department tasks. Typically, the permit technician is the first point of contact when a permit applicant or citizen comes into the building department to apply for a permit, request an inspection or just to ask a code-related or procedural question.*

Discussion and Commentary: In larger departments a permit technician may specialize in only one or two duties while in smaller departments they may handle all of the front counter-related responsibilities. In most cases, the department relies on the permit technician to verify that the submittal documents are complete during the permit application process and to maintain accurate records throughout the permitting and inspection process. In some cases, permit technicians perform preliminary plan review, and may be authorized to issue permits for some small, routine projects.

A permit technician may also be referred to as a development services technician, permit clerk, administrative assistant, permit coordinator, projects coordinator, plan and permit technician or permit expediter.

Study Session 2

Topic: Building Official Duties **Category:** Building Department Operations
Reference: *Basic Code Enforcement, 2.4* **Subject:** Authority of the Building Official

Text: *It is important to remember that a building code is a legal document. A building official is a law enforcement officer with four basic duties: 1. Review applications and conduct preliminary inspection of new construction and equipment installation (if deemed necessary); 2. Issue permits; 3. Perform periodic inspections, and; 4. Gain compliance with the code and related ordinances.*

Discussion and Commentary: The building official must verify that all information initially submitted for a permit is complete, signed and all fees are paid. Verification of compliance with ordinance administered by other departments, such as zoning, fire and engineering must also be conducted.

The documents then must proceed through the review process and, once approved and fees are paid, the permit is issued.

During construction, periodic inspections are conducted to ensure compliance with the approved construction documents, and once full compliance is achieved a certificate of occupancy is issued. Again, it is imperative that detailed and accurate records are kept throughout the entire process.

BUILDING PERMIT
CITY OF ANYTOWN

PERMIT NUMBER _____
DATE ISSUED _____
CONTRACTOR _____
HOMEOWNER _____
DESCRIPTION/SCOPE OF WORK _____
_____
_____

NEW ☐ EXISTING/REPAIR ☐ REPLACEMENT ☐

REQUIRED INSPECTIONS _____
_____
_____
_____

FEES _____

_____
BUILDING CODE OFFICIAL
24-HOURS' NOTICE REQUIRED

The building official has a multitude of duties and responsibilities as established by the code. These will be discussed further in Study Session 4.

Topic: Fees	**Category:** Building Department Operations
Reference: *Basic Code Enforcement,* 2.5	**Subject:** Offsetting Operational Costs

Text: *Generally, fees are collected to offset the cost of department operations. Ideally, the code enforcement department should be self-supporting. Once the department is established and has a financial history, fees are based on budgetary requirements. The budgeting process is the cornerstone of the fee process; each community should decide what constitutes an acceptable fee structure. To establish a budget, the department should evaluate the services needed and establish a cost for each service.*

Discussion and Commentary: There are many methods of establishing fees for services rendered, but the department should at least cover the majority of its costs through appropriate and defensible fees. Many of the department's functions can generate revenue, but there are other operations that do not, such as training, code research, processing code violations on existing properties, hiring staff, department meetings and just answering general questions from the public. In any event, fees should be justified and reviewed at least at every code adoption.

Direct Costs

Personnel:
- **Wages**
- **Benefits** (vacation, insurance, sick leave, pensions)
- **Employer's share of FICA taxes**

Other:
- **Equipment** (automobiles, tools, test equipment, computers)
- **Supplies** (fuel, paper products)
- **Contact Services** (consulting fees, outside plan reviews, third-party inspection services, expert witness services)

Indirect Costs

Administrative:
- **General Government** (manager's office, accounting, finance, purchasing, personnel, data process, mail room, attorney)
- **Department Administration** (administrative assistants, supervisors, department supervisors)
- **Facilities** (janitorial services, maintenance costs)
- **Operating Costs** (utilities)
- **Capital Costs** (space use, building or space rental)

Some departments feel that it is necessary to cover all costs of operation through user fees, while others look to cover the majority of costs through fees and the remainder through taxes collected by the jurisdiction.

Study Session 2

Topic: Calculating the Permit Fee **Category:** Building Department Operations
Reference: *Basic Code Enforcement,* 2.5.2 **Subject:** Offsetting Operational Costs

Text: *Permit fees are intended to cover the cost of the service provided. The provisions of the IBC and the other I-Codes do not provide any guidance for establishing permit fees, such as a fee schedule (a sample fee schedule does appear in Appendix L of the IRC). Authorization is simply given to the jurisdiction for the establishment and adoption of a schedule of permit fees based on their individual needs.*

Discussion and Commentary: Many jurisdictions have utilized a standardized method of determining fees for many years and continue with their former schedule of fees by merely updating them to reflect current costs. Most permits fees are calculated based on the cubic feet, square feet or valuation of the building under consideration. Typically, the permit fee covers the costs of conducting inspections and an additional plan review fee may be charged to cover the costs of processing the permit. All building department fees must be legally adopted by the jurisdiction's legislative body.

ICC Building Valuation Data

Square Foot Construction Costs [a, b, c, d]

Group (2012 International Building Code)	IA	IB	IIA	IIB	IIIA	IIIB	IV	VA	VB
A-1 Assembly, theaters, with stage	224.49	217.12	211.82	202.96	190.83	185.33	196.14	174.43	167.83
A-1 Assembly, theaters, without stage	205.71	198.34	193.04	184.18	172.15	166.65	177.36	155.75	149.15
A-2 Assembly, nightclubs	177.15	172.12	167.31	160.58	150.83	146.74	154.65	136.68	132.81
A-2 Assembly, restaurants, bars, banquet halls	176.15	171.12	165.31	159.58	148.83	145.74	153.65	134.68	131.81
A-3 Assembly, churches	207.73	200.36	195.06	186.20	174.41	168.91	179.38	158.02	151.41
A-3 Assembly, general, community halls, libraries, museums	173.36	165.99	159.69	151.83	138.90	134.40	145.01	122.50	116.89
A-4 Assembly, arenas	204.71	197.34	191.04	183.18	170.15	165.65	176.36	153.75	148.15
B Business	179.29	172.71	166.96	158.70	144.63	139.20	152.43	126.93	121.32
E Educational	192.11	185.49	180.05	171.90	160.09	151.62	165.97	139.90	135.35
F-1 Factory and industrial, moderate hazard	108.42	103.32	97.18	93.38	83.24	79.62	89.22	68.69	64.39
F-2 Factory and industrial, low hazard	107.42	102.32	97.18	92.38	83.24	78.62	88.22	68.69	63.39
H-1 High Hazard, explosives	101.53	96.44	91.29	86.49	77.57	72.95	82.34	63.02	N.P.
H234 High Hazard	101.53	96.44	91.29	86.49	77.57	72.95	82.34	63.02	57.71
H-5 HPM	179.29	172.71	166.96	158.70	144.63	139.20	152.43	126.93	121.32
I-1 Institutional, supervised environment	177.76	171.50	166.52	159.45	146.31	142.45	159.13	131.29	126.72
I-2 Institutional, hospitals	302.44	295.85	290.11	281.84	266.80	N.P.	275.58	249.09	N.P.
I-2 Institutional, nursing homes	209.38	202.79	197.05	188.78	175.72	N.P.	182.52	158.01	N.P.
I-3 Institutional, restrained	204.27	197.68	191.94	183.67	171.10	164.68	177.41	153.40	145.80
I-4 Institutional, day care facilities	177.76	171.50	166.52	159.45	146.31	142.45	159.13	131.29	126.72
M Mercantile	132.04	127.01	121.20	115.47	105.47	102.39	109.54	91.33	88.45
R-1 Residential, hotels	179.14	172.89	167.90	160.83	147.95	144.10	160.52	132.93	128.36
R-2 Residential, multiple family	150.25	143.99	139.01	131.94	119.77	115.91	131.62	104.74	100.18
R-3 Residential, one- and two-family	141.80	137.90	134.46	131.00	125.88	122.71	128.29	117.71	110.29
R-4 Residential, care/assisted living facilities	177.76	171.50	166.52	159.45	146.31	142.45	159.13	131.29	126.72
S-1 Storage, moderate hazard	100.53	95.44	89.29	85.49	75.57	71.95	81.34	61.02	56.71
S-2 Storage, low hazard	99.53	94.44	89.29	84.49	75.57	70.95	80.34	61.02	55.71
U Utility, miscellaneous	75.59	71.22	66.78	63.37	56.99	53.22	60.41	44.60	42.48

a. Private Garages use Utility, miscellaneous
b. Unfinished basements (all use group) = $15.00 per sq. ft.
c. For shell only buildings deduct 20 percent
d. N.P. = not permitted

As with establishing a budget for the department, many formulas are used for arriving at permit and plan review fees. Using a nationally recognized method is more defensible than generating a "home grown" method of arriving at these fees. The ICC website, www.iccsafe.org, provides periodically updated versions of the Building Valuation Data Table.

Topic: Zones **Category:** Zoning Ordinances
Reference: *Basic Code Enforcement*, 3.1 **Subject:** Zoning Defined

Text: *A Zone is an area or district in a city or town under special restrictions as to the types of buildings that may be erected. Zoning is the act of dividing a city or town into zones in order to determine land use restrictions.*

Discussion and Commentary: Just as building codes regulate the uses of buildings, zoning codes regulate the uses of land. Where building codes may require certain fire buffers between different building uses, zoning codes require land buffers between various land uses.

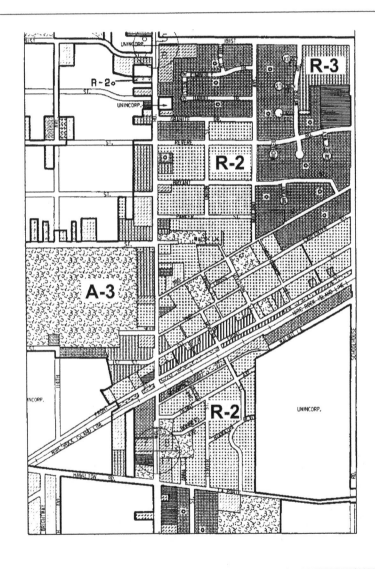

Typical land use zones may include agricultural, residential, commercial and industrial. Each of these would be further broken down into more detailed uses. For example, residential may be further categorized as single-family, one- and two-family and multifamily.

Study Session 2

Topic: Objectives
Reference: *Basic Code Enforcement*, 3.2
Category: Zoning Ordinances
Subject: Purpose of Zoning

Text: *The objectives of zoning are to provide economical, efficient land use and a well-blended community of buildings where the structures complement rather than hinder each other. No one would want to build a house next to a petroleum refinery. By the same token, no homeowner would want a petroleum company building a refinery next door. Zoning ordinances keep these kinds of situations from happening. Therefore, the purpose of zoning is to protect the general welfare of the public.*

Discussion and Commentary: Well-planned zoning ordinances maintain property values by separating various land uses from other incompatible land uses. A typical scenario may be a single family district abutted by a one- and two-family district, abutted by a multifamily district, abutted by a light commercial district, abutted by a regional commercial district, abutted by an industrial district.

Benefits of Zoning

Regulation	Benefit
Controlling the height, area and bulk of buildings ...	... provides standards for healthful housing by ensuring: - adequate natural lighting; - ventilation; - privacy; and - recreation areas for children.
Regulating off-street parking and loading ...	... reduces street congestion.
Placing conflicting uses in separate districts ...	... controls noise, vibration, glare, pollution and odor.
Restricting building and preserving existing trees ...	... prevents flooding and erosion.

Although a use such as a church may not be considered residential in character, it may become compatible through a special or conditional use if certain criteria are met such as parking, light and noise restrictions. More information on conditional uses will be discussed in Study Session 10.

Topic: Enabling Legislation **Category:** Zoning Ordinances
Reference: *Basic Code Enforcement,* 3.6 **Subject:** Adopting a Zoning Ordinance

Text: *In 1924, the US Department of Commerce established A Standard Zoning Enabling Act. This act was and still is the basis for most local zoning ordinances. The act addresses the need to divide municipalities into districts to help provide for population density, building use, light, ventilation, appropriate height and area, and other zoning elements. State enabling legislation grants local political subdivisions the authority to adopt and enforce zoning ordinances.*

Discussion and Commentary: The jurisdiction's zoning or planning commission is responsible for drafting a zoning ordinance. Because the members of this commission typically reside in the jurisdiction, they are familiar with the community and use local economic, demographic and land use studies to lay out the regulations. Public hearings are also held throughout the process so that affected property owners can provide needed input.

Typical 4-Step Process When Drafting a Zoning Code

The municipal zoning or planning commission is responsible for designing the zoning ordinance. When drafting a community's zoning regulations, the commission generally follows a four-step process:

1	By conducting current economic, demographic and land use studies, tailor the ordinance to the needs of the community.
2	Draft regulations that comply with the provisions of state enabling legislation.
3	Find reason for the ordinance which directly relates to the public health, safety and welfare.
4	Hold public hearings to solicit citizen input.

Zoning ordinances are under constant review so as to maintain up-to-date uses of the land within the jurisdiction's planning boundaries. Certain districts may be rezoned to allow new land uses while other districts may be rezoned to prohibit undesirable types of businesses. Many types of unwanted businesses may not legally be prohibited from locating within the jurisdiction, but they may be restricted as to their location by the zoning ordinance.

Topic: Ordinance Map and Text
Reference: *Basic Code Enforcement,* 3.7
Category: Zoning Ordinances
Subject: Parts of a Zoning Ordinance

Text: *A zoning ordinance is divided into two parts. The map of the ordinance shows the district boundaries. The text of the ordinance describes how land may be used in each district. Every zoning ordinance must contain a text and a map to be complete and enforceable.*

Discussion and Commentary: A zoning map usually shows the layout of the jurisdiction as it is at the present time as well as the undeveloped areas that are planned and what the various zoning districts will be for those areas. The text in the zoning ordinance will explain in detail how the various districts can be used or what conditions must be met to allow a certain use within a district. It will also establish requirements for parking, signs, accessory buildings and setback lines.

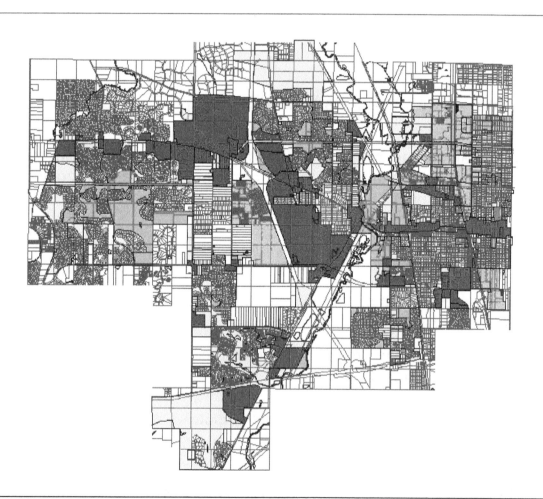

In some cases, jurisdictions may establish a planning area, which may extend a mile or more outside of the jurisdiction's actual boundaries. In the event two or more jurisdictions start annexing land and growing closer together, these planning areas are used to guide the development of land within the annexation.

Topic: Nonconforming Uses	**Category:** Zoning Ordinances
Reference: *Basic Code Enforcement*, 3.8.1	**Subject:** Adjustments for Inequities

Text: *Zoning ordinances are not retroactive; therefore they must include provisions for nonconforming uses, that is, uses that existed before the zoning ordinance was enacted. Nonconforming-use provisions generally prohibit the following: enlarging or expanding the nonconforming use, rebuilding the nonconforming use if more than a certain portion is destroyed, resuming the use after it has been abandoned for a specified period of time and/or changing the use to a higher classification or to another nonconforming use. Some ordinances also state that a nonconforming use must also be phased out during a period of amortization.*

Discussion and Commentary: In most cases, zoning ordinances allow an existing use to remain even though it may not conform to the new ordinance. However, certain stipulations will apply. Primarily, the nonconforming use must have lawfully existed at the time the new ordinance was enacted. If a building code was in effect at the time of construction a record of a permit and/or a certificate of use or occupancy would verify the legal use of the building. If no permit or certificate was issued, and there is no other means to determine that the use was legal at the time of construction, there may be no legal record of the existing use. The jurisdiction could then require it to comply with the new zoning regulations unless a variance is granted to allow it to continue.

The *International Zoning Code*, Section 1102, stipulates when a nonconforming structure must come into compliance with the new zoning regulations.

Topic: Variance **Category:** Zoning Ordinances
Reference: *Basic Code Enforcement,* 3.8.2 **Subject:** Adjustments for Inequities

Text: *Another way that zoning ordinances try to adjust for possible inequities is by providing for variances. A variance is an easing of the terms of the zoning ordinance to relieve individual hardship while protecting the public interest.*

Discussion and Commentary: There are times when the letter of the zoning code cannot strictly be complied with because of unusual terrain, previous property line layouts, nonconforming uses adjacent to conforming uses or any number of circumstances beyond the property owner's control. In such cases, the zoning board of appeals, or a similar body, will weigh the situation and determine if granting a variance would be in the best interest of all concerned.

Before the variance can be granted, an individual must show

- Practical hardship
- That a reasonable return on the property requires a variance
- That the character and appearance of the neighborhood is not changed
- That the public safety and welfare is protected

Typically, a variance to the zoning ordinance will not be granted based on hardship if the property owner created the hardship.

Topic: Determining Compliance	**Category:** Zoning Ordinances
Reference: *Basic Code Enforcement*, 3.9	**Subject:** Enforcing a Zoning Ordinance

Text: *State enabling legislation permits local political subdivisions to appoint zoning officials. Like the building official, the zoning official is considered a law enforcement officer. By comparing actual land use against that shown on a zoning map, the zoning official determines compliance or noncompliance with the zoning ordinance. If a request does not comply with the zoning ordinance, the zoning official checks department records to see if the property was a nonconforming use when the ordinance was passed.*

Discussion and Commentary: Just as the building official reviews construction documents when submitted for a permit, the zoning official reviews the permit application to determine if the use is allowed in the proposed location. He or she also checks the site plan to verify that the location of the structure on the lot in relation to the property lines is in compliance and that any height limitations are not exceeded.

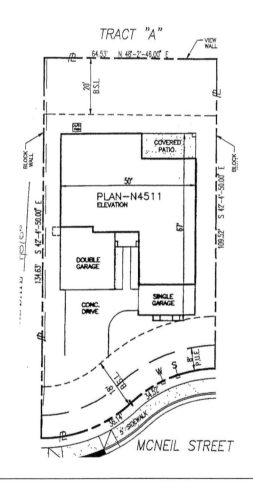

As part of the approval process, certain properties or subdivisions may have additional stipulations that must be complied with in addition to, or in lieu of, the zoning ordinance, such as garage locations, variations in building facades, building heights adjacent to designated streets and off-street parking requirements. These must all be reviewed by the zoning official before the building permit can be issued.

Study Session 2

Topic: License to Build **Category:** Building Permits
Reference: *Basic Code Enforcement,* 4.1 **Subject:** Building Permit Required

Text: *A building permit is a license that grants legal permission to construct or alter a structure. It is, then, a license to build.*

Discussion and Commentary: A building permit is issued by the jurisdiction to construct or alter a building or structure in compliance with the building code and other adopted ordinances. Once it is issued, it becomes a binding legal document and cannot be altered except by the issuing body.

A building permit is typically required for the following:

New Construction
Additions
Renovation
Alteration
Repair
Demolition
Relocation
Equipment
Use and Occupancy
Prefabricated Structures
Mobile Homes
Electrical Systems
Plumbing Systems
HVAC Systems (heating, ventilating, air conditioning)
Temporary Buildings
Miscellaneous for Residential (fireplaces, pools, decks, fences)
Miscellaneous for Commercial (parking, health, food handling, signs)

In many instances, a permit is not required for minor ordinary repairs to structures. However, the IBC has certain stipulations which may apply.

Topic: Protecting Public Welfare
Reference: *Basic Code Enforcement, 4.2*
Category: Building Permits
Subject: Why is a Building Permit Required?

Text: *Building permits and the permit process provide means for code officials to protect the public health, safety and welfare by reducing the potential hazards of unsafe construction; help the public understand local laws and ordinances affecting building construction and; provide the means for building officials to inspect construction to ensure that work complies with the minimum standards for materials and methods as adopted in the jurisdiction.*

Discussion and Commentary: Building permits also provide documentation that allows verification, through plan review and field inspections, that any work covered under the permit is proceeding per code. Permits also allow for the issuance of a Certificate of Occupancy once all work is properly completed. This assists the present owner, insurance companies and future owners of the building by providing a formal record of code compliance.

Notice
Building Permit

Building Department
City Of

Permit No. 00-0000

Has been issued to

Owner _____

Contractor _____

For (Work Description) _____

At (Project Address) _____

(Date) _____ (Building Official Signature) _____
Issue Date   Building Official

The issuance or granting of a permit shall not be construed to be a permit for, or an approval of, any violation of any of the provisions of the city building code or of any other ordinance of the jurisdiction.

A copy of this building permit shall be kept on the site of the work until the completion of the project.

The permit holder or authorized agent is responsible for calling for all required inspections before work is covered and for providing access to the work. Do not occupy this building, or portion of building as described, until final inspection, approval and issuance of the certificate of occupancy.

This permit expires ___/___/___

City Building Department
(000) 000-0000

In most areas of the United States, a building permit also gives notice to the tax assessor that improvements on a property are being made that may affect the assessed valuation of the property and ensure that the local municipality will receive its fair share of revenue. It is also important for a property owner to obtain a demolition permit when necessary so as to formally notify the assessor that an improvement is no longer there.

Study Session 2

Topic: Permit Technician Duties
Reference: *Basic Code Enforcement,* 4.3
Category: Building Permits
Subject: Building Permit Process

Text: *The building permit process is the primary method by which a governmental agency verifies that construction complies with the minimum requirements of the code to protect the health, safety and welfare of the public. The code is explicit in describing the progressive steps in this permitting process and gives the building official broad authority to carry out these duties. Many of the duties in this process fall to the permit technician, though procedures vary by department.*

Discussion and Commentary: Typically, an application for a permit by the owner or owner's agent starts the permit process. Building departments today typically rely on permit software to generate permit forms. Copies are distributed as required, often electronically. Processes have become more automated, with some larger departments transacting many functions digitally.

The permit technician:

1. Assists the applicant with the permit application and receives two sets of construction documents.
2. Verifies the submittal documents and permit application are complete.
3. Generates a permit number and stamps or marks submittal documents as appropriate.
4. Receives building permit and plan review fees based on the permit fee schedule and the estimated construction value.
5. Has the applicant sign the application.
6. Gives the applicant a copy of the application and other information.
7. Forwards the application to the plan reviewer.
8. Processes the permit when issued and maintains the permit file.
9. Sends the issued permit, approved construction documents, job site card and other information to the applicant.
10. Distributes the issued permit to the tax assessor and other departments.
11. Issues the certificate of occupancy when final inspection is approved.

Procedures vary by department, but the list above illustrates some typical administrative functions carried out by the permit technician in the building permit process.

Quiz

Study Session 2
Basic Code Enforcement, **Chapters 2 through 4**

1. Which of the following is not under the authority of the building official?

    a. issue permits

    b. perform inspections

    c. grant variances

    d. review applications

    Reference _____

2. Permit and plan review fees are collected to _____.

    a. provide prevailing wages to the building department staff

    b. provide a minimum profit for the jurisdiction

    c. abate dangerous buildings within a jurisdiction

    d. offset the cost of departmental operations

    Reference _____

3. Which of the following is not typically a function of a building department?

    a. enforce building codes

    b. protect the public health, safety and welfare

    c. act as a law enforcement agency

    d. prohibit specific construction methods and materials

    Reference _____

4. Which of the following is not a typical consideration when calculating a building permit fee?

   a. type of construction

   b. square foot construction costs

   c. value of land

   d. occupancy group

   Reference _____

5. ICC's Building Valuation Data table is based on _____.

   a. geographical location of the building

   b. type of construction and occupancy group

   c. size and occupant load of the building

   d. tax assessor valuations

   Reference _____

6. When recieving a building permit application, the building official is authorized to waive the requirement for _____ if the work is of a very minor nature.

   a. building permit fees

   b. construction documents

   c. a signature on the application

   d. a description of work

   Reference _____

7. A building permit may be revoked for all of the following reasons except _____.

   a. false information on the application

   b. disagreeing with the code official's interpretation

   c. incorrect information on the plans

   d. failure to follow the code

   Reference _____

8. An area or district in a city or town under special restrictions as to the types of buildings that may be constructed is known as a _____.
   a. Home Owners Association
   b. zone
   c. fire district
   d. subdivision

   Reference _____

9. Which of the following is not generally considered a benefit of a zoning code?
   a. provides adequate ventilation and privacy
   b. reduces street congestion
   c. establishes maximum speed regulations in residential districts
   d. controls noise, glare, pollution and odor

   Reference _____

10. The two parts of a zoning ordinance are _____.
    a. the building code and the zoning code
    b. a map and the text
    c. zoning districts and fees for conditional uses
    d. lot coverage and height restrictions

    Reference _____

11. If the setbacks for a proposed building do not meet the zoning ordinance because of an irregular shaped lot, the citizen may _____.
    a. pay a surcharge and proceed with construction
    b. appeal to the zoning board of appeals for a variance
    c. seek an injunction from the courts
    d. request a variance from the city council

    Reference _____

12. Generally, nonconforming use provisions in the zoning code do not prohibit _____.

    a. the sale of the nonconforming property to another owner
    b. changing the use to another nonconforming use
    c. enlarging or expanding the nonconforming use
    d. resuming the use after it has been abandoned for a specified time period

    Reference _____

13. An easing of the terms of the zoning ordinance is known as a _____.

    a. variance   b. nonconforming use
    c. conditional use   d. modification

    Reference _____

14. Typically, when there is a conflict between the building code and the zoning ordinance, the _____ is enforced.

    a. building code   b. zoning ordinance
    c. intent of both codes   d. most stringent requirement

    Reference _____

15. The Standard Zoning Enabling Act was established by the US Department of Commerce in _____.

    a. 1901   b. 1924
    c. 1952   d. 1955

    Reference _____

16. Which of the following is not generally part of the four-step process when drafting a zoning ordinance?

    a. hold a general election to adopt the zoning ordinance
    b. hold public hearings to solicit citizen input
    c. draft regulations that comply with state enabling legislation
    d. conduct current economic, demographic and land use studies of the community

    Reference _____

17. All of the following are typically considered one of the three major zoning districts except _____.
    a. industrial
    b. residential
    c. entertainment
    d. commercial

    Reference _____

18. Zoning ordinances must include provisions for nonconforming uses, which are _____.
    a. uses permitted over the objections of affected neighbors
    b. buildings constructed prior to the adoption of a building code
    c. uses that existed before the zoning ordinance was in effect
    d. buildings without a certificate of occupancy

    Reference _____

19. A building permit is _____.
    a. a license to build
    b. required for any type of repair or improvement
    c. not required if a business license is obtained and kept current
    d. a constitutional right granted by the US Commerce Department

    Reference _____

20. Which of the following would not be considered one of the typical functions of the permit technician in processing building permits?
    a. Verifies the submittal documents are complete
    b. Has the applicant sign the application
    c. Distributes issued permits to the tax assessor and other departments
    d. Follows the plan review checklist

    Reference _____

21. One of the primary reasons for requiring a building permit is to _____.
    a. compute future property taxes fairly
    b. inform adjacent neighbors of the project
    c. provide additional revenue to the jurisdiction
    d. verify compliance with minimum construction standards

    Reference_____

22. If the building official rejects a permit application based on his or her interpretation of the code, the permit applicant can accept the ruling or _____.
    a. request a variance to waive the code requirements
    b. file a formal complaint with the jurisdiction's chief administrator
    c. appeal the ruling to the jurisdiction's board of appeals
    d. seek an injunction from the courts

    Reference_____

23. The building code does not permit an appeal based on which of the following?
    a. The building official may have incorrectly interpreted the code.
    b. The code section in question does not apply to the project.
    c. An equal or better material or method is being proposed.
    d. Full compliance would cause a hardship.

    Reference_____

24. Construction documents are reviewed for completeness, code conformance and _____.
    a. compliance with all applicable ordinances
    b. compliance with the most recently published model codes
    c. use of the most modern construction techniques
    d. use of the most modern construction materials

    Reference_____

25. Which of the following is not one of the typical steps in the permit process?
    a. issuance of a certificate of occupancy
    b. receiving permit and plan review fees
    c. submission of an application
    d. holding a public hearing

    Reference_____

Basic Code Enforcement, Chapters 5 through 7
Reading Construction Documents, Performing a Plan Review and Conducting Inspections

OBJECTIVE: To become familiar with the technical aspects of code enforcement: first, by learning to recognize the basic construction documents necessary for a building plan review; then, by examining the construction documents for compliance with zoning ordinances and building code requirements; and finally, by learning the various types of inspections and the procedures for verifying code compliance.

REFERENCE: *Basic Code Enforcement,* Chapters 5 through 7

KEY POINTS:
- What are construction documents?
- What are some typical architectural symbols and abbreviations?
- What are some of the typical views in a set of architectural plans?
- What scales are used for the various elements in a set of plans?
- What are specifications and engineering details?
- What is the purpose of plan review?
- What are the responsibilities of the building official, the plan reviewer and the inspector in respect to building plan review?
- Why is a plan review record necessary?
- What code requirements must generally be checked during building plan review?
- Why inspect a building?
- What are the various types of inspections?
- What is the typical sequence of inspections during the course of construction?
- Why is it important to document inspections?
- What are field correction notices and notices of violation?
- How are complaint inspections handled?

Topic: Plans and Specifications **Category:** Reading Construction Documents
Reference: *Basic Code Enforcement,* 5.2 **Subject:** What are Construction Documents?

Text: *In order for the building official to determine that proposed construction is in compliance with code requirements, it is necessary that sufficient information be submitted for review. This information typically consists of drawings and specifications describing the proposed work. These are the construction documents. Construction documents is the term that replaces the less descriptive "plans and specifications" used in earlier codes.*

Discussion and Commentary: Construction documents assist the staff of the Building Safety Department in determining if a building or structure is in compliance with the jurisdiction's regulations. The Zoning Department will review the site plans for compliance with minimum setbacks and other zoning regulations. The building plans examiner will review the submitted building plans to see if the project complies with maximum height and area, means of egress, light and ventilation, HVAC, plumbing, electrical, structural, accessibility and fire suppression/detection. The specifications will also be reviewed to determine types of materials, window and door hardware and other detailed information not shown on the plans. Structural calculations and soils reports may also be submitted as part of the construction documents.

Drawings are graphic representations of the proposed work and serve to illustrate the physical relationship of materials to each other, including sizes, shapes, quantity, locations and connections. Drawings also include schedules of structural elements, equipment, finishes and similar items.

Specifications are written descriptions which specify the qualitative requirements for products, materials and workmanship for the proposed work, including installation, testing and performance criteria.

It is important that those responsible for accepting construction documents, typically permit technicians, ensure that a complete submittal is received. Otherwise those that are conducting the review will not be able to properly complete their tasks, which will result in delays.

Topic: Symbols and Abbreviations **Category:** Reading Construction Documents
Reference: *Basic Code Enforcement,* 5.3 **Subject:** Architectural Material Symbols

Text: *When the building official reviews construction documents to determine if a proposed building conforms to the building code, he or she will be reading architectural symbols which are pictorial representations of construction materials. Properly identifying the materials being represented is essential to determine construction materials being proposed for use.*

Discussion and Commentary: In addition to architectural symbols, standard abbreviations are used to describe various structural, architectural and mechanical systems. Abbreviations assist in keeping the plans less cluttered. Plans should include a legend that will identify what each of the abbreviations represents.

Legend

Above finished floor	AFF	Lavatory	LAV
Anchor bolt	AB	On center	OC
Concrete masonry unit	CMU	Polyvinyl chloride	PVC
Diameter	DIA	Property line	PL
Elevation	ELEV	Roof drain	RD
Finished floor level	FFL	Smoke detector	SD
Footing	FTG	Square feet	SQ FT or SF
Foundation	FDN	Switch	SW
Gypsum wallboard	GWB	Underwriters Laboratories	UL
Height	HT or HGT	Weatherproof	WP
Junction box	JB	Welded wire fabric	WWF

Some abbreviations such as ftg, fdn, dia, sf and oc are fairly typical whereas others such as ffcl, (finish floor change line), apc (as per code) and cbif (carpenter-built in field) may be unique to a specific set of plans. A legend is often necessary for an accurate review of the plans.

Topic: Plan View
Reference: *Basic Code Enforcement,* 5.4.1

Category: Reading Construction Documents
Subject: Architectural Views

Text: *In the context of construction documents, the term "plan" applies to various types of architectural and engineering drawings that are used by the builder, building official and plan reviewer. But it has another meaning, too. When speaking of the various elements of architectural drawings, "plan" refers to the way we are looking at, or viewing, the proposed construction. The "plan view" shows the proposed construction as if it were being viewed from above.*

Discussion and Commentary: Floor plans are probably the most important of all construction documents because they represent the layout, dimensions and uses of the rooms and include window locations, beams and header locations, plumbing fixtures and other required information. Certain areas on the floor plan may be circled to indicate that there will be a detailed drawing of the area located on the Details page of the plans.

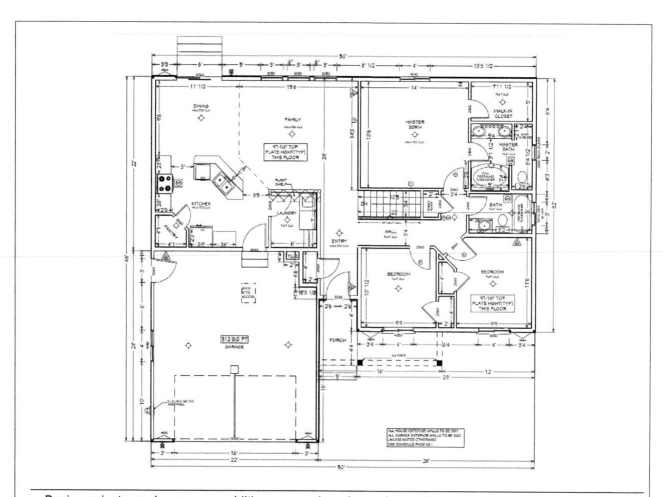

Basic projects such as room additions may also show electrical receptacles, lights and switches, plumbing lines and heat ducts on the floor plan instead of on separate drawings for each type of work. Furniture and other movable items do not typically need to be shown on a floor plan.

Topic: Elevation View **Category:** Reading Construction Documents
Reference: *Basic Code Enforcement*, 5.4.2 **Subject:** Architectural Views

Text: *Another way of viewing the proposed construction is to stand on the ground and look at it. This is called the elevation view. Exterior elevation views may be viewed from the front, sides and rear. The designer prepares elevations views to help the builder visualize the proposed construction from the outside.*

Discussion and Commentary: If a building section view is similar to the open side of a dollhouse, an elevation drawing would be similar to looking at the front or the sides of a dollhouse. Like the cover of a jigsaw box, it shows what the project is intended to look like once it is completed.

On some elevation drawings, the designer may show lines indicating where the various floor levels (basement, crawl space, first, second, attic) may occur. This is helpful when a project has multiple floor levels.

Topic: Building Section View
Reference: *Basic Code Enforcement,* 5.4.3
Category: Reading Construction Documents
Subject: Architectural Views

Text: *A building section is a cutaway view of the entire building or portion of the building. Building sections are sometimes called longitudinal sections or transverse sections. A longitudinal section is cut through the long axis of the structure and a transverse (or cross) section is cut through the short axis. In practice, the terms "section" and "cross section" are used interchangeably, and may be either longitudinal or transverse.*

Discussion and Commentary: Although a building section may be drawn at 1/4" = 1'-0", most detailed section drawings are drawn at a larger scale than floor plans, such as 1/2" = 1'-0", so greater detail can be shown. These drawings can show various connections, anchorage, header and beam details, thicknesses of finish materials (drywall and exterior coverings), wall and roof sheathing type and thickness, flashing and other information that would not be depicted on a floor or foundation plan. The floor plans should indicate the location where the sections are taken.

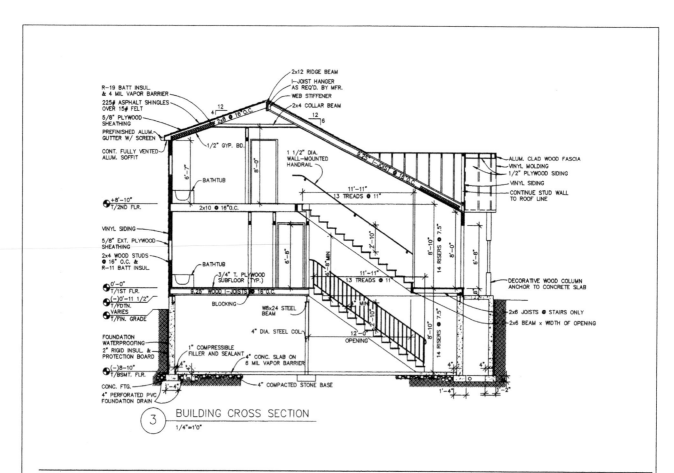

Section drawings are important because they show the builder, plans examiner and inspector in detail how certain aspects of the building will be connected or framed in. They also show various dimensions pertaining to window and door heights as well as ceiling heights.

Topic: Details **Category:** Reading Construction Documents
Reference: *Basic Code Enforcement, 5.4.6* **Subject:** Architectural Views

Text: *Detail drawings show a building element on a larger scale, and therefore in much greater detail and accuracy than can be conveyed on the building plan or section drawings. This level of detail provides information necessary for the correct installation of an element of the building.*

Discussion and Commentary: Typically, the designer will circle certain areas on the floor plans to indicate that there are blow-ups or details. The circled area on the floor plan will be labeled to indicate what the detail number is and on what page the detail will appear. This is known as a reference symbol. (See below.)

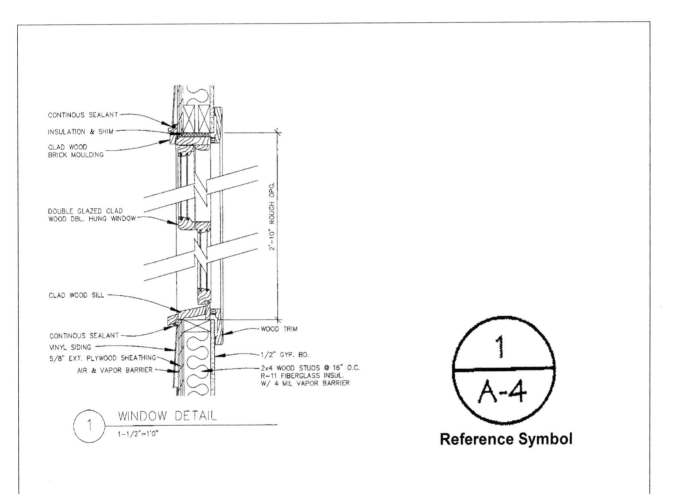

Reference Symbol

Typical details will show connections at wall and foundation, roof and wall, stairways, structural elements such as beam connections, window/door headers and any other areas that may need special attention during building or inspection.

Study Session 3

Topic: Use of Scales
Reference: *Basic Code Enforcement,* 5.5

Category: Reading Construction Documents
Subject: Drawing to Scale

Text: *Drawing to scale has the advantage of showing various elements in correct proportion to one another and helps the user accurately visualize completed construction. The scale may also be used to approximate dimensions for estimating or area calculation purposes, for example. However, the scale should not be used to figure out critical dimensions. Instead, the dimensions indicated on the drawings should be used. If a dimension is missing, it can often be determined by adding and subtracting other dimensions that are given on the drawings.*

Discussion and Commentary: Most floor plans, elevations and foundations plans will be drawn at ¼" = 1'-0". This scale is usually sufficient to view these types of plans. However, for clarity, many details will use a larger scale so that drawing will be larger and capable of showing more specifics. For example, the window detail on the previous page was drawn at 1½" = 1'-0".

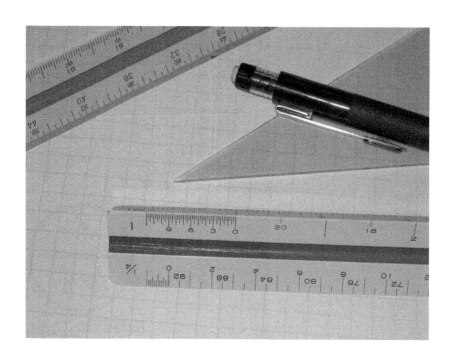

Most site plans are drawn using an Engineer's Scale. This type of scale is broken down in increments of tenths of a foot. Example: 20.5' would equal 20'-6" and 20.75' would equal 20'-9".

Topic: Site Plan
Reference: *Basic Code Enforcement,* 5.6.1
Category: Reading Construction Documents
Subject: Typical Plans

Text: *A site plan depicts the location of the building on the lot, the size of the lot, the distance from the property lines to the building and the outline of the building. It does not show any interior building details.*

Discussion and Commentary: The site plan, or plot plan, is important to the zoning code official to verify that the building use is appropriate for the zone and that the building is located properly on the lot. Front, side and rear yard setbacks will be checked, as well as driveway location, sufficient off-street parking areas and locations of utility easements. Some site plans, known as landscaping plans, will show what plants will be on the property and where they are located.

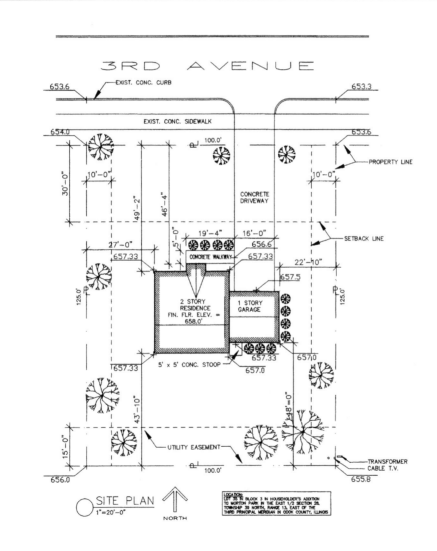

The building inspector will also review this plan in the field upon conducting a footing inspection to determine if the location of the building in the field complies with that of the approved site plan.

Study Session 3 63

Topic: Foundation Plan
Reference: *Basic Code Enforcement*, 5.6.2
Category: Reading Construction Documents
Subject: Typical Plans

Text: *Checking the foundation plan is an important part of a building official's job. Foundation construction, basement floor construction and wall openings are indicated on the foundation plan. Also, unexcavated areas are marked on the plan.*

Discussion and Commentary: If a foundation is installed incorrectly, all additional work on the project will suffer. A proper foundation plan is critical for a plans examiner so that he or she can verify if footings are large enough based on local soil conditions, if proper reinforcing bars are installed based on soil or seismic conditions, if foundation or stem walls are sufficient to carry the anticipated loads, and if the location and sizes of interior footings that may be carrying loads from columns or bearing walls are proper.

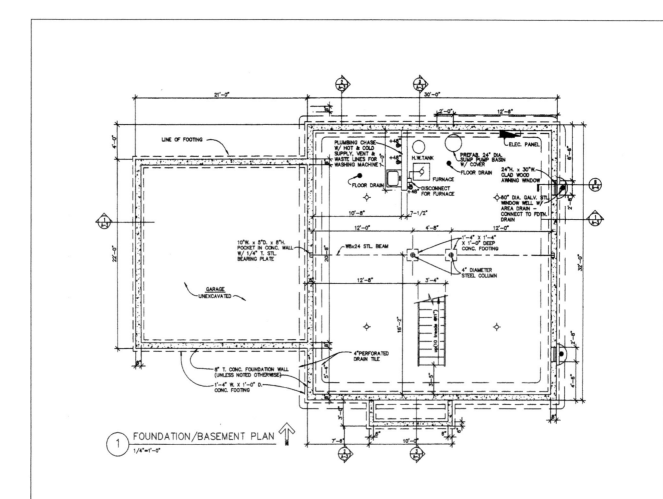

A foundation plan will also show if a foundation is continuous around the perimeter of the project, or if sections will be omitted such as under the garage door or other large openings.

Topic: Specifications
Reference: *Basic Code Enforcement, 5.7.1*
Category: Reading Construction Documents
Subject: Specifications and Engineering

Text: *Building designers try to make their instructions as clear and complete as possible. One way they do this is to provide specifications, which are instructions that come along with the construction documents. Specifications usually cover methods of construction and standards for materials that are not covered in the drawings. Where it is not practical for the design professional to include sufficient notes on the drawings to describe detailed products, materials and methods proposed for use, separate and detailed descriptions or specifications are provided.*

Discussion and Commentary: The building official must review these specifications, or specs, to determine if the proper methods and materials are going to be used or if certain types of hardware or fittings not specifically called for on the drawings will be in compliance with the code.

SAMPLE PORTION OF PLUMBING SPECIFICATIONS

A. General Requirements—-Plumbing
  1. All penetrations of poured concrete or precast walls and floors shall be done by the use of sleeves manufactured or fabricated for that purpose.
     a) Materials:
        1. Plastic
        2. Steel pipe
        3. Terra cotta for underground sleeves
        4. Manufactured sheet metal
     b) Installation:
        1. Sleeves entering building below grade to be made water tight.
        2. Sleeves to be of sufficient size to permit covering of insulated pipe.

  2. Subsurface drainage piping shall have at least two rows of $1/4$-inch diameter perforations on 3-inch centers and the perforations shall be directed toward the bottom of the trench. All pipes shall be laid on a fall of $1/16$- inch per foot unless otherwise noted on plans. Cover top of rock with two layers of 15 pound felt.

  3. Domestic water pipe and fittings inside the building shall either be Type M copper, Type L copper, Type K copper, galvanized steel or brass as noted on the plans. All pipe and fittings below grade are to be wrapped with approved wrappings.

Specifications for a small building may be printed on the plans, whereas a larger building typically requires a more detailed set of specifications, which are printed separately.

Topic: Engineering Details
Reference: *Basic Code Enforcement,* 5.7.2
Category: Reading Construction Documents
Subject: Specifications and Engineering

Text: *Engineering details, which may be test results or engineering calculations, provide the verification the code may require to support the proposed design indicated on the construction documents. Both types of engineering details are important because they provide the specific information that is often needed to verify that code requirements are satisfied.*

Discussion and Commentary: Two examples of engineering details are the soils, or geotechnical, report and structural calculations. The soils report lists the bearing capacities of the soil so the designer is able to design a foundation capable of supporting the proposed structure. The structural calculations typically indicate what forces or loads will be affecting the structure and how those forces will be counteracted. Forces such as wind, snow, earthquake (seismic), the weight of furnishings and people, and the structure itself must all be taken into account and spelled out in the structural calculations.

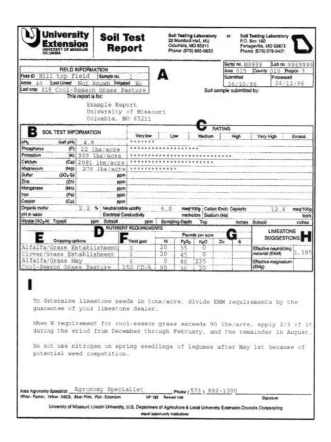

Energy calculations are another type of engineering report that must be submitted in many jurisdictions. Most energy calculations as well as structural calculations are now done with software programs that allow the user to enter certain information and parameters for the project and receive immediate and accurate results.

Topic: Purpose of Plan Review		**Category:** Performing a Plan Review	
Reference: *Basic Code Enforcement,* 6.2.2		**Subject:** Building Plan Review	

Text: *The purpose of a building plan review is to check the construction documents for compliance with the code. This process applies to commercial structures as well as single-family dwellings. The responsibility of the building official extends only to monitoring the performance of the designer and does not supplant the designer's direct responsibility for code compliance. The building official's job is to exercise reasonable and lawful checking of certain design aspects for code compliance, not to perform an exacting and comprehensive design review which guarantees full code compliance.*

Discussion and Commentary: Designers may spend several months or more preparing a set of plans that will be submitted for a permit, and they become therefore intimately acquainted with all aspects of the project. Depending on the workload, a plans examiner may only have a few days to conduct a review of the construction documents to determine if the plans as submitted generally comply with the code. Major deficiencies should be discovered, noted and corrected before the permit is issued. Additional detailed items may not become visible until the project is under construction and discovered by the building inspector. It is imperative that plans examiners and inspectors are qualified for the discipline(s) they are reviewing or inspecting.

Approved plans issued by the jurisdiction are legal documents and cannot be changed or revised until resubmitted to the jurisdiction for additional review. Some building officials will allow minor field deviations to the plans if the changes do not involve structural or life safety systems.

Study Session 3

Topic: ICC Plan Review Record **Category:** Performing a Plan Review
Reference: *Basic Code Enforcement*, 6.4 **Subject:** Plan Review Record

Text: *For consistency and accuracy, building departments typically use some type of checklist when conducting a plan review. For example, the* International Building Code *Plan Review Record fully and accurately covers each item that must be checked before plans are approved.*

Discussion and Commentary: The International Code Council publishes a Plan Review Record that can be used when reviewing plans. Some jurisdictions develop their own checklists based on the various types of plans that are being reviewed. A checklist for a commercial building typically will be lengthier and cover different code items than a checklist for a single-family dwelling.

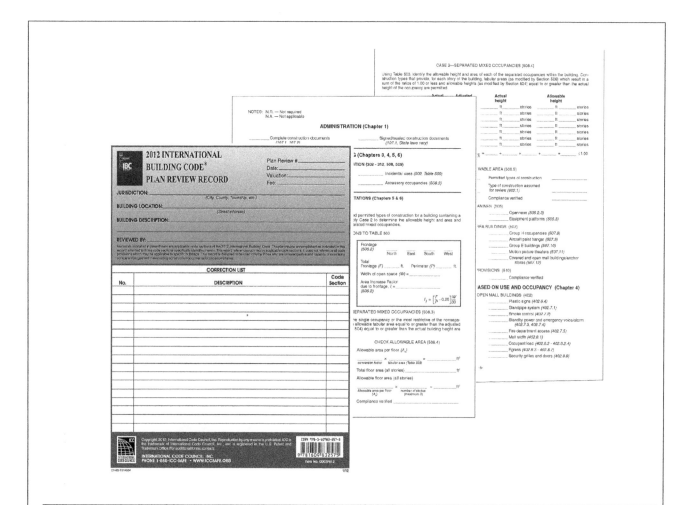

Whatever type of checklist is used for plan review, it should contain the code sections that pertain to each comment. Requiring corrections that do not correspond to an adopted code section is not legal.

Topic: Summary of Steps
Reference: *Basic Code Enforcement*, 6.5
Category: Performing a Plan Review
Subject: Building Code Requirements

Text: *A plan reviewer has to review many aspects of the design of a building or structure to determine compliance with the building code. The steps in the plan review process include: Administration, Building Planning, Fire Protection, Occupant Needs, Building Envelope, Structural Systems, Structural Materials, Nonstructural Materials, Building Mechanical Services, and Special Construction.*

Discussion and Commentary: Just about every building will need to be checked for these requirements whether it is a large commercial building or a single-family dwelling. The permit application must be accompanied by complete and accurate construction documents indicating the building is located properly on the lot, meets the requirements for fire resistance, provides a healthy and safe environment for the occupants, is structurally sound and contains safe electrical, plumbing and HVAC systems.

- ✔ **Administration** requirements, which include the submittal of complete construction documents.
- ✔ **Building Planning** requirements, which consist of classifying the building according to use group, reviewing height and area limitations, and verifying the type of construction. Special use and occupancy requirements also fall under this heading.
- ✔ **Fire Protection** requirements, which cover fire-resistant materials and construction and fire protection systems.
- ✔ **Occupant Needs** requirements including means of egress, accessibility and interior environment.
- ✔ **Building Envelope** requirements, which are exterior wall coverings and roofs and roof structures.
- ✔ **Structural Systems** requirements, which cover structural loads, structural tests and inspections, and foundations and retaining walls.
- ✔ **Structural Materials** requirements, which include concrete, masonry steel and wood.
- ✔ **Nonstructural Materials** requirements, which include glass and glazing, gypsum board and plaster, and plastic.
- ✔ **Building Services** requirements including mechanical systems and elevators and conveying systems.
- ✔ **Special Construction** requirements including membrane structures and temporary structures.

Some minor structures such as storage sheds, gazebos and detached carports typically do not require the same level of review as larger structures, but they still must be properly located and structurally safe.

Study Session 3

Topic: Verifying Compliance
Reference: *Basic Code Enforcement*, 7.1
Category: Conducting Inspections
Subject: Why Inspect a Building?

Text: *A building permit is actually a license to build. The permit is based on approved construction documents that have been reviewed for compliance with the code. Inspections are necessary to ensure that the permit holder does not deviate from approved drawings during the course of construction.*

Discussion and Commentary: At least one set of construction documents must be on the job site so the inspector can verify that construction is proceeding in accordance with the plans. Very rarely does a building get constructed exactly as indicated on the plans, but the inspector must verify that all code-related items are present. Inspections are conducted periodically through the various stages of construction.

The number of required inspections varies from jurisdiction to jurisdiction but most, at a minimum, require inspections before any concrete is poured, before any walls are covered up and at project completion before the building is used or occupied.

Topic: Summary
Reference: *Basic Code Enforcement, 7.2*
Category: Conducting Inspections
Subject: Types of Inspections

Text: *Typically, there are three types of inspections handled by building departments. The first type, known as called inspections, are routine visits to a construction site to check for code compliance during specific phases of construction as part of the permit process.*

Complaint inspections are the second type. These result when complaints about code or zoning matters are initiated by someone outside of the building department. Building officials check the complaint, gather information in the field and make their recommendations.

Survey and periodic inspections are the third type. These typically relate to property maintenance, housing or fire codes adopted by the local jurisdiction. Survey inspections may include all existing buildings in a block or neighborhood. Periodic inspections, in contrast, focus on specific types of buildings such as schools, apartments or commercial buildings.

Discussion and Commentary: Another type of inspection is the special inspection, which is covered in Chapter 17 of the IBC. A special inspection is typically conducted by a third party on behalf of the owner. It involves expertise not usually available in a typical building department, such as welding, structural concrete and masonry, special soil conditions and high-strength bolts inspections. Inspection reports from the special inspector must be filed with the building official.

Many jurisdictions have a separate code enforcement division, which may or may not report directly to the building official, that handles complaints involving work without a permit, dangerous buildings, weeds, abandoned vehicles and other property maintenance issues.

Study Session 3

Topic: Work in Progress
Reference: *Basic Code Enforcement*, 7.3
Category: Conducting Inspections
Subject: Called Inspections

Text: *The applicant copy of the building permit informs the applicant that construction work will be inspected. The building permit signifies that the plans have been approved and construction may begin. A notice on the permit or jobsite card tells the builder to notify the building department to arrange for inspections. These are known as "called" inspections.*

Discussion and Commentary: In accordance with IBC Section 110.5, it is the responsibility of the building permit holder to contact the building department for required inspections. Section 110.3 lists the required inspections but, as mentioned previously, some jurisdictions, through their adopting ordinances or administrative procedures, require more inspections than those listed in the IBC and some may require less. They may also combine several inspections into a single trip to the jobsite.

Inspection Record

Building Department City Of

Permit No. _____
Name _____
Address _____

INSPECTOR SHALL SIGN ALL SPACES WHICH APPLY TO THIS JOB

Inspection Category	Date	Comment	Inspector
Foundation Inspection:			
Setbacks, Footings			
Under Slab Inspections:			
Plumbing			
Mechanical			
Electrical			
Utility Inspections:			
Electrical Service			
Gas Piping/Air Test			
Rough-In Inspections:			
Plumbing			
Mechanical (HVAC)			
Electrical			
Framing			

DO NOT COVER WORK
UNTIL IT IS INSPECTED, APPROVED AND ABOVE SPACES ARE SIGNED

Inspection Category	Date	Comment	Inspector
Final Inspection			

DO NOT OCCUPY
Final Inspection Approval and Certificate of Occupancy issued by the building department are required before occupying this building

In the field, inspectors may use checklists to verify that code issues are covered during the inspection. Also, many jurisdictions require a job weather card to be posted at the site so that it is visible from the street. The inspector will verify that the permit number on the job weather card matches the number on the approved permit.

Topic: Footings **Category:** Conducting Inspections
Reference: *Basic Code Enforcement,* 7.3.1 **Subject:** Called Inspections

Text: *The first inspection takes place when the contractor has completed all excavations for the building footings and forms for the footings are in place. The contractor calls to have this inspection performed before the concrete is placed.*

Discussion and Commentary: The inspector will first check to verify that the footings are located in accordance with the approved site plan. He or she will then check the condition of the soil within the footing forms and determine if the soil is suitable for proper bearing. If the soil appears inadequate, the inspector will require an engineering report from a soils engineer prior to allowing the footing to be poured. The footing area must be clean and free of any standing water or debris. The inspector will also check to see if there are any reinforcing steel bars, or rebar, required per the plan. The depth and width of the footing forms will also be checked against the approved plans. Pipes passing under or through the footings must also be protected from damage. In some cases, a grounding electrode, know as an Ufer, may be present, and the inspector will check its size, length and location.

Some jurisdictions may conduct a site inspection to verify conditions as they exist before construction starts. For additions to existing buildings, this is especially important to determine if the new addition will interfere with any existing exits, drainage swales or utility meters, or if there are any other structures that may not have received a permit.

Topic: Foundations **Category:** Conducting Inspections
Reference: *Basic Code Enforcement,* 7.3.2 **Subject:** Called Inspections

Text: *A second inspection takes place after the footings are installed and the forms for the foundation walls are in place. The contractor shall call to have this inspection performed before the concrete for the foundation walls is placed or after the masonry foundation walls are erected.*

Discussion and Commentary: As with the footings, the inspector will verify the thickness and depth of the foundation wall forms and determine if any required rebar is properly installed. If any window or door openings are to appear in the foundation, the inspector will check the plans for conformity. If anchor bolts will be placed in the wet concrete after it is poured, the inspector will check bolts that are on site and verify that they are the proper diameter and length. Any pipes that will be passing through the foundation wall must be protected.

Foundation walls may be basement walls or stem/knee walls (typically less than four feet tall).

Topic: Concrete Slab-on-Grade **Category:** Conducting Inspections
Reference: *Basic Code Enforcement*, 7.3.3 **Subject:** Called Inspections

Text: *The third inspection takes place after the forms are removed from the foundation walls. Once approval is given, the builder may place the concrete slabs, backfill the excavation around the foundation and begin framing.*

Discussion and Commentary: For concrete slabs the inspector will check the subgrade, base fill, vapor barrier and any reinforcing wire mesh or rebar. The subgrade must be firm and free of any foreign debris and vegetation. All wire mesh must be installed and tied together, and the vapor barrier must be installed without openings and lapped at the seams. Usually, the contractor will have the top of the slab marked with a snapped chalk line on the foundation wall so that the inspector can verify the final slab thickness.

Any electrical or plumbing pipes as well as any in-slab heating ducts will be checked for proper size, placement and protection against damage. Rigid foam insulation may also be present, and the inspector will verify its thickness and location.

Slab inspections may be conducted in phases, especially if there is a large surface area, insofar as concrete finishers can only work with a limited amount of concrete at a time before it begins to harden and cure. In some cases the foundation and slab are poured at the same time. This is known as a monolithic pour.

Topic: Framing
Reference: *Basic Code Enforcement,* 7.3.4
Category: Conducting Inspections
Subject: Called Inspections

Text: *The fourth inspection is made when all the framing is complete and all electrical wiring, plumbing, heating ducts, and other mechanical equipment that will be concealed by wallboard have been installed and fireblocked.*

Discussion and Commentary: The framing, or rough, inspection typically takes the longest amount of time to conduct because there is so much to look for. All framing members are checked for proper nailing, size and spacing and to ensure that they are not overspanned. The inspector will also check to see that they have not been weakened by cutting, notching or drilling for plumbing or electrical pipes. Because roof trusses are engineered, the inspector will verify that they have not been damaged or weakened after having been set in place. If they have been damaged, the inspector will require that an engineer submit a report recommending proper repair or replacement. Wall bracing and shear walls, which provide rigidity for the structure, will be checked for proper nailing, use of materials and placement as per the approved plans. Concealed spaces in stud walls, partitions, stair stringers and soffits must be fireblocked to prevent fire from passing from one concealed space to the next. In addition, spaces around vents, ducts, chimneys and pipes must be sealed with approved draft-stopping materials to prevent or reduce the spread of smoke or fire.

In addition to inspecting the framing, the inspector will also check the electrical, plumbing and HVAC installations to confirm compliance with the code and approved plans. Many jurisdictions also require an insulation or energy inspection to confirm that all energy-saving provisions of the code are properly installed. Depending on the jurisdiction, all these inspections may be conducted by one inspector during the framing inspection, or they may be conducted separately by different inspectors before the framing inspector is called.

A framing inspection may have many different names, such as rough, pre-drywall, top-out, four-way or intermediate.

Topic: Final
Reference: *Basic Code Enforcement,* 7.3.5
Category: Conducting Inspections
Subject: Called Inspections

Text: *The fifth and final inspection is made when the building is completely enclosed and weather-tight, including the installation of windows, exterior doors, siding and roofing. All glazing including safety glazing has been installed and construction is complete to the extent required by code. Additionally, all plumbing, electrical and mechanical equipment must be installed and in operating condition. Exterior stairs, walks and driveways must be installed. The lot must be graded to conform to the approved drainage plan before a certificate of occupancy can be issued.*

Discussion and Commentary: A final inspection is just as its name implies. All work has been completed, and the building is safe to use and occupy. The certificate of occupancy certifies that, to the best of the building official's knowledge through periodic inspections, the building complies with the adopted codes and regulations. IBC Section 111 lists specific information that must be included on the certificate of occupancy.

Although some jurisdictions require carpeting, painting, trim board and cabinetry to be installed at the final inspection, the code does not require these items to be completed.

In colder climates where exterior concrete or grading may not be able to be completed, the building official may issue a conditional or temporary certificate of occupancy with the stipulation that all work will be completed when weather permits.

Study Session 3

Topic: Inspection Record
Reference: *Basic Code Enforcement,* 7.4.1
Category: Conducting Inspections
Subject: Called Inspection Records

Text: *The inspector uses an inspection record form, which may be a card posted at the job site to note compliance and noncompliance with the code.*

Discussion and Commentary: Just as it is important to keep a plan review record, it is also important to maintain an accurate inspection record for each project. This documentation keeps track of each visit made by the inspector and what conditions he or she found upon conclusion of the inspection. If a deficiency was found, it should be noted. Typically a reinspection is necessary, and the inspector will revisit the site to determine if the deficiency was corrected. If the violation has not been corrected, construction cannot proceed and, in some extreme instances, the inspector may place a stop work order on the project. Once the violation has been corrected, it also should be documented.

INSPECTION RECORD

DATE	NOTE PROGRESS - CORRECTIONS AND REMARKS	INSPECTOR
6/15	Footings O.K.	N. Pagano
7/1	Basement wall forms O.K.	N. Pagano
7/23	O.K. To Backfill footing drains & dampproofing O.K.	N. Pagano
8/12	Violations: (1) Stairway not fireblocked	
	(2) Split joist north of stairwell	
	Correction notice to superintendent	N. Pagano
8/18	Violation Complied	N. Pagano

Although the code is silent on charging fees for reinspections, many jurisdictions will place provisions for such fees in their adopting ordinance to encourage contractors to be ready for inspection when the inspector arrives. Other jurisdictions do not charge a fee but require a 24 or 48 hour waiting period before the contractor can call for another inspection. Still other jurisdictions use both methods.

Topic: Procedures **Category:** Conducting Inspections
Reference: *Basic Code Enforcement, 7.5* **Subject:** Complaint Inspections

Text: *Besides handling violations at the site of a called building inspection, building officials make inspections that are initiated by citizen complaints. These complaints may range from an illegal alteration, such as converting an attic into an apartment or starting construction of an addition without a permit, to zoning violations. While called inspections focus on construction in progress, complaint inspections focus on existing buildings and the current use of those buildings.*

Discussion and Commentary: Handling complaint inspections properly is extremely important. Following procedures and maintaining accurate records is imperative in the event a case must be taken to court. Before and during the establishment of a formal procedure, the jurisdiction's legal counsel should be consulted in order to verify that all legal areas are covered. Below is a generic procedure for handling a complaint report.

1	A correction notice or stop work order is issued.
2	Reinspection is made on or before the compliance date.
3	If violations are corrected, compliance is noted.
4	In case of noncompliance, a notice of violation is sent.
5	If the responsible party has been repeatedly contacted in person or by phone and noncompliance continues, then further legal action is appropriate.

The *International Property Maintenance Code*® (IPMC®) establishes minimum maintenance standards for the regulation and safe use of existing structures.

Study Session 3

Basic Code Enforcement, Chapters 5 through 7

1. Plans and specifications necessary for obtaining a permit are known as _____.

    a. engineering details
    b. architectural drawings
    c. construction documents
    d. application forms

    Reference_____

2. A written description that spells out the qualitative requirements for products, materials and workmanship including installation, testing and performance criteria for a proposed project is known as a(n) _____.

    a. architectural legend
    b. building code
    c. building standard
    d. specification

    Reference_____

3. Architectural material symbols are _____.

    a. pictorial representations of construction materials
    b. shown on each page of the submitted plans
    c. identical for each set of submitted plans
    d. required by the *International Building Code* (IBC)

    Reference_____

4. The architectural abbreviation "FFL" signifies _____.
   a. furniture and fixture locations
   b. first floor location
   c. finished floor level
   d. furniture and fixture load

   Reference_____

5. "HVAC" stands for _____.
   a. height variance above curb
   b. heating, ventilation and air conditioning
   c. high velocity air circulation
   d. home vacuuming system

   Reference_____

6. A(n) _____ view of a construction drawing shows the proposed construction as if it were being viewed from above.
   a. elevation
   b. framing
   c. plan
   d. section

   Reference_____

7. A cross-sectional view through the short axis of a building is also known as a _____.
   a. transverse section
   b. detail
   c. longitudinal section
   d. side elevation

   Reference_____

8. A drawing showing a particular building element on a larger scale is known as a _____.
   a. section
   b. framing plan
   c. perspective drawing
   d. detail

   Reference_____

9. A reference symbol indicates _____.
   a. what number the detail is and on what page it appears
   b. the type of glazing used and its size
   c. what code section applies to a specific detail
   d. what type of soil is referenced in the soils report

   Reference_____

10. If a dimension is missing from the floor plans, the plans examiner should first _____.
    a. use an architect's scale to measure the missing dimension
    b. add or subtract the existing dimension to determine the missing dimension
    c. contact the architect or designer
    d. use an engineer's scale to measure the missing dimension

    Reference_____

11. Which of the following is not typically shown on a foundation plan?
    a. unexcavated areas
    b. wall openings
    c. thickness of foundation walls
    d. height of foundation walls

    Reference_____

12. A site plan does not typically show _____.
    a. finished roof elevation
    b. property lines
    c. building location on the lot
    d. distance between the building and property lines

    Reference_____

13. A roof plan does not typically show the _____.
    a. trusses or rafters
    b. type of roof covering
    c. roof drainage system
    d. items which penetrate or are mounted to the roof

    Reference_____

14. Structural calculations or soils reports are examples of _____.
    a. engineering details
    b. standard specifications
    c. plans specifications
    d. requirements for special inspections

    Reference_____

15. A parcel of land bounded by a lot line or a designated portion of a public right-of-way is known as a _____.
    a. zoning district   b. site
    c. site plan   d. zoning map

    Reference_____

16. Which of the following is not typically one of the first three items to check in a zoning review?
    a. use   b. construction type
    c. zoning district   d. location

    Reference_____

17. The primary purpose of conducting a building plan review is to _____.
    a. generate revenue to cover operating costs
    b. determine if the proposed structure can be built in a specific zoning district
    c. determine what impact the building will have on traffic flow
    d. check the construction documents for compliance with the code

    Reference_____

18. Which one of the following is not considered one of the three types of inspections performed by building departments?

    a. special inspections
    b. called inspections
    c. complaint inspections
    d. survey and periodic inspections

    Reference_____

19. All of the following are verified during a footing inspection except _____.

    a. top of foundation clearance above grade
    b. soil conditions at the bottom of the excavation
    c. size and location of rebar, if required
    d. location, width and depth of the forms

    Reference_____

20. During the _____ inspection, the inspector checks base fill material type and thickness, and vapor barrier placement.

    a. foundation
    b. framing
    c. concrete slab-on-grade
    d. special

    Reference_____

21. At the framing inspection, all concealed spaces are checked to determine if _____ is required.

    a. additional nailing or strapping
    b. sway bracing
    c. termite-proofing
    d. fireblocking or draftstopping

    Reference_____

22. All of the following must be present at the final inspection except _____.

    a. carpeting
    b. completed HVAC system
    c. exterior stairs
    d. exterior siding

    Reference_____

23. A correction notice informs the contractor of _____.
    a. what the reinspection fee will be
    b. what the penalty will be for not calling in the next inspection
    c. what must be done to bring inspected work into compliance with the code
    d. who is responsible for correcting any violations noted during inspection

    Reference_____

24. When compliance cannot be obtained through a correction notice alone, a written _____ may be the next formal step for enforcing the code.
    a. cease and desist
    b. court order
    c. notice to appear
    d. notice of violation

    Reference_____

25. Which of the following is not typically part of the administrative procedure for handling a citizen complaint inspection?
    a. A correction notice or stop work order is issued
    b. A notice of violation is sent
    c. The minimum and maximum penalties are established
    d. Reinspection is made on or before the compliance date

    Reference_____

Study Session

2018 IBC Sections 101 through 104
Scope and Administration

OBJECTIVE: To obtain an understanding of the administrative provisions of the *International Building Code®* (IBC®), including the scope and purpose of the code, duties of the building official, issuance of permits, inspection procedures, special inspections, existing buildings and referenced standards.

REFERENCE: Sections 101 through 104, 2018 *International Building Code*

KEY POINTS:
- What is the purpose and scope of the *International Building Code*?
- What are the limitations for use of the *International Residential Code®* (IRC®)?
- When do the provisions of the appendices apply?
- What other construction codes are referenced throughout the IBC?
- When materials, methods of construction or other requirements are specified differently in separate provisions, which requirement governs?
- When there is a conflict in the code between a general requirement and a specific requirement, which provision is applicable?
- How do the standards referenced in the IBC relate to the provisions of the code?
- Where a difference occurs between the code and a referenced standard, which provisions are applicable?
- How does the IBC identify the agency charged with the enforcement of the IBC?
- What is the IBC designation for the individual in charge of the code enforcement agency?
- What are the powers and duties of the building official in regard to the application and interpretation of the code?
- What is the building official's authority in regard to the waiving of requirements?
- When is the building official required to carry appropriate identification?
- Under what conditions is the building official authorized to enter an occupied building to enforce the provisions of the code? An unoccupied building?

KEY POINTS (Cont'd):

- What level of personal liability is undertaken by the building official in the performance of his or her duties?
- What are the responsibilities of the jurisdiction when a lawsuit is instituted against an employee?
- Under what conditions may used materials and equipment be utilized?
- Under what conditions may the building official grant modifications to the code?
- How may alternate materials, designs and methods of construction be approved? What type of supporting data is required?

Topic: Scope
Reference: IBC 101.2
Category: Scope and Administration
Subject: General Requirements

Code Text: *The provisions of this code shall apply to the construction, alteration, relocation, enlargement, replacement, repair, equipment, use and occupancy, location, maintenance, removal and demolition of every building or structure or any appurtenances connected or attached to such buildings or structures.*

Discussion and Commentary: The *International Building Code* (IBC) is intended to regulate the broad spectrum of construction activities associated with buildings and structures other than those specifically exempted from this code. The provisions cover many aspects including construction types, use of buildings and structures, occupancy loads, means of egress, light and ventilation, existing buildings, energy conservation and fire protection.

Fundamental purposes of the provisions of the *International Building Code*:

- Safety of building occupants
- Prevent panic
- Safety and protection of others' property
- Safety and protection of own property
- Safety of fire fighters and emergency responders

The appendices of the IBC address a diverse number of issues that may be of value to a jurisdiction in developing a set of construction regulations. However, the provisions contained in the appendices do not apply unless specifically adopted.

Topic: Scope
Reference: IBC 101.2, Exception
Category: Scope and Administration
Subject: General Requirements

Code Text: *Detached one- and two-family dwellings and multiple single-family dwellings (townhouses) not more than three stories above grade plane in height with a separate means of egress, and their accessory structures not more than three stories above grade plane in height, shall comply with this code or the* International Residential Code.

Discussion and Commentary: The exception establishes that typical residential buildings, including houses and their accessory structures such as sheds and detached garages are regulated under the *International Residential Code* (IRC). Multiple-family dwelling units such as apartments are covered under the IBC unless they qualify as townhouses as defined by the code and regulated by the IRC.

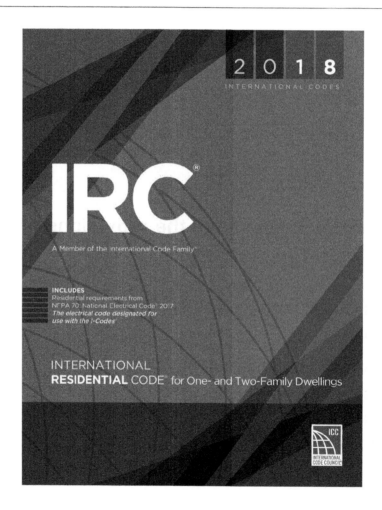

The IBC references the IRC for construction of typical residential structures. The IRC contains prescriptive requirements for the construction of detached single-family dwellings, detached duplexes, townhouses and all structures accessory to such buildings.

Topic: Appendices
Reference: IBC 101.2.1
Category: Scope and Administration
Subject: General Requirements

Code Text: *Provisions in the appendices shall not apply unless specifically adopted.*

Discussion and Commentary: The appendices are specialized topics that may be considered optional when adopting the IBC. If a jurisdiction adopts the IBC and does not specifically include these appendices, they are not considered part of the adopted code. Some appendices are actually extensions of the requirements established in the IBC, and a jurisdiction may adopt any or all of the appendices when it adopts the IBC.

IBC Appendix Chapters

Appendix A	Employee Qualifications
Appendix B	Board of Appeals
Appendix C	Group U—Agricultural Buildings
Appendix D	Fire Districts
Appendix E	Supplementary Accessibility Requirements
Appendix F	Rodentproofing
Appendix G	Flood-Resistant Construction
Appendix H	Signs
Appendix I	Patio Covers
Appendix J	Grading
Appendix K	Administrative Provisions
Appendix L	Earthquake Recording Instrumentation
Appendix M	Tsunami-Generated Flood Hazard
Appendix N	Replicable Buildings

Appendix chapters, where not adopted as a portion of a jurisdiction's building code, may still be of value in the application of the code. Provisions in the appendices may provide some degree of assistance or guidance in evaluating proposed alternative designs, methods or materials of construction.

Topic: Intent
Reference: IBC 101.3
Category: Scope and Administration
Subject: General Requirements

Code Text: *The purpose of this code is to establish the minimum requirements to provide a reasonable level of safety, public health and general welfare through structural strength, means of egress facilities, stability, sanitation, adequate light and ventilation, energy conservation, and safety to life and property from fire, explosion and other hazards, and to provide a reasonable level of safety to fire fighters and emergency responders during emergency operations.*

Discussion and Commentary: The code is to be considered a minimum set of requirements to protect the occupants of a building, particularly during emergency conditions such as fire incidents. In many cases, enforcement of the IBC may rely on what the code is trying to accomplish (intent). It would be impossible to create a document to address all life safety, health and welfare issues that may arise during the design and construction of a building.

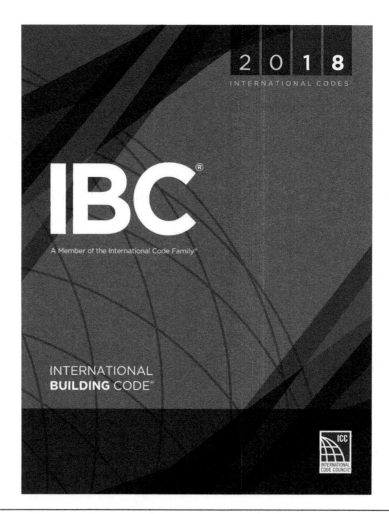

There are multiple code sections that refer to the "intent of the code," insofar as strict application of the letter of the code may be impractical and, at times, impossible. The code's intent should always be considered when evaluating proposed alternative designs, methods or materials of construction.

Topic: Referenced Codes
Reference: IBC 101.4
Category: Scope and Administration
Subject: General Requirements

Code Text: *The other codes listed in Sections 101.4.1 through 101.4.7 and referenced elsewhere in this code shall be considered part of the requirements of this code to the prescribed extent of each such reference.*

Discussion and Commentary: The applicable portions of the referenced codes are considered part of the IBC because it would be impractical to enumerate all requirements that are covered in other documents. The application of the other code documents referenced in the IBC is limited to the extent to which they are addressed in the IBC.

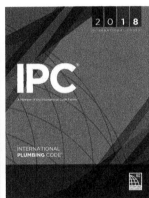

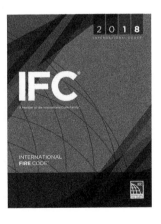
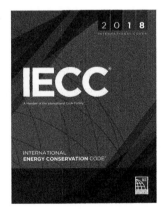
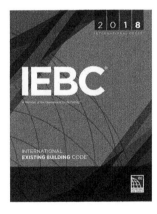

The *International Building Code* is but one document in a set of interrelated regulations, often described as the family of International Codes. These referenced codes provide a greater degree of detail that may, for example, apply specifically to plumbing and mechanical systems, existing structures, fire-related issues, property maintenance and energy conservation.

Topic: General Provisions
Reference: IBC 102.1
Category: Scope and Administration
Subject: Applicability

Code Text: *Where there is a conflict between a general requirement and a specific requirement, the specific requirement shall be applicable. Where, in any specific case, different sections of this code specify different materials, methods of construction or other requirements, the most restrictive shall govern.*

Discussion and Commentary: Insofar as many code sections may apply to a single building, it is inherent that several sections may come in conflict with one another. When this occurs, the most restrictive code requirement shall apply. In addition, where the code sets forth a general requirement and elsewhere addresses the same topic in greater detail, the more specific requirement applies.

Although it is at times difficult to determine the hierarchy of code requirements regarding their level of specificity, it is important that the relationship of such requirements be determined. Where a specific requirement and a general requirement conflict, the specific requirement is always applicable.

Topic: Other Laws	**Category:** Scope and Administration
Reference: IBC 102.2	**Subject:** Applicability

Code Text: *The provisions of this code shall not be deemed to nullify any provisions of local, state or federal law.*

Discussion and Commentary: The *International Building Code* does not override local or state ordinances, amendments or additional provisions.

State, county and municipal jurisdictions routinely enact ordinances that address the built environment. These laws may conflict with a portion of a code provision. In addition, jurisdictions may amend or replace certain provisions of the IBC. In all cases, the local requirements must be met.

Study Session 4

Topic: Referenced Codes and Standards **Category:** Scope and Administration
Reference: IBC 102.4 **Subject:** Applicability

Code Text: *The codes and standards referenced in this code shall be considered to be part of the requirements of this code to the prescribed extent of each such reference. Where conflicts occur between provisions of this code and referenced codes and standards, the provisions of this code shall apply. Where the extent of the reference to a referenced code or standard includes subject matter that is within the scope of this code or the International Codes listed in Section 101.4, the provisions of this code or the International Codes shall take precedence over the provisions in the referenced code or standard.*

Discussion and Commentary: Although limited in their scope, standards define more precisely many of the general provisions in the code. The IBC references many standards, each addressing a specific aspect of building design or construction. In general terms, the standards referenced by the IBC are primarily materials, testing and installation standards. The requirements of a referenced standard are intended to supplement the IBC provisions in those areas not already addressed by the code. If a requirement is addressed in both the IBC and the standard, the IBC provision applies.

Chapter 35 Referenced Standards

AA	BHMA	NCMA
AAMA	CEN	NFPA
ACI	CGSB	PCI
AISC	CPA	PTI
AISI	CPSC	RMI
ALI	CSA	SBCA
AMCA	CSSB	SDI
ANSI	DASMA	SJI
APA	DOC	SPRI
APSP	DOL	SRCC
ASABE	DOTn	TIA
ASCE/SEI	FEMA	TMS
ASME	FM	TPI
ASSE	GA	UL
ASTM	HPVA	ULC
AWC	ICC	USC
AWCI	ISO	WCLIB
AWPA	MHI	WDMA
AWS	NAAMM	WRI

The codes and standards referenced in the IBC are an extension of the code, but only to the degree prescribed by the IBC. Where a standard is referenced, the IBC typically states what is required and the standard indicates how full compliance is to be achieved. Where there is a conflict between the provisions of the IBC and any referenced standard, the provisions of the IBC shall apply.

Topic: Existing Structures
Reference: IBC 102.6

Category: Scope and Administration
Subject: Applicability

Code Text: *The legal occupancy of any structure existing on the date of adoption of this code shall be permitted to continue without change, except as otherwise specifically provided in this code, the* International Existing Building Code, *the* International Property Maintenance Code *or the* International Fire Code.

Discussion and Commentary: If a structure was legally constructed prior to the adoption of a newer code, it will be permitted to remain without further updates. In the event it is improperly maintained or falls into an unsafe condition for the building's occupants or the general public, the applicable provisions of the *International Existing Building Code*, the *International Property Maintenance Code* or the *International Fire Code* may require repair or, in some instances, demolition.

The *International Existing Building Code* (IEBC) covers existing buildings in detail and discusses how renovations and additions to existing buildings are to be addressed, as well as how the code applies to buildings that are moved into the jurisdiction.

Study Session 4

Topic: Buildings Not Previously Occupied
Reference: IBC 102.6.1
Category: Scope and Administration
Subject: Applicability

Code Text: *A building or portion of a building that has not been previously occupied or used for its intended purpose in accordance with the laws in existence at the time of its completion shall comply with the provisions of the* International Building Code *or* International Residential Code, *as applicable, for new construction or with any current permit for such occupancy.*

Discussion and Commentary: Buildings or portions of buildings that have not been used for their intended purpose must meet the provisions of the *International Building Code*.

A building that is completed and waiting for tenants must meet requirements of the current adopted building code when tenant improvements are made.

Topic: Buildings Previously Occupied
Reference: IBC 102.6.2

Category: Scope and Administration
Subject: Applicability

Code Text: *The legal occupancy of any building existing on the date of adoption of this code shall be permitted to continue without change, except as otherwise specifically provided in this code, the* International Fire Code *or* International Property Maintenance Code, *or as is deemed necessary by the building official for the general safety and welfare of the occupants and the public.*

Discussion and Commentary: Occupancy of a building is allowed to continue as is unless there is a danger to the welfare of the public or the occupants of the structure. Typically, requirements affecting an existing building not applying for a permit for construction are requirements focused on property maintenance or fire requirements enforced by the fire marshal.

Existing buildings, new or historical, may continue their current occupancy if they are maintained and present no danger to the public or their current occupants.

Study Session 4

Topic: Creation of Enforcement Agency
Reference: IBC 103.1
Category: Scope and Administration
Subject: Department of Building Safety

Code Text: *The Department of Building Safety is hereby created and the official in charge thereof shall be known as the building official.*

Discussion and Commentary: An enforcement agency must be created to enforce the ordinances regulating buildings and structures within a jurisdiction. Although designated the Department of Building Safety by the IBC, the agency is often known by various other designations as determined by the individual jurisdictions. By whatever name, the role of the agency is the administration of the adopted construction codes and related activities.

DEPARTMENT OF BUILDING SAFETY
Mission Statement

We promote the health, safety and welfare of the community by ensuring that existing and future buildings and structures are safe for use. This is accomplished through quality plan review, inspections and the application of state-of-the-art technology and up-to-date codes.

Although the IBC references the building official as the official in charge, in actuality the person may hold a different title. Such titles include Chief Building Inspector, Building Commissioner, Superintendent of Central Inspection or Director of Code Enforcement. However, for purposes of the code, the term *building official* is used.

Topic: Deputies
Reference: IBC 103.3
Category: Scope and Administration
Subject: Department of Building Safety

Code Text: *In accordance with the prescribed procedures of this jurisdiction and with the concurrence of the appointing authority, the building official shall have the authority to appoint a deputy building official, the related technical officers, inspectors, plan examiners and other employees. Such employees shall have the powers as delegated by the building official. For the maintenance of existing properties, see the* International Property Maintenance Code.

Discussion and Commentary: The IBC frequently refers to the building official as the individual who is charged with making all decisions regarding the administration and application of the code provisions. However, the building department employees (deputies) are, by extension, also considered building officials when discharging their assigned duties

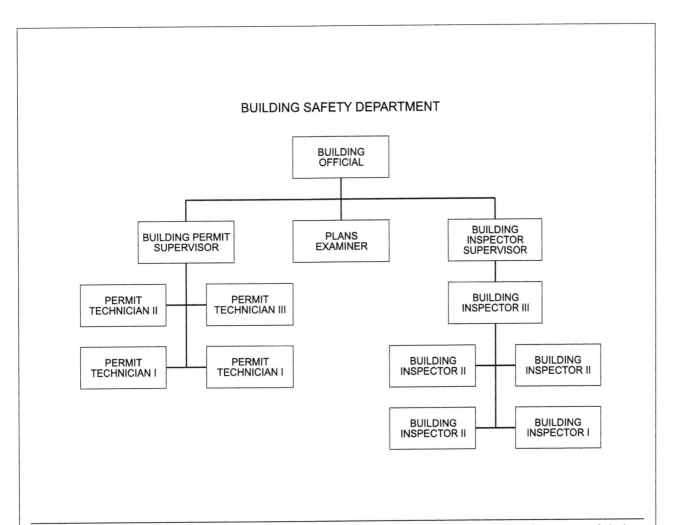

Departmental employees must be advised of the limits to their authority in the performance of their duties and responsibilities, as their actions are considered to be one and the same as those of the designated building official.

Topic: General Provisions	**Category:** Scope and Administration
Reference: IBC 104.1	**Subject:** Duties and Powers of Building Official

Code Text: *The building official is hereby authorized and directed to enforce the provisions of this code. The building official shall have the authority to render interpretations of this code and to adopt policies and procedures in order to clarify the application of its provisions. Such interpretations, policies and procedures shall be in compliance with the intent and purpose of this code. Such policies and procedures shall not have the effect of waiving requirements specifically provided for in this code.*

Discussion and Commentary: The building official must be knowledgeable to the extent that he or she can rule on those issues that are not directly addressed or are unclear in the code. The basis for such a determination is the intent and purpose of the IBC, which often takes some research to discover. The intent of the IBC as set forth in Section 101.3 can assist the building official and is extremely important when weighing decision options.

IBC APPENDIX A
SECTION A101
BUILDING OFFICIAL QUALIFICATIONS

A101.1 Building Official. The building official shall have at least 10 years' experience or equivalent as an architect, engineer, inspector, contractor or superintendent of construction, or any combination of these, five years of which shall have been supervisory experience. The building official should be certified as a building official through a recognized certification program. The building official shall be appointed or hired by the applicable governing authority.

Although the building official is charged with interpreting and clarifying the provisions in the IBC, no authority is granted to allow the building official to provide variances to code requirements. Many resources are available to assist the building official in matters of interpretation.

Topic: Application and Records
Reference: IBC 104.2, 104.7
Category: Scope and Administration
Subject: Duties and Powers of Building Official

Code Text: *The building official shall receive applications, review construction documents and issue permits for the erection, and alteration, demolition and moving of buildings and structures, inspect the premises for which such permits have been issued and enforce compliance with the provisions of this code. The building official shall keep official records of applications received, permits and certificates issued, fees collected, reports of inspections, and notices and orders issued. Such records shall be retained in the official records for the period required for retention of public records.*

Discussion and Commentary: The code enforcement process is normally initiated with an application for a permit. The building official is responsible for processing applications and issuing permits for the construction or alteration of buildings in accordance with all of the adopted codes.

The task of maintaining department records is critical in the successful operation of the building department. Proper record keeping assists in the efficiency of the business practice and provides a valuable resource of information if questions arise regarding the department's actions with respect to a project.

Study Session 4

Topic: Substantially Improved or Damaged
Reference: IBC 104.2.1
Category: Scope and Administration Existing Buildings
Subject: Duties and Powers of Building Official

Code Text: *For . . . repair, alteration, addition or other improvement of existing buildings or structures located in flood hazard areas, the building official shall determine if the proposed work constitutes substantial improvement or repair of substantial damage. [The] building official shall require the building to meet the requirements of Section 1612.*

Discussion and Commentary: The building official determines whether proposed work is a substantial improvement or repair, that is, whether the project will cost more than 50 percent of the market value of the structure. If a project is deemed substantial, the design must meet the flood load requirements of Section 1612 of the IBC. This section only applies buildings in flood hazard areas.

Buildings damaged by any event, in this case fire, in a flood hazard area must meet flood zone requirements in the IBC when repairs will cost more than 50 percent of the market value of the building.

Topic: Right of Entry
Reference: IBC 104.6

Category: Scope and Administration
Subject: Duties and Powers of Building Official

Code Text: *Where it is necessary to make an inspection to enforce the provisions of this code, or where the building official has reasonable cause to believe that there exists in a structure or on a premises a condition that is contrary to or in violation of this code that makes the structure or premises unsafe, dangerous or hazardous, the building official is authorized to enter the structure or premises at reasonable times to inspect or to perform the duties imposed by this code, provided that if such structure or premises be occupied that credentials be presented to the occupant and entry requested. If such structure or premises is unoccupied, the building official shall first make a reasonable effort to locate the owner or other person having charge or control of the structure or premises and request entry. If entry is refused, the building official shall have recourse to the remedies provided by law to secure entry.*

Discussion and Commentary: The building official has a right and responsibility to enter a structure believed to be unsafe. When the building is occupied, the official will present credentials and request entry. If the building is unoccupied, the building official must first attempt to contact the owner or manager to request entry.

In the photo, entry is unnecessary to determine an unsafe condition in one portion of the structure. But in the long, narrow building, the rest of the structure must be determined unsafe or of limited use.

Study Session 4

Topic: Liability
Reference: IBC 104.8

Category: Scope and Administration
Subject: Duties and Powers of Building Official

Code Text: *The building official, member of the board of appeals or employee charged with the enforcement of this code, while acting for the jurisdiction and in good faith and without malice in the discharge of the duties required by this code or other pertinent law or ordinance, shall not thereby be civilly or criminally rendered liable personally and is hereby relieved from personal liability for any damage accruing to persons or property as a result of any act or by reason of an act or omission in the discharge of official duties. Any suit or criminal complaint instituted against an officer or employee because of an act performed by that officer or employee in the lawful discharge of duties and under the provisions of this code shall be defended by legal representatives of the jurisdiction until the final termination of the proceedings. The building official or any subordinate shall not be liable for cost in any action, suit or proceeding that is instituted in pursuance of the provisions of this code.*

Discussion and Commentary: This important section allows building safety employees to conduct their duties with the reasonable expectation that legal action against them will not be initiated as long as they are performing their assigned duties in good faith and without malice. In the event action is brought against the employee, the jurisdiction must absorb the costs to defend the employee. There seems to be an increasing trend in the courts to find civil officers personably liable for careless acts.

Case law regarding tort liability of building safety employees is in a state of flux, and old doctrines may not now be applicable. Therefore, the legal officer of the jurisdiction should always be consulted when there is any question about liability.

Topic: Modifications
Reference: IBC 104.10
Category: Scope and Administration
Subject: Duties and Powers of Building Official

Code Text: *Wherever there are practical difficulties involved in carrying out the provisions of this code, the building official shall have the authority to grant modifications for individual cases, upon application of the owner or owner's authorized agent, provided the building official shall first find that special individual reason makes the strict letter of this code impractical, the modification is in compliance with the intent and purpose of this code and that such modification does not lessen health, accessibility, life and fire safety or structural requirements. The details of action granting modifications shall be recorded and entered in the files of the department of building safety.*

Discussion and Commentary: Although the building code is a fairly comprehensive document, it does not always anticipate unforeseen difficulties. When strict adherence to the code is impractical, the building official is authorized, in individual cases, to modify the provisions for the specific application. It is important that the intent and purpose of the code be maintained in respect to the health, accessibility, life safety, fire safety and structural stability; and that the details of all decisions are placed in the department files as provided for in the code.

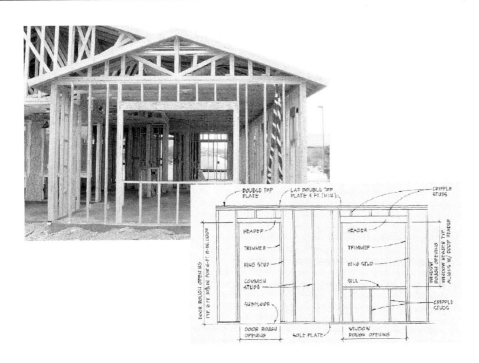

The building official should ensure that any necessary substantiating data or other evidence that shows the modification meets the intent of the code is submitted and recorded in writing. Moreover, where tests are performed, the reports of such tests and all other supporting material and documents must be filed and retained by the building official.

Study Session 4

Topic: Alternative Materials and Methods **Category:** Scope and Administration
Reference: IBC 104.11 **Subject:** Duties and Powers of Building Official

Code Text: *The provisions of this code are not intended to prevent the installation of any material or to prohibit any design or method of construction not specifically prescribed by this code, provided that any such alternative has been approved.*

Discussion and Commentary: The building official is granted broad authority in the acceptance of alternative materials, designs and methods of construction. Arguably the most important provision of the IBC, the intent is to implement the adoption of new technologies. Furthermore, it gives the code even more of a performance character. The provisions encourage state-of-the-art concepts in construction, design and materials—as long as they meet the performance level intended by the IBC. If an alternative material is denied, the reason for disapproval must be given in a written response.

Building official shall approve alternative materials, design and methods of construction, if

  Proposed alternative is satisfactory

  Proposed alternative complies with intent of code

  Material, method or work is equivalent in:

  1. **Quality**
  2. **Strength**
  3. **Effectiveness**
  4. **Fire Resistance**
  5 **Durability**
  6. **Safety**

Advisable for building official to

  Require sufficient evidence or proof

  Record any action granting approval

  Enter information into the files

The building official should ensure that any necessary substantiating data or other evidence that shows the alternative to be equivalent in performance is submitted. Moreover, where tests are performed, the building official must retain the reports of such tests in the department files.

Study Session 4
IBC Sections 101 through 104

1. Which of the following conditions is not specifically listed in the *International Building Code* for the establishment of minimum standards to safeguard the public health, safety and welfare?

    a. structural strength

    b. light and ventilation

    c. sanitation

    d. accessibility

    Reference _____

2. The scope of the *International Building Code* does not typically regulate what general category of buildings?

    a. hotels

    b. museums

    c. offices

    d. houses

    Reference _____

3. Which of the following codes is not specifically referenced as part of the *International Building Code* to the extent prescribed?

    a. *International Zoning Code®*

    b. *International Fuel Gas Code®*

    c. *International Property Maintenance Code®*

    d. *International Energy Conservation Code®*

    Reference _____

4. Where, in a specific situation, different provisions of the code specify differing requirements, the _____ provision shall govern.

   a. least restrictive
   b. most restrictive
   c. most genera
   d. most detailed

   Reference _____

5. The person charged with the administration and enforcement of the code is the _____.

   a. fire chief
   b. city manager
   c. building official
   d. plans examiner

   Reference _____

6. Where there is a conflict between a general requirement and a specific requirement, the _____ requirement shall be applicable.

   a. least restrictive
   b. most restrictive
   c. general
   d. specific

   Reference _____

7. The standards referenced in the IBC are considered _____.

   a. in whole as an extension of the code
   b. as optional criteria provided for informational purposes only
   c. in effect only when specifically adopted
   d. a part of the code only to the extent prescribed

   Reference _____

8. As it applies to construction under the *International Building Code*, where a referenced standard contains provisions that are within the scope of the *International Fire Code*, the _____ provisions take precedence.

   a. standard
   b. *International Fire Code*
   c. more specific
   d. most restrictive

   Reference _____

9. The code does not recognize which of the following as an official department record?
   a. fees collected
   b. reports of inspections
   c. notices issued
   d. operating expenses

   Reference _____

10. Official department records shall be retained _____.
    a. until the project has been completed
    b. for 180 days after the project has been completed
    c. for the period required for retention of public records
    d. for 90 days after the certificate of occupancy is issued

    Reference _____

11. The appendices of the code shall _____.
    a. be strictly enforced
    b. only be considered guidelines
    c. not apply unless specifically adopted
    d. apply only to existing buildings or structures

    Reference _____

12. When permitted, a modification to the code must be in compliance with the _____ of the code.
    a. intent and purpose
    b. fire and life safety provisions
    c. accessibility provisions
    d. flood hazard provisions

    Reference _____

13. The building official, through the development of policies and procedures, shall not have the authority to _____.

    a. allow the use of used materials

    b. permit alternative methods of construction

    c. waive the provisions of the code

    d. render interpretations based on the code's intent

    Reference _____

14. Inspections performed by an approved agency must be documented by reports certified by _____.

    a. the owner

    b. the general contractor

    c. a responsible officer of the agency

    d. the design professional in responsible charge

    Reference _____

15. Employees of the jurisdiction who are delegated authority by the building official to serve in his or her behalf are described by the IBC as _____.

    a. deputies   b. inspectors

    c. designees   d. technical officers

    Reference _____

16. All representatives of the building safety department shall carry proper identification _____.

    a. when dealing with the public

    b. during business hours

    c. when inspecting structures

    d. describing the employee's job function

    Reference _____

17. Generally, the building official will not be rendered liable while _____.
    a. conducting nonrequired inspections
    b. acting for the jurisdiction in good faith
    c. following orders of the board of appeals
    d. complying with the attorney for the jurisdiction

    Reference_____

18. The building official is authorized to enter an occupied structure at reasonable times to make an inspection, provided _____.
    a. a valid permit is in effect
    b. credentials are presented and entry is requested
    c. an official complaint has been lodged
    d. an unusual condition exists

    Reference_____

19. If a building is unoccupied and the building official finds it necessary to make an inspection to enforce the provisions of the code, the building official must first _____.
    a. obtain a search warrant
    b. determine the extent of the hazard
    c. seek approval from the board of appeals
    d. make a reasonable effort to locate the owner and request entry

    Reference_____

20. Who is responsible for providing legal representation to a building department employee being sued because of the performance of their lawful duty?
    a. the employee
    b. the jurisdiction
    c. the state
    d. the department

    Reference_____

21. Under what conditions may used materials be reused?

    a. when approved by the design professional

    b. none; used materials may not be reused

    c. if they meet the code requirements for new materials

    d. if their original use was compliant at the time of such use

    Reference_____

22. When determining the adequacy of alternative materials or methods of construction through testing, such tests shall be performed _____.

    a. by an approved agency

    b. at the expense of the jurisdiction

    c. under the direction of the design professional in responsible charge

    d. in accordance with a valid evaluation report

    Reference_____

23. Supporting data utilized in the approval of materials or assemblies not specifically addressed in the code shall consist of _____ from approved sources.

    a. shop drawings   b. research reports

    c. manufacturer's instructions   d. technical brochures

    Reference_____

24. In general, the legal occupancy of any structure existing on the date of adoption of a new code is _____.

    a. pending until the issuance of a new certificate of occupancy

    b. invalid until the building is re-inspected

    c. permitted to continue without change

    d. subject to review by the board of appeals

    Reference_____

25. A determination by the building official to allow construction below the level prescribed by the flood hazard provisions requires written notice to the applicant stating that _____.

    a. construction below the design flood elevation increases risks to life and property

    b. flood insurance is not available because of the reduced floor elevation

    c. the variance will not result in increased flood heights

    d. the topography of the site render the elevation standards of the code inappropriate

Reference_____

26. In flood hazard areas, who determines whether proposed work is a substantial repair?

    a. design engineer of record

    b. building official

    c. registered design professional

    d. plans examiner

Reference_____

27. If an office building is built and then sits vacant for six years, new permit applications for tenant improvements, additions and alterations must meet which code plus local amendments?

    a. 1997 *Uniform Building Code*

    b. 2000 *International Building Code*

    c. The edition of the *International Building Code* adopted at the time of construction

    d. The currently adopted edition of the *International Building Code*

Reference_____

28. A state amendment to the building code allows a day care run in a facility that is primarily a residence to have up to seven children in the day care. The IBC limits the number of children to five or fewer. If there are six children in the day care, should the day care be classified as an educational occupancy?

    a. Yes, the number of children is greater than the number allowed in the IBC for a non-educational occupancy.

    b. No, the structure is classified as a business occupancy.

    c. No, the state amendment overrides the IBC; the structure remains a residential occupancy

    d. No, answers b and c apply.

    Reference_____

29. When a building is deemed a substantial improvement by the building official in a flood hazard region, the structure must meet the requirements of _____.

    a. Section 1612 of the currently adopted IBC

    b. Section 1612 of the code adopted at the time of the original construction

    c. 25 percent of the loads of Section 1612 of the currently adopted IBC

    d. 50 percent of the loads of Section 1612 of the code adopted at the time of the original construction

    Reference_____

30. The fire marshal reviews a school's fire alarm system and hazardous materials storage in the science closet. The school does not meet the current fire requirements. According to the *International Building Code*, does the school need to meet all currently adopted building and fire provisions?

    a. No, the *International Building Code* does not require the school to meet adopted provisions of the building and fire codes at the time of the fire marshal's inspection.

    b. No, the school must meet provisions of the fire and building codes adopted when the school was built.

    c. Yes, the school must meet all the requirements within the adopted codes at the time of the fire marshal's visit.

    d. It depends; the school does not need to meet requirements in the current edition of the building code or fire code unless a specific provision requires existing construction to meet a specific requirement.

    Reference_____

Study Session

5

2018 IBC Sections 105 and 107
Scope and Administration

OBJECTIVE: To develop an understanding of the administration provisions of the *International Building Code* relating to the issuance of permits, permit exemptions, expiration of permits and submission of construction documents.

REFERENCE: Sections 105 and 107, 2018 *International Building Code*

KEY POINTS:
- When is a permit required? What types of work are exempted from permits?
- What is an annual permit? Under what conditions can an annual permit be issued?
- Is work that is exempted from a permit required to comply with the provisions of the code?
- Are repairs exempted from permits? What about emergency repairs?
- What process is outlined for obtaining a permit?
- What information is required on the permit application?
- What conditions or circumstances might bring the validity of the permit into question?
- When does a permit expire? What must occur when a permit expires before completion? What is the time limitation of an application for permit?
- What circumstances can cause a permit to be suspended or revoked?
- Where should a building permit be posted?
- When are construction documents required?
- What information is required on the construction documents? What should the site plan entail?
- When must plans be prepared by a registered design professional? Under what conditions is such an individual required?
- How shall an approved set of construction documents be identified?
- How many sets of construction documents must be submitted to the building department?
- Can permits be issued in phases?

KEY POINTS (Cont'd):
- Can approved construction documents be amended?
- Who is a "design professional in responsible charge"? What are their duties and responsibilities? What is their role in dealing with deferred submittals?
- How long must approved construction documents be retained by the Department of Building Safety?

Topic: Required Permits
Reference: IBC 105.1, 105.2
Category: Scope and Administration
Subject: Permits

Code Text: *Any owner or owner's authorized agent who intends to construct, enlarge, alter, repair, move, demolish or change the occupancy of a building or structure . . . shall first make application to the building official and obtain the required permit. Exemptions from permit requirements of this code shall not be deemed to grant authorization for any work to be done in any manner in violation of the provisions of this code or any other laws or ordinances of this jurisdiction.* See the thirteen exceptions where a building permit is not required.

Discussion and Commentary: Except in those few cases specifically listed in the code, such as small accessory structures and finish work, all construction-related work requires a permit and is subject to subsequent inspections. Emergency repairs may be performed, but the permit application shall be submitted for processing within the next business day. Some ordinary repairs to structures are also exempted with certain stipulations.

Whether or not a building permit is required by the code, all work must be done in accordance with the code requirements. The owner is responsible for all construction being done properly and safely.

Study Session 5

Topic: Annual Permit
Reference: IBC 105.1.1

Category: Scope and Administration
Subject: Permits

Code Text: *Instead of an individual permit for each alteration to an already approved electrical, gas, mechanical or plumbing installation, the building official is authorized to issue an annual permit upon application therefor to any person, firm or corporation regularly employing one or more qualified tradepersons in the building, structure or on the premises owned or operated by the applicant for the permit.*

Discussion and Commentary: Typically, a permit is required each time a distinct code-related activity occurs. However, when acceptable to the building official, certain alterations to specific, previously approved systems can be performed by qualified trades persons when they are employed by the permit applicant. The permit applicant must also keep detailed records that are accessible to the building official at all times. An annual permit is especially useful for large factory, industrial or commercial buildings where minor changes such as adding a few outlets, lighting fixtures or minor mechanical or plumbing revisions are routine.

The allowance for annual permits simplifies the permit application procedure; however, it only applies to specific systems and does not include structural alterations, fire protection work, means of egress modifications or the addition of floor area.

Topic: Application for Permit
Reference: IBC 105.3
Category: Scope and Administration
Subject: Permits

Code Text: *To obtain a permit, the applicant shall first file an application therefor in writing on a form furnished by the department of building safety for that purpose.*

Discussion and Commentary: Before the permit process can begin, one must submit a completed, signed permit application to the Building Safety Department. The IBC identifies seven important items that must be included on the application. The application for permit is the first of many procedural requirements for work regulated by the IBC.

An application for permit shall

1. Identify and describe the work to be covered by the permit for which the application is made.
2. Describe the land by address or legal description on which the proposed work is to be done.
3. Indicate the use and occupancy for which the proposed work is intended.
4. Be accompanied by construction documents and other information as required in Section 107.
5. State the valuation of the proposed work.
6. Be signed by the applicant or the applicant's authorized agent.
7. Give such other data and information as required by the building official.

The permit application is extremely important, as it identifies many aspects of the proposed project, including what is going to be constructed, where the project will be located and its estimated value. Because it is a legal document, the permit application must be signed by the applicant or applicant's authorized agent.

Study Session 5

Topic: Action on Permit Application
Reference: IBC 105.3.1
Category: Scope and Administration
Subject: Permits

Code Text: *The building official shall examine or cause to be examined applications for permits and amendments thereto within a reasonable time after filing. If the application or the construction documents do not conform to the requirements of pertinent laws, the building official shall reject such application in writing, stating the reasons therefor. If the building official is satisfied that the proposed work conforms to the requirements of this code and laws and ordinances applicable thereto, the building official shall issue a permit therefor as soon as practicable.*

Discussion and Commentary: It is important that the application for permit be examined in an expedient manner. Failure to do so will reflect negatively on the building department, possibly resulting in legal action if substantial harm is caused that is due to an unnecessary delay. If it is determined that the submittal documents do not conform to the code, a written report of the deficiencies must be provided.

Once the building official determines that the work described conforms with the code and other applicable laws, the permit must be issued upon the payment of any required fees.

Topic: Time Limitation of Application
Reference: IBC 105.3.2
Category: Scope and Administration
Subject: Permits

Code Text: *An application for a permit for any proposed work shall be deemed to have been abandoned 180 days after the date of filing, unless such application has been pursued in good faith or a permit has been issued; except that the building official is authorized to grant one or more extensions of time for additional periods not exceeding 90 days each. The extension shall be requested in writing and justifiable cause demonstrated.*

Discussion and Commentary: Once an application has been submitted, the applicant has 180 days to pick up that permit or it will be considered abandoned, unless the delay was not the fault of the applicant or where the applicant has been diligently pursuing permit issuance. The applicant needs to sufficiently demonstrate compliance, usually in writing. Where the applicant can show a justifiable cause why the application has not been pursued, the building official is authorized, but not compelled, to grant one or more 90-day extension. Section 105.3.1 essentially mandates the building official to issue a permit as soon as practicable, when it is shown that all proposed work conforms to the code and all other applicable laws.

January

Su	Mo	Tu	We	Th	Fr	Sa
1	2	3	4	5	6	7
8	9	10	11	12	13	14
15	16	17	18	19	20	21
22	23	24	25	26	27	28
29	30	31				

February

Su	Mo	Tu	We	Th	Fr	Sa
			1	2	3	4
5	6	7	8	9	10	11
12	13	14	15	16	17	18
19	20	21	22	23	24	25
26	27	28				

March

Su	Mo	Tu	We	Th	Fr	Sa
			1	2	3	4
5	6	7	8	9	10	11
12	13	14	15	16	17	18
19	20	21	22	23	24	25
26	27	28	29	30	31	

April

Su	Mo	Tu	We	Th	Fr	Sa
						1
2	3	4	5	6	7	8
9	10	11	12	13	14	15
16	17	18	19	20	21	22
23	24	25	26	27	28	29
30						

May

Su	Mo	Tu	We	Th	Fr	Sa
	1	2	3	4	5	6
7	8	9	10	11	12	13
14	15	16	17	18	19	20
21	22	23	24	25	26	27
28	29	30	31			

June

Su	Mo	Tu	We	Th	Fr	Sa
				1	2	3
4	5	6	7	8	9	10
11	12	13	14	15	16	17
18	19	20	21	22	23	24
25	26	27	28	29	30	

Date Permit Was Applied For + 180 Days = Abandoned (Or Must Request a 90-day Extension)

The terms *pursued in good faith* and *justifiable cause* elude strict definitions. Therefore, the building official has the challenge of determining, on a case-by-case basis, when an application for permit should be extended or terminated.

Topic: Validity of Permit
Reference: IBC 105.4

Category: Scope and Administration
Subject: Permits

Code Text: *The issuance or granting of a permit shall not be construed to be a permit for, or an approval of, any violation of any of the provisions of this code or of any other ordinance of the jurisdiction. Permits presuming to give authority to violate or cancel the provisions of this code or other ordinances of the jurisdiction shall not be valid. The issuance of a permit based on construction documents and other data shall not prevent the building official from requiring the correction of errors in the construction documents and other data. The building official is authorized to prevent occupancy or use of a structure where in violation of this code or of any other ordinances of this jurisdiction.*

Discussion and Commentary: The code intends that the issuance of a permit shall not be construed as permitting work to be done in violation of the code or any other laws or ordinances. Therefore, the building official is authorized to invalidate the permit when it was issued in error or if approval was based on incorrect, inaccurate or falsified information. This should be done carefully and accurately, as there can be legal ramifications to stopping or slowing work on projects that have an open permit.

UNDER PENALTY OF INTENTIONAL MISREPRESENTATION AND/OR PERJURY, I DECLARE that I have examined and/or made this application and it is true and correct to the best of my knowledge and belief. I agree to construct said improvement in compliance with all provisions of the Ordinances of the City of . . . I realize that the information that I have stated heron forms a basis for the issuance of the Building Permit herein applied for and approval of any plans in connection therewith shall not be construed to permit any construction upon said premises or use thereof in violation of any provision of the City Code or any other ordinance or to excuse the owner or his successors in from complying therewith. **WHERE NO WORK HAS BEEN STARTED WITHIN 180 DAYS AFTER THE ISSUANCE OF A PERMIT OR WHEN MORE THAN 180 DAYS LAPSES BETWEEN APPROVAL OF REQUIRED INSPECTIONS, SUCH PERMIT SHALL BE VOID.**

I hereby certify that I am the OWNER at this address or that, for the purposes of obtaining this approval, I am acting on behalf of the owner. All contract work on this project will be done by a contractor holding a valid privilege tax license and contractor's license issued by the State of . . . and the City of . . .

The building official should require modifications to the permit application or construction documents to correct any errors that are identified.

Topic: Expiration
Reference: IBC 105.5

Category: Scope and Administration
Subject: Permits

Code Text: *Every permit issued shall become invalid unless the work on the site authorized by such permit is commenced within 180 days after its issuance, or if the work authorized on the site by such permit is suspended or abandoned for a period of 180 days after the time the work is commenced. The building official is authorized to grant, in writing, one or more extensions of time, for periods not more than 180 days each. The extension shall be requested in writing and justifiable cause demonstrated.*

Discussion and Commentary: The code intends that, once a permit is issued, the work should begin and proceed within a reasonable time that is typical for construction projects, or the permit will become invalid. Where extenuating circumstances may occur, the building official is authorized, but not obligated, to grant one or more 180-day time extensions, in writing, where justifiable cause can be demonstrated. Once a permit has expired, additional fees may be required to reinstate or renew the permit. There are several reasons why the building official may not grant extensions. One reason is economical. Fees are paid to support a service at today's costs. Another reason is that codes change, and new construction must comply with current codes. If a project is not built until years after approval, it is unlikely to meet the most current regulations.

Date Permit Was Issued + 180 Days = Invalid

(Or Must Request a 180-day Extension)

OR

Date Work Was Abandoned + 180 Days = Invalid

(Or Must Request a 180-day Extension)

The terms *suspended* and *abandoned* and *justifiable cause* do not have strict definitions and therefore must be established, usually on a case-by-case basis, by the building official.

Study Session 5

Topic: General Provisions
Reference: IBC 107.1
Category: Scope and Administration
Subject: Submittal Documents

Code Text: *Submittal documents consisting of construction documents, statement of special inspections, geotechnical report and other data shall be submitted in two or more sets with each permit application. The construction documents shall be prepared by a registered design professional where required by the statutes of the jurisdiction in which the project is to be constructed. Where special conditions exist, the building official is authorized to require additional construction documents to be prepared by a registered design professional. (See the exception authorizing the building official to waive the submission of construction documents based on the limited extent of the work proposed.)*

Discussion and Commentary For an application for a permit to be properly processed, certain detailed construction documents must be submitted for review to determine compliance with all applicable codes and laws. When required by statute, these documents shall be prepared by a registered design professional, such as an architect or engineer.

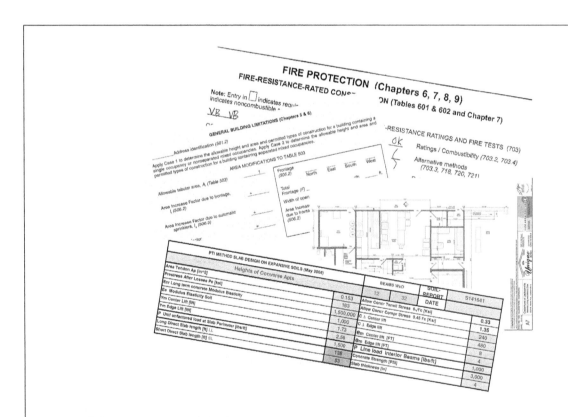

The building official has the authority to waive the submission of construction documents if the nature of the project does not necessitate the review of such documents to determine code compliance and such documents are not required to be prepared by a registered design professional.

Topic: Information on Construction Documents **Category:** Scope and Administration
Reference: IBC 107.2.1 **Subject:** Submittal Documents

Code Text: *Construction documents shall be dimensioned and drawn upon suitable material. Electronic media documents are permitted to be submitted where approved by the building official. Construction documents shall be of sufficient clarity to indicate the location, nature and extent of the work proposed and show in detail that it will conform to the provisions of this code and relevant laws, ordinances, rules and regulations, as determined by the building official.*

Discussion and Commentary: Submittal documents may include, but are not limited to, construction drawings, structural calculations, soils reports, fire protection system plans, details of special equipment, means of egress plans, hazardous materials identification, site plans, grading and drainage plans and other civil engineering drawings.

Please check the type of plans submitted for review. (Check all that apply.)
NOTE! No plans will be accepted for review until all appropriate information is submitted.

TYPE OF PLANS	NUMBER OF SETS	
	Single Family Residential	All Others
__ Sign Plans	0	2
__ Pool/Spa Plans	2	2
__ Approved Site Plan	1	3
__ Architectural Plans	1	3
__ Structural Plans	1	3
__ Structural Calculations	*	2
__ Soils Report	*	1
__ Specifications	0	2
__ Plumbing	1	3
__ Electrical	1	3
__ Mechanical	1	3
__ Truss Specifications	1	2

__ Retaining Walls Over 4' in Height Require a Separate Permit. Drawings to
Have an Engineer's Seal.   2   2

__ **For Engineering Permits Please Call Engineering Department**

__ Construction Fire Safety (access/water supply)	*Noted on construction documents*	
__ Building Construction Plans (with Fire Submittal)		1
__ Fire Sprinkler Construction Plans	**	3
__ Fire Sprinkler Shop Drawings	**	3
__ Fire Alarm/Monitoring Systems (ANSI 117.1)	0	3
__ Exhaust Hood/extinguishing system details	0	3
__ Spray Booth/extinguishing system details	0	3
__ Liquid Petroleum Gas Installation	2	3
__ Process Piping Plans	0	3
__ Hazardous Materials Inventory/Report	0	3
__ Flammable/Combustible Liquid Tanks	0	3
__ Fire Department Key Box Locations *Must be noted on construction documents*		
__ Other _____		

General statements on construction documents, such as "all work shall comply with the *International Building Code*," are not an acceptable substitute for providing the required information.

Topic: Site Plan
Reference: IBC 107.2.6
Category: Administration
Subject: Submittal Documents

Code Text: *The construction documents submitted with the application for permit shall be accompanied by a site plan . . . and it shall be drawn in accordance with an accurate boundary line survey . . . The building official is authorized to waive or modify the requirement for a site plan where the application for permit is for alteration or repair or where otherwise warranted.*

Discussion and Commentary: Most zoning laws address to some detail the location of buildings and structures on a lot; for example, building setbacks are often mandated. In addition, a number of building code provisions focus on a building's relationship to the site, both in terms of open space surrounding a building and the topography of the lot. Such issues include exterior wall and opening protection, allowable area increases, unlimited area buildings, the location of exterior stairways and balconies, as well as accessible routes of travel for individuals with physical disabilities.

---

2. <u>SITE PLANS</u> (To be attached to Building Plans)

Three sets of City "Approved" site plans to scale (24" x 36" minimum, with the City Planning Division's "Approved" stamp), showing all setbacks, parking layout, existing and proposed structures, lot and building dimensions, easements, storage tanks (above and below ground, if any), signs, lighting layouts, fire hydrants, adjacent street names and North arrow. Please note that signs, storage tanks, some retaining walls, etc., will require separate permits.

When a building is to be demolished, a permit is required and a site plan must be submitted. The site plan must indicate the construction to be demolished, as well as the size and location of other existing structures that will remain on the lot.

Topic: Approval of Construction Documents
Reference: IBC 107.3.1
Category: Scope and Administration
Subject: Submittal Documents

Code Text: *When the building official issues a permit, the construction documents shall be approved, in writing or by stamp, as "Reviewed for Code Compliance." One set of construction documents so reviewed shall be retained by the building official. The other set shall be returned to the applicant, shall be kept at the site of work and shall be open to inspection by the building official or a duly authorized representative.*

Discussion and Commentary: As a part of the permit process, the submittal documents are to be reviewed and approved. Once the approval is granted, the construction documents must, in some manner, be identified as to this fact. One set of approved construction documents shall be kept on the construction site to serve as the basis for all subsequent inspections. In addition, the contractor cannot determine compliance with the approved plans unless they are readily available.

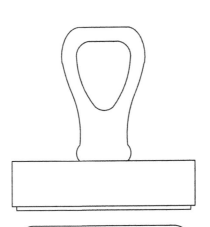

At least one set of approved construction documents shall be maintained by the building department for their use. This will allow department personnel to review the documents should any questions arise during the course of the construction project.

Study Session 5

Topic: Phased Approval
Reference: IBC 107.3.3
Category: Scope and Administration
Subject: Submittal Documents

Code Text: *The building official is authorized to issue a permit for the construction of foundations or any other part of a building or structure before the construction documents for the whole building or structure have been submitted, provided that adequate information and detailed statements have been filed complying with the pertinent requirements of this code. The holder of such permit for the foundation or other parts of a building or structure shall proceed at the holder's own risk with the building operation and without assurance that a permit for the entire structure will be granted.*

Discussion and Commentary: In many instances, major projects may be designed in phases and necessitate that several permits be issued in order for the work to proceed on schedule without waiting for the entire set of plans to be completed and submitted. As long as the building official is satisfied that certain portions can be issued in scheduled phases, the code authorizes this process to occur.

The permit holder is not guaranteed that the remainder of the permit for the entire structure will be issued and should be advised that work can proceed only at the holder's own risk.

Topic: Design Professional in Charge
Reference: IBC 107.3.4
Category: Scope and Administration
Subject: Submittal Documents

Code Text: *Where it is required that documents be prepared by a registered design professional, the building official shall be authorized to require the owner or the owner's authorized agent to engage and designate on the building permit application a registered design professional in responsible charge.*

Discussion and Commentary: The function of the design professional in responsible charge is to review and coordinate submittal documents prepared by others and, if necessary, coordinate any phased or deferred submittal items.

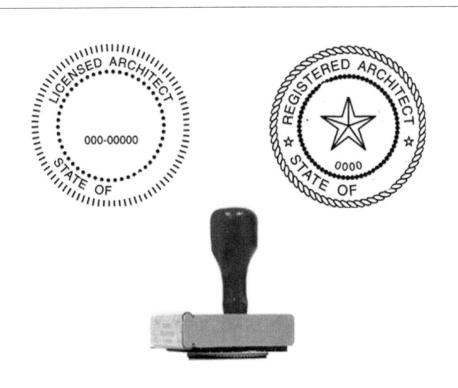

In some cases, the design of some portions of the building are not complete and may be dependent on the manufacture of proposed prefabricated elements. Therefore, the code specifically allows deferring the submittal of portions of plans and specifications. Roof truss drawings are a good example of a deferred submittal.

Study Session 5

Topic: Amended Construction Documents
Reference: IBC 107.4

Category: Scope and Administration
Subject: Submittal Documents

Code Text: *Work shall be installed in accordance with the approved construction documents, and any changes made during construction that are not in compliance with the approved construction documents shall be resubmitted for approval as an amended set of construction documents.*

Discussion and Commentary: Once the building official approves a set of construction drawings or other construction documents, they must remain unchanged except for any revisions that are submitted for review and approval. Typically, these changes must be prepared under the direction of the design professional in responsible charge.

Many times, actual field conditions dictate that plans be modified somewhat from the original design. Sometimes the changes are minor in nature, such as moving a window several inches to avoid a structural column, and can be reviewed by the building inspector on the job site. The building official should establish a policy that guides inspectors when such changes occur.

Topic: Retention of Construction Documents **Category:** Scope and Administration
Reference: IBC 107.5 **Subject:** Submittal Documents

Code Text: *One set of approved construction documents shall be retained by the building official for a period of not less than 180 days from date of completion of the permitted work, or as required by state or local laws.*

Discussion and Commentary: Approved construction documents must be retained for a certain period of time in case they are needed for referral. However, many states have certain retention schedules that supersede the code unless permission is granted from state authorities. The state or other authority may also dictate what retention method is acceptable if documents are to be retained longer than the 180 days established by the IBC.

Usually, the Clerk's Office of the jurisdiction should be consulted to determine which documents must be retained and for how long they must be retained. The approved method of retention (hard copies, microfilm, electronic storage, etc.) should also be determined.

Study Session 5

Study Session 5
IBC Sections 105 and 107

1. An application for permit shall be considered abandoned _____ days after filing, unless the application has been pursued in good faith or a permit has been issued.

    a. 60
    b. 90
    c. 180
    d. 365

    Reference _____

2. Which one of the following types of work is specifically allowed to be covered under an annual permit?

    a. nonstructural alterations
    b. alteration to an already approved mechanical installation
    c. relocation of interior walls or partitions
    d. expansion of automatic fire sprinkler system

    Reference _____

3. If no work is commenced on an approved permit, it shall expire after _____ days.

    a. 90
    b. 120
    c. 180
    d. 365

    Reference _____

4. Which of the following types of work does not require a building permit?

    a. driveway located 4 feet above adjacent grade
    b. 7-foot-high solid masonry fence
    c. 3-foot-high retaining wall supporting a surcharge
    d. 180-square-foot one-story detached accessory building

    Reference _____

5. The _____ shall keep a detailed record of alterations made under an annual permit?

   a. fire marshal
   b. municipal clerk
   c. building official
   d. permit holder

   Reference _____

6. According to the *International Building Code*, "approved" means acceptable to the _____.

   a. project owner
   b. building official
   c. testing laboratory
   d. design professional in responsible charge

   Reference _____

7. An application for a permit that exceeds the time limit from the date of filing may be extended for maximum periods of _____ days when authorized by the building official.

   a. 60
   b. 90
   c. 180
   d. 365

   Reference _____

8. The maximum allowed area for an accessory storage structure that does not require a permit is _____ square feet.

   a. 100
   b. 120
   c. 150
   d. 200

   Reference _____

9. A permit is not required for _____.

   a. connection of approved portable electrical equipment
   b. alteration of a means of egress element
   c. replacement of a section of plumbing vent piping
   d. cutting a doorway in a wall or partition

   Reference _____

10. Which of the following is not specifically required on the application for permit?

    a. intended use or occupancy

    b. valuation of the work

    c. general contractor of record

    d. description of the work to be performed

    Reference _____

11. Which of the following conditions is not specified in the code as a reason to revoke or suspend a permit?

    a. The contractor's license was suspended.

    b. The permit was issued in error.

    c. The permit was based on incomplete information.

    d. The permit was issued in violation of a municipal ordinance.

    Reference _____

12. In the submission of construction documents, which of the following is not specifically required by the code to be included on the site plan?

    a. distances from lot lines

    b. proposed finish grades

    c. location of existing structures

    d. roof height of new construction

    Reference _____

13. The building official is responsible for examining applications for permits within _____ after filing.

    a. 15 calendar days   b. 30 business days

    c. a reasonable time   d. a department-established time

    Reference _____

14. Changes made during construction that are not in compliance with the approved construction documents shall be _____.

    a. approved by the inspector in the field
    b. denied and a stop work order posted on the job site
    c. permitted by sole approval of the design professional in responsible charge
    d. resubmitted for approval as an amended set of construction documents

    Reference _____

15. Deferral of any submittal items shall have prior approval of the _____.

    a. project owner
    b. building official
    c. inspector assigned to the project
    d. design professional in responsible charge

    Reference _____

16. When repairs must be performed in an emergency situation, the permit application shall be submitted to the building official within _____.

    a. 24 hours
    b. 7 business days
    c. the next working business day
    d. the same week as the repairs occurred

    Reference _____

17. When construction documents are approved in the issuance of a permit, the documents shall be identified, in writing or by stamp, as _____.

    a. APPROVED AS SUBMITTED
    b. ACCEPTED AND REVIEWED
    c. APPROVED SUBJECT TO FIELD COMPLIANCE
    d. REVIEWED FOR CODE COMPLIANCE

    Reference _____

18. The registered design professional in responsible charge shall be responsible for _____.

    a. requesting all inspections
    b. scheduling all work on the project
    c. verifying code compliance of the applicable design elements
    d. reviewing submittal documents prepared by others

    Reference_____

19. Which of the following requires a permit?

    a. portable heating appliance
    b. portable cooling appliance
    c. replacing a section of leaking plumbing pipe
    d. clearing of a major stoppage in an underground sewer pipe

    Reference_____

20. Which one of the following sequence of events is correct?

    a. receipt of permit application; review of construction documents; issue of permit
    b. inspection of construction; receipt of appeal; issuance of violation notice
    c. review of site plan; denial of permit; issuance of certificate of occupancy
    d. receipt of construction documents; issuance of certificate of occupancy; approval of permit

    Reference_____

21. The building official is authorized to waive the submission of construction documents if the _____.

    a. work will be inspected as required by the code
    b. contractor has previously done work in the jurisdiction
    c. review of construction documents is not necessary to obtain code compliance
    d. design professional in responsible charge signs an affidavit of compliance

    Reference_____

22. Fire protection system shop drawings shall be _____.

    a. prepared by a design professional
    b. submitted to the fire department upon completion of system installation
    c. approved prior to the start of system installation
    d. under the control of the fire protection system installer

    Reference_____

23. The building permit or a copy shall be _____.

    a. visible from the street
    b. kept on the site of the work
    c. posted with the inspection record
    d. made available to the inspector

    Reference_____

24. For an above-ground prefabricated swimming pool accessory to a Group R-3 dwelling to be exempt from the permit requirements, the code limits the pool to a water depth less than _____ inches and a capacity not greater than _____ gallons.

    a. 30; 4,000   b. 18; 6,000
    c. 18; 5,000   d. 24; 5,000

    Reference_____

25. Unless state or local law mandates a different time period, at least one set of approved construction documents shall be retained by the building official for at least _____ days after completion of the permitted work.

    a. 30
    b. 90
    c. 180
    d. 120

    Reference_____

Study Session 5

Study Session 6

2018 IBC Sections 108 through 116
Scope and Administration

OBJECTIVE: To develop an understanding of the administrative provisions of the *International Building Code,* addressing temporary structures, permit fees, inspection procedures, certificate of occupancy, board of appeals, existing buildings and unsafe structures.

REFERENCE: Sections 108 through 116, 2018 *International Building Code*

KEY POINTS:
- What is the time limit for use of a temporary structure?
- How are temporary structures addressed? To what levels of conformance must they comply?
- What fees are set forth in the code? How are fees determined?
- How are permit valuations determined? Who establishes the final valuation?
- What should occur when work is started without a valid permit?
- For what period of time must work remain exposed and accessible for inspection purposes? How are violations not identified during an inspection to be addressed?
- What types of inspections are specifically required by the code? When are such inspections required?
- Who is required to notify the building official when work is ready for an inspection?
- When is a certificate of occupancy required? For what reasons is revocation permitted?
- What information must be provided on the certificate of occupancy?
- When may a temporary certificate of occupancy be issued?
- Under what authority may service utilities be connected or disconnected?
- What is the purpose of the board of appeals? Who is eligible to serve on the board?
- What limitations are placed on the authority of the board of appeals?
- Under what conditions should a notice of violation be issued?
- When should a stop work order be issued?

KEY POINTS (Cont'd):
- What are the consequences of continuing work after issuance of a stop work order?
- How are unsafe structures addressed?

Topic: General Provisions
Reference: IBC 108.1

Category: Scope and Administration
Subject: Temporary Structures and Uses

Code Text: *The building official is authorized to issue a permit for temporary structures and temporary uses. Such permits shall be limited as to time of service, but shall not be permitted for more than 180 days. The building official is authorized to grant extensions for demonstrated cause.*

Discussion and Commentary: Temporary structures, like permanent structures, must conform to the code requirements for structural strength, fire safety, means of egress, accessibility, light, ventilation and sanitary requirements. Authority is granted to the building official to terminate the permit for a temporary structure and order its use to be discontinued.

Additional requirements for temporary structures are found in IBC Section 3103. For example, tents and other membrane structures erected for a period less than 180 days must also comply with the applicable provisions of the *International Fire Code*.

Study Session 6

Topic: Payment of Fees
Reference: IBC 109.1
Category: Scope and Administration
Subject: Fees

Code Text: *A permit shall not be valid until the fees prescribed by law have been paid, nor shall an amendment to a permit be released until the additional fee, if any, has been paid.*

Discussion and Commentary: The Department of Building Safety must establish a fee schedule to allow for fees to be charged to cover necessary costs involved in its operation, including overhead. Many permit fees are based on the proposed project's valuation, which is required to be submitted by the applicant; however, the final valuation is determined by the building official. Other related fees should be established to cover work commencing before the permit is issued, repeat inspections, plan review and any additional work involved in the permit or inspection process.

SAMPLE FEE SCHEDULE

TOTAL VALUATION	FEE
$1.00 to $500.00	$34.00
$501.00 to $2,000.00	$34.00 for the first $500.00 plus $5.00 for each additional $100.00 or fraction thereof, to and including $2,000.00.
$2,001.00 to $25,000.00	$98.00 for the first $2,000.00 plus $19.00 for each additional $1,000.00 or fraction thereof, to and including $25,000.00.
$25,001.00 to $50,000.00	$554.00 for the first $25,000.00 plus $14.00 for each additional $1,000.00 or fraction thereof, to and including $50,000.00.
$50,001.00 to $100,000.00	$912.00 for the first $50,000.00 plus $10.00 for each additional $1,000.00 or fraction thereof, to and including $100,000.00.
$100,001 to $500,000.00	$1408.00 for the first $100,000.00 plus $8.00 for each additional $1,000.00 or fraction thereof, to and including $500,000.00.
$500,001.00 to $1,000,000.00	$4579.00 for the first $500,000 plus $7.00 for each additional $1,000.00 or fraction thereof, to and including $1,000,000.00.
$1,000,001.00 and up	$7042.00 for the first $1,000,000.00 plus $5.00 for each $1,000.00 or fraction thereof.

The IBC authorizes, but does not compel, the building official to establish a refund policy. Refunds for building permits should only be issued for good cause based upon a consistent equitable policy for all permit holders.

Topic: Schedule of Permit Fees	Category: Scope and Administration
Reference: IBC 109.2	Subject: Fees

Code Text: *On buildings, structures, electrical, gas, mechanical, and plumbing systems or alterations requiring a permit, a fee for each permit shall be paid as required, in accordance with the schedule as established by the applicable governing authority.*

Discussion and Commentary: The provisions of the IBC do not provide any guidance for establishing permit fees, such as a fee schedule. Authorization is simply given to the jurisdiction for the establishment and adoption of a schedule of permit fees based upon their individual needs. Many jurisdictions have utilized a standardized method of determining fees for many years and continue with their former schedule of fees by merely updating them to reflect current costs. Permit fees are often calculated based on the cubic feet, square feet or valuation of the building under consideration.

Example: If a jurisdiction establishes that a 2,000-sq ft single-family dwelling is valued at $72 per square foot for the living area and $44 per square foot for the 400-sq ft attached garage, the total valuation, for permit calculation purposes, would be: 2,000 sf x $72 = $144,000 plus 400 sf x $44 = $17,600. $144,000 plus $17,600 = a total valuation of $161,600. In looking at the sample table below, it should be noted that it is a graduated scale based on the total valuation of the project. For a valuation of $161,100 we would first round the valuation up to the nearest $1,000 because the table states "or fraction thereof" and then go to line 6 in the table. Because the rounded valuation would now be $162,000, we would calculate the first $100,000 at a total of $1408. The remaining $62,000 would then be calculated at $8 for each remaining $1,000, which would be $496 (62 x $8). If we total the two numbers together, we would arrive at a permit fee of $1,904 ($1,408 + $496). As another example, a project valued at $500,020 would be rounded to the nearest $1,000, which would be $501,000. Calculations would continue as above, arriving at a permit fee of $4,586

TOTAL VALUATION	FEE
$1.00 to $500.00	$34.00
$501.00 to $2,000.00	$34.00 for the first $500.00 plus $5.00 for each additional $100.00 or fraction thereof, to and including $2,000.00.
$2,001.00 to $25,000.00	$98.00 for the first $2,000.00 plus $19.00 for each additional $1,000.00 or fraction thereof, to and including $25,000.00.
$25,001.00 to $50,000.00	$554.00 for the first $25,000.00 plus $14.00 for each additional $1,000.00 or fraction thereof, to and including $50,000.00.
$50,001.00 to $100,000.00	$912.00 for the first $50,000.00 plus $10.00 for each additional $1,000.00 or fraction thereof, to and including $100,000.00.
$100,001 to $500,000.00	$1408.00 for the first $100,000.00 plus $8.00 for each additional $1,000.00 or fraction thereof, to and including $500,000.00.
$500,001.00 to $1,000,000.00	$4579.00 for the first $500,000 plus $7.00 for each additional $1,000.00 or fraction thereof, to and including $1,000,000.00.
$1,000,001.00 and up	$7042.00 for the first $1,000,000.00 plus $5.00 for each $1,000.00 or fraction thereof.

In the calculation of fees based on most schedules being utilized, it is important to first round the valuation up to the nearest thousand to obtain a consistent determination of the fees to be imposed.

Topic: General Provisions
Reference: IBC 110.1
Category: Scope and Administration
Subject: Inspections

Code Text: *Construction or work for which a permit is required shall be subject to inspection by the building official and such construction or work shall remain visible and able to be accessed for inspection purposes until approved. Approval as a result of an inspection shall not be construed to be an approval of a violation of the provisions of this code or of other ordinances of the jurisdiction. It shall be the duty of the owner or the owner's authorized agent to cause the work to remain visible and able to be accessed for inspection purposes.*

Discussion and Commentary: The inspection function is possibly the most critical activity in the entire code enforcement process. At the varied stages of construction, an inspector often performs the final check of the building for safety-related compliance. It is the responsibility of the holder of the permit or their duly authorized agent to notify the building official when work is ready for inspection and to provide access for all inspections.

Required inspections (where applicable):
- **Footing and foundation**
- **Concrete slab or under-floor**
- **Lowest floor elevation**
- **Frame**
- **Lath or gypsum board**
- **Weather-exposed balcony waterproofing**
- **Fire- and smoke-resistant penetrations**
- **Energy efficiency**
- **Others as required by the building official**
- **Special inspections**
- **Final**

The code requires that certain inspections be conducted where applicable. In the event the portion of the building or structure is covered or otherwise inaccessible, the responsibility rests with the permit applicant to remove the material to make the work available for inspection, with no expense to be borne by the jurisdiction.

Topic: Change of Occupancy
Reference: IBC 111.1

Category: Scope and Administration
Subject: Certificate of Occupancy

Code Text: *A building or structure shall not be used or occupied, and a change of occupancy of a building or structure or portion thereof shall not be made, until the building official has issued a certificate of occupancy therefor as provided herein. Issuance of a certificate of occupancy shall not be construed as an approval of a violation of the provisions of this code or of other ordinances of the jurisdiction.* Note the exception for work exempt from permits under Section 105.2.

Discussion and Commentary: The certificate of occupancy is the tool with which the building official can regulate and control the uses and occupancies of the various buildings and structures within the jurisdiction, and it is unlawful to use or occupy a building unless a certificate of occupancy has been issued for that specific use. The building official is authorized to issue a temporary certificate of occupancy under certain circumstances where the building or portion thereof can be occupied safely before being fully completed.

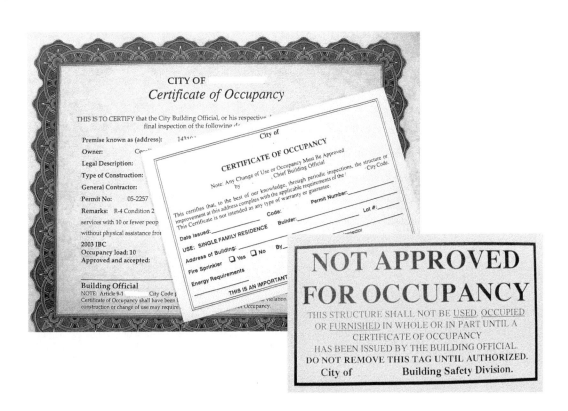

The building official is authorized to suspend or revoke the certificate of occupancy for any of the following reasons: (1) when the certificate is issued in error, (2) when incorrect information is supplied or (3) when the building is in violation of the code.

Study Session 6

Topic: General Provisions
Reference: IBC 113.1

Category: Scope and Administration
Subject: Board of Appeals

Code Text: *In order to hear and decide appeals of orders, decisions or determinations made by the building official relative to the application and interpretation of this code, there shall be and is hereby created a board of appeals.*

Discussion and Commentary: The IBC intends for the board of appeals to have very limited authority. This authority is granted to hear and decide appeals of orders and interpretations of the code. The board shall have no authority to waive specific requirements of the code, only to determine if the intent of the code has been incorrectly interpreted, that the code provision does not apply or that an equally good or better form of construction as that mandated by the code is proposed.

Typically, specific and concise code requirements are not subject to appeal. An appeal may be filed on those provisions that are imprecise or unclear, or where alternative methods may be used to perform equivalent to the code requirements. More detailed information on the qualifications and duties of the board of appeals can be found in Appendix B of the IBC.

Topic: Authority for Issuance
Reference: IBC 115.1
Category: Scope and Administration
Subject: Stop Work Order

Code Text: *Where the building official finds any work regulated by this code being performed in a manner either contrary to the provisions of this code or dangerous or unsafe, the building official is authorized to issue a stop work order.*

Discussion and Commentary: The stop work order, a written notice usually issued only in rare cases, is a tool that enables the building official to temporarily suspend work on a building or structure. It must state the reason or reasons for the work to be suspended as well as the remedy necessary in order for the work to resume.

It is important that the owner of the subject property, their authorized agent or the person doing the work be presented with the stop work order. It is also important that the jurisdiction has a clear and justifiable reason for stopping the work. Only after the terms of the stop work order have been satisfied may work continue.

Study Session 6

Topic: Conditions
Reference: IBC 116.1

Category: Scope and Administration
Subject: Unsafe Structures and Equipment

Code Text: *Structures or existing equipment that are or hereafter become unsafe, insanitary or deficient because of inadequate means of egress facilities, inadequate light and ventilation, or that constitute a fire hazard, or are otherwise dangerous to human life or the public welfare, or that involve illegal or improper occupancy or inadequate maintenance, shall be deemed an unsafe condition.*

Discussion and Commentary: Unsafe buildings and structures are considered public nuisances and require repair or abatement. The abatement procedures are established in this section, including the creation of a report, providing written notice listing the unsafe conditions and remedies necessary, and the method of service required for service of such notice.

Where restoration or repair of the building is desired, the provisions of the *International Existing Building Code* are applicable.

Quiz

Study Session 6
IBC Sections 108 through 116

1. It shall be the duty of the _____ to notify the building official that work is ready for inspection.

    a. owner
    b. contractor
    c. architect of record
    d. permit holder

    Reference _____

2. Who is authorized to revoke a certificate of occupancy?

    a. the fire chief
    b. the city manager
    c. the building official
    d. the board of appeals

    Reference _____

3. Which of the following is not specifically identified as a required inspection under the *International Building Code* (IBC)?

    a. footing
    b. roof covering
    c. under-floor
    d. lath and gypsum board

    Reference _____

4. The building official has the authority to authorize disconnection of utility service to the building _____.

    a. for occupying a building without a certificate of occupancy
    b. for violations related to fire and life safety or structural requirements
    c. to eliminate an immediate hazard to life or property
    d. when temporary connection authorization has expired

    Reference _____

5. In flood hazard areas, documentation of the elevation of the lowest floor shall be submitted to the building official prior to _____.

   a. concrete slab and under-floor inspection

   b. placement of the lowest floor

   c. final inspection

   d. issuance of a certificate of occupancy

   Reference _____

6. The required energy efficiency inspection specifically includes verifying all of the following except _____.

   a. sealing against air leakage

   b. envelope insulation R-values

   c. fenestration U-values

   d. duct system R-values

   Reference _____

7. Gypsum board that is part of a fire-resistance-rated assembly must be inspected prior to _____.

   a. lathing   b. fastening

   c. taping   d. sealing

   Reference _____

8. Final building permit valuation shall be set by the _____.

   a. owner   b. building official

   c. general contractor d. architect or engineer

   Reference _____

9. The code specifically requires temporary structures to conform to the requirements for all of the following except _____.

   a. means of egress   b. fire safety

   c. light and ventilation d. life safety

   Reference _____

10. The members of the board of appeals shall be appointed by the _____.
    a. zoning official
    b. building official
    c. governing body
    d. city, town or county manager
    Reference _____

11. Which of the following information is not required on the certificate of occupancy?
    a. name of the building official
    b. name and address of the owner
    c. name of the architect in responsible charge
    d. code edition under which the permit was issued
    Reference _____

12. Which of the following is not a reason to revoke a certificate of occupancy?
    a. It was issued in error.
    b. It was issued based on incorrect information.
    c. The owner has sold the building to a new owner.
    d. A portion of the building is in violation of the building code.
    Reference _____

13. Which of the following is not required to be completed at the time of a framing inspection?
    a. insulation
    b. fireblocking
    c. roof sheathing
    d. rough electrical
    Reference _____

14. Causing work to remain accessible and exposed for inspection purposes shall be the responsibility of the _____.
    a. contractor
    b. permit applicant
    c. owner
    d. design professional
    Reference _____

15. The building official is authorized to accept the reports of approved inspection agencies, provided they are _____.

    a. qualified and reliable   b. insured
    c. certified   d. listed

    Reference_____

16. A stop work order shall be in writing and given to any of the following individuals except the _____.

    a. owner of the property   b. plans examiner
    c. owner's agent   d. person doing the work

    Reference_____

17. The board of appeals shall have no authority to _____.

    a. adopt rules of procedure
    b. waive code requirements
    c. rule on interpretations of the code
    d. hear appeals of administrative decisions

    Reference_____

18. For building permit purposes, a 2,135-square-foot house has a valuation of $89.00 per square foot, plus $51.00 per square foot for a 450-square-foot attached garage. The permit fee based on the following table would be $_____.

    a. 1,408   b. 1,512
    c. 2,312   d. 2,465

    Reference_____

TOTAL VALUATION	FEE
$1.00 to $500.00	$34.00
$501.00 to $2,000.00	$34.00 for the first $500.00 plus $5.00 for each additional $100.00 or fraction thereof, to and including $2,000.00.
$2001.00 to $25,000.00	$98.00 for the first $2,000.00 plus $19.00 for each additional $1,000.00 or fraction thereof, to and including $25,000.
$25,001.00 to $50,000.00	$554.00 for the first $25,000.00 plus $14.00 for each additional $1,000.00 or fraction thereof, to and including $50,000.
$50,001.00 to $100,000.00	$912.00 for the first $50,000.00 plus $10.00 for each additional $1,000.00 or fraction thereof, to and including $100,000.
$100,001.00 to $500,000.00	$1,408.00 for the first $100,000.00 plus $8.00 for each additional $1,000.00 or fraction thereof, to and including $500,000.
$500,001.00 to $100,000,00.00	$4,579.00 for the first $500,000.00 plus $7.00 for each additional $1,000.00 or fraction thereof, to and including $100,000,000.00.
$100,001.00 and up	$7,042.00 for the first $100,000,000.00 plus $5.00 for each additional $1,000.00 or fraction thereof.

19. A 5,673-square-foot sales building has a valuation of $92.00 per square foot, plus a valuation of $65.00 per square foot for the 620-square-foot attached vehicle service area. The permit fee, based on the previous table, would be $_____.

    a. 4,579   b. 5,014

    c. 5,020   d. 5,202

    Reference_____

20. Unsafe conditions in a structure include _____.

    a. inadequate light and ventilation

    b. a fire hazard

    c. unsanitary conditions

    d. all of the above

    Reference_____

2018 IBC Chapter 3 and Sections 508 and 509
Occupancy Classification

OBJECTIVE: To gain an understanding of the approach to classifying a building based on its intended use and the various methods for addressing buildings with multiple occupancy classifications.

REFERENCE: Chapter 3 and Sections 508 and 509, 2018 *International Building Code*

KEY POINTS:
- What are the ten specific occupancy groups?
- How is a space that is intended to be occupied at different times for different purposes to be addressed?
- How is an occupancy that is not specifically described to be classified?
- Which types of activities are considered assembly uses? What is their general classification?
- How are small assembly uses classified where accessory to a different occupancy?
- What is the classification for restaurants and cafés? Theaters? Churches, conference rooms and libraries? Arenas? Grandstands?
- What is the most common use classified as Group B?
- Group E occupancies describe educational uses for individuals of what age group?
- Which types of day care are considered Group E occupancies?
- Manufacturing operations fall into what occupancy group? How do the two divisions of factory use differ from each other?
- What types of operations or materials cause a use to be considered Group H?
- Which occupancies address explosion hazards? Physical hazards? Health hazards?
- Which characteristics are typical of a Group I occupancy?
- In which institutional occupancies are the occupants considered incapable of self-preservation?
- For which types of institutional uses may the *International Residential Code* be utilized?

KEY POINTS (Cont'd):

- What general type of building is considered a Group M occupancy?
- How are residential occupancies classified?
- What is the key difference between Group R-1 and Group R-2 occupancies?
- What do the storage occupancies have in common with those of the manufacturing uses?
- What is a utility occupancy? How does its classification differ from that of other occupancies?
- What is an incidental use area? How are hazards presented by an incidental use addressed?
- How must such an incidental use area be separated from the remainder of the building?
- When can sprinklers be used as an alternative to fire separations? When is sprinkler protection required?
- Which options are available for addressing multiple occupancies within a building?
- What is an accessory use occupancy? What benefit is derived from such a designation?
- How is a mixed-occupancy building regulated when utilizing the provisions for nonseparated occupancies?
- When is a physical occupancy separation needed? What occupancy must always be isolated from other uses by an occupancy separation?

Topic: Occupancy Classification
Reference: IBC 302.1

Category: Occupancy Classification
Subject: Classification and Use

Code Text: *Structures shall be classified into one or more of the occupancy groups listed ... Where a structure is proposed for a purpose that is not specifically listed in this section, such structure shall be classified in the occupancy it most nearly resembles based on the fire safety and relative hazard.*

Discussion and Commentary: The perils contemplated by the occupancy groupings are divided into two general categories: those related to people and those related to content. People-related hazards include the number and density of the occupants, their age or mobility, and their awareness of surrounding conditions. Content-related hazards include the storage and use of hazardous materials, as well as the presence of large quantities of combustible materials. Some uses may not fit neatly into a specific category. The building official must therefore make the determination as to what occupancy group the use is to be classified as, based on certain criteria.

Assembly
Educational
Hazardous
Mercantile
Storage

Business
Factory
Institutional
Residential
Utility

Proper occupancy classification is critical in making appropriate code determinations throughout a project. In the classification process, the building official must use appropriate judgment in the determination of the potential hazards of an affected occupancy.

Study Session 7

Topic: Assembly Uses
Reference: IBC 303.1
Category: Occupancy Classification
Subject: Group A Occupancies

Code Text: *Assembly Group A occupancy includes, among others, the use of a building or structure, or a portion thereof, for the gathering of persons for purposes such as civic, social or religious functions; recreation, food or drink consumption or awaiting transportation. See exceptions for rooms or spaces used for assembly purposes by less than 50 persons.*

Discussion and Commentary: The conditions related to a typical Group A occupancy suggest a higher level of moderate-hazard use. This often includes sizable numbers of people who are generally mobile and aware of the surrounding conditions. The extremely high occupant density level often present in an assembly occupancy is what distinguishes the Group A from other occupancies.

Group A-1
Motion picture theaters
Performance theaters
Symphony and concert halls

Group A-2
Banquet halls
Casino gaming areas
Night clubs
Restaurants
Taverns

Group A-3
Amusement arcades
Art galleries
Bowling alleys
Community halls
Courtrooms
Dance halls (not including food or drink consumption)
Exhibition halls
Funeral parlors
Greenhouses for the conservation and exhibition of plants that provide public access.
Gymnasiums (without spectator seating)
Indoor swimming pools (without spectator seating)
Indoor tennis courts (without spectator seating)
Lecture halls
Libraries
Museums
Places of religious worship
Pool and billiard parlors
Waiting areas in transportation terminals

Group A-4
Arenas
Skating rinks
Swimming pools
Tennis courts

Group A-5
Amusement park structures
Bleachers
Grandstands
Stadiums

Unique conditions are represented by the classification of Groups A-1, A-2, A-4 and A-5. However, the category Group A-3 includes a variety of broad and diverse assembly uses. It is not uncommon to find high combustible loading in Group A-3 occupancies.

Topic: Business Uses
Reference: IBC 304.1

Category: Occupancy Classification
Subject: Group B Occupancies

Code Text: *Business Group B occupancy includes, among others, the use of a building or structure, or a portion thereof, for office, professional or service-type transactions, including storage of records and accounts.*

Discussion and Commentary: Business occupancies typically have a low to moderate fire load, a moderate density level, and occupants who are usually mobile and have a general awareness of the surrounding conditions. As such, business occupancies are grouped into a classification based upon a relatively moderate fire hazard level. Group B occupancies are not restricted by occupant load, as the number of people in a business use, such as an office, can range from one person to thousands of people.

Group B
Airport traffic control towers
Ambulatory care facilities
Animal hospitals, kennels and pounds
Banks
Barber and beauty shops
Car wash
Civic administration
Clinic, outpatient
Dry cleaning and laundries: pickup, delivery and self service
Educational occupancies for students above the 12th grade
Electronic data processing
Food processing establishments and commercial kitchens ≤ 2,500 square feet
Laboratories: testing and research
Motor vehicle showrooms
Post offices
Print shops
Professional services
Radio and television stations
Telephone exchanges
Training and skill development not in a school or academic program

As is the case for many of the occupancy groups, a review of the building's intended uses is necessary to determine the amount of hazardous materials that may be stored, handled or used. If the amounts exceed a specified quantity, then a Group H classification will be in order.

Topic: Educational Uses
Reference: IBC 305.1, 305.2

Category: Occupancy Classification
Subject: Group E Occupancies

Code Text: *Educational Group E occupancy includes, among others, the use of a building or structure, or a portion thereof, by six or more persons at any one time for educational purposes through the twelfth grade. This group includes buildings and structures or portions thereof occupied by more than five children older than $2^1/_2$ years of age who receive educational, supervision or personal care services for fewer than 24 hours per day.*

Discussion and Commentary: Educational occupancies address classroom uses for students of high school age and younger. Educational facilities limited to use by older students, such as college classrooms, are classified as Group B occupancies. Assembly areas that are accessory to the educational uses are not considered separate assembly occupancies.

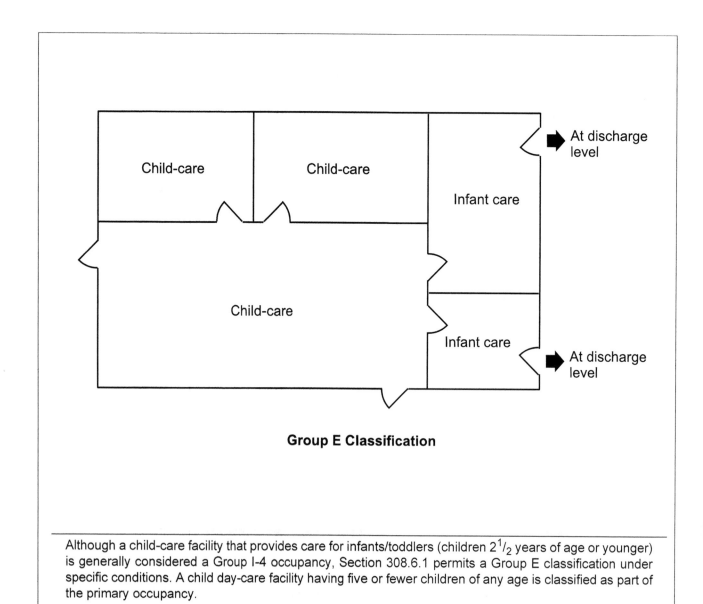

Group E Classification

Although a child-care facility that provides care for infants/toddlers (children $2^1/_2$ years of age or younger) is generally considered a Group I-4 occupancy, Section 308.6.1 permits a Group E classification under specific conditions. A child day-care facility having five or fewer children of any age is classified as part of the primary occupancy.

Topic: Factory Uses	**Category:** Occupancy Classification
Reference: IBC 306.1	**Subject:** Group F Occupancies

Code Text: *Factory Industrial Group F occupancy includes, among others, the use of a building or structure, or portion thereof, for assembling, disassembling, fabricating, finishing, manufacturing, packaging, repair or processing operations that are not classified as a Group H hazardous or Group S storage occupancy.*

Discussion and Commentary: Although the potential hazard and fire severity varies among the many uses categorized as Group F occupancies, the uses still share elements in common. The occupants are adults who are awake and who generally have enough familiarity with the premises to be able to exit the building with reasonable efficiency. The presence of combustible materials in the industrial process causes a classification of Group F-1, which is by far the most common factory use.

Group F-1	Group F-2
Aircraft Appliances Automobiles Athletic equipment Bakeries Beverages with > 16% alcohol Bicycles, boats Business machines Canvas and leather Carpets and rugs Clothing Construction machinery Dry cleaning and dyeing Electric generation plants Electronics Engines Food processing > 2,500 sq ft Furniture Hemp, jute and tobacco Laundries Machinery, metals and millwork Motion pictures Musical instruments Paper mills or products Plastic products Printing or publishing Refuse incineration Soaps and detergents Textiles Trailers Wood distillation Woodworking	Beverages with ≤ 16% alcohol Brick and masonry Ceramic products Foundries Glass products Gypsum Ice Metal products

Classification as a Group F-2 occupancy is limited to the fabrication or manufacturing of noncombustible materials, which during the finishing, packaging or processing operations cannot involve a significant fire hazard.

Topic: High-Hazard Uses
Reference: IBC 307.1
Category: Occupancy Classification
Subject: Group H Occupancies

Code Text: *High-hazard Group H occupancy includes, among others, the use of a building or structure, or portion thereof, that involves the manufacturing, processing, generation or storage of materials that constitute a physical or health hazard in quantities in excess of those allowed in control areas complying with Section 414, based on the maximum allowable quantity limits for control areas set forth in Tables 307.1(1) and 307.1(2). Hazardous occupancies are classified in Groups H-1, H-2, H-3, H-4 and H-5 and shall be in accordance with this section, the requirements of Section 415 and the* International Fire Code. *(See the fourteen listed exemptions for conditions where a Group H classification is not required.)*

Discussion and Commentary: There is only one fundamental type of Group H occupancy—that which is designated based solely on excessive quantities of hazardous material contained therein. The quantities of hazardous materials that necessitate a Group H classification vary, based on the type, quantity, condition (use or storage) and environment of the materials. Where the use does not exceed the maximum allowable quantities set forth in the code, a classification other than the Group H is appropriate. Many mercantile (Group M) occupancies, for example, may contain hazardous products but they are usually in relatively small amounts and distributed around the sales area.

Where Hazardous Materials and Processes Are Involved

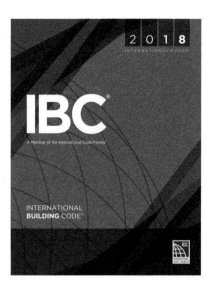

Referenced for Detailed Provisions
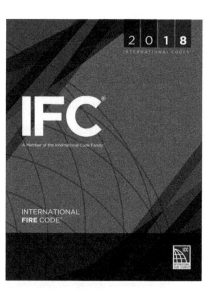

Although the IBC is limited to general construction regulations and occupancy-specific requirements, the *International Fire Code* sets forth special detailed provisions relating to specific materials and the specific conditions of storage, use and handling.

Topic: Institutional Uses
Reference: IBC 308.1

Category: Occupancy Classification
Subject: Group I Occupancies

Code Text: *Institutional Group I occupancy includes, among others, the use of a building or structure, or a portion thereof, in which care or supervision is provided to persons who are or are not capable of self-preservation without physical assistance or in which people are detained for penal or correctional purposes or in which the liberty of the occupants is restricted.*

Discussion and Commentary: The institutional uses classified as Group I occupancies are of three broad types. The first is a facility in which the care is provided for the very young, sick or injured. The second category includes those facilities in which the personal liberties of the inmates or residents are restricted. The primary hazard is people-related. Thirdly, supervised care facilities are regulated. Though the hazard that is due to combustible contents is typically quite low, the occupants' lack of mobility limits their egress ability and defines the primary difference between Group I-1 and Group I-2 occupancies.

Group I-1
- Alcohol and drug centers
- Assisted living facilities
- Congregate care facilities
- Group homes
- Halfway houses
- Residential board and care facilities
- Social rehabilitation facilities

Group I-2
- Foster care facilities
- Detoxification facilities
- Hospitals
- Nursing homes
- Psychiatric hospitals

Group I-3
- Correctional centers
- Detention centers
- Jails
- Prerelease centers
- Prisons
- Reformatories

Group I-4
- Adult day care (> 5 persons)
- Child day care (> 5 children)

Where the number of children, patients or residents in institutional uses is five or fewer, the hazards are similar in nature to a residential use. In most cases, an institutional facility with such a low occupant load would be considered a Group R-3 occupancy. Day care in other than a dwelling unit for five or fewer persons is classified as part of the primary occupancy.

Topic: Mercantile Uses
Reference: IBC 309.1
Category: Occupancy Classification
Subject: Group M Occupancies

Code Text: *Mercantile Group M occupancy includes, among others, the use of a building or structure, or a portion thereof, for the display and sale of merchandise, and involves stocks of goods, wares or merchandise incidental to such purposes and accessible to the public.*

Discussion and Commentary: A Group M occupancy is a retail or wholesale facility, or a store. An entire building can be classified as a Group M occupancy, such as a department store, or a portion of a building can be considered a mercantile use, such as a sales room in a manufacturing facility. A service station, including a canopy over the pump islands, is also classified as a Group M occupancy. In limited instances, a sales operation is designated a Group B occupancy, as in the case of automobile showrooms.

Group M

- Department stores
- Drug stores
- Greenhouses for display and sale of plants that provide public access
- Markets
- Motor fuel-dispensing facilities
- Retail or wholesale stores
- Sales rooms

When classifying the occupancy of a storage area adjacent to the sales area in a retail store, the provisions that address the specific hazards of the use must be applied. A space used for storage that is accessory to the Group M occupancy is classified as part of that occupancy.

Topic: Residential Uses
Reference: IBC 310.1
Category: Occupancy Classification
Subject: Group R Occupancies

Code Text: *Residential Group R occupancy includes, among others, the use of a building or structure, or portion thereof, for sleeping purposes when not classed as an Institutional Group I or when not regulated by the* International Residential Code.

Discussion and Commentary: Residential occupancies are characterized by: (1) their use by people for living and sleeping purposes, (2) a relatively low potential fire severity, and (3) the worst fire record of all use categories. Because occupants of these types of buildings spend up to one-third of each day sleeping, there is a high potential for a fire to rage out of control before the occupants awaken. After awakening, the residents will typically be disoriented for a short period of time, further decreasing the opportunity for immediate egress.

Group R-1

Boarding houses (transient) > 10 occupants

Congregate living facilities (transient) > 10 occupants

Hotels (transient)

Motels (transient)

Group R-2

Apartment houses

Congregate living facilities (nontransient) > 16 occupants
- Boarding houses (nontransient)
- Convents
- Dormitories
- Fraternities and sororities
- Monasteries

Hotels (nontransient)

Live/work units

Motels (nontransient)

Vacation timeshare properties

Group R-3

Buildings ≤ 2 dwelling units

Care facilities: accomodations for ≤ 5 persons

Congregate living facilities (nontransient) ≤ 16 occupants
- Boarding houses (nontransient)
- Convents
- Dormitories
- Fraternities and sororities
- Monasteries

Congregate living facilities (transient) ≤ 10 occupants
- Boarding houses (transient)

Lodging houses (transient) with ≤ 5 guest rooms and ≤ 10 occupants

Group R-4

For 6–16 persons receiving custodial care on a 24-hour basis:

Alcohol and drug centers

Assisted living facilities Congregate care facilities

Group homes

Halfway houses

Residential board and care facilities

Social rehabilitation facilities

Detached one- and two-family dwellings, as well as townhouses, are regulated by the IRC. They are also permitted to be constructed under the IBC.

Study Session 7

Topic: Storage Uses
Reference: IBC 311.1
Category: Occupancy Classification
Subject: Group S Occupancies

Code Text: *Storage Group S occupancy includes, among others, the use of a building or structure, or a portion thereof, for storage that is not classified as a hazardous occupancy.*

Discussion and Commentary: Where a warehouse or other storage facility does not contain significant amounts of hazardous commodities (as determined by Section 307), it should be considered a Group S occupancy. A facility used for the storage of combustible goods is classified as a Group S-1, whereas a Group S-2 occupancy is to be used only for the storage of noncombustible materials.

Group S-1
Aerosol products, Levels 2 and 3
Aircraft hangar (storage and repair)
Bags: cloth, burlap and paper
Bamboos and rattan
Baskets
Belting: canvas and leather
Books and paper in rolls or packs
Boots and shoes
Buttons, including cloth covered, pearl or bone
Cardboard and cardboard boxes
Clothing, woolen wearing apparel
Cordage
Dry boat storage (indoor)
Furniture
Furs
Glues, mucilage, pastes and size
Grains
Horns and combs, other than celluloid Leather
Linoleum
Lumber
Motor vehicle repair garages
Photo engravings
Resilient flooring
Self-service storage facility (mini-storage)
Silks
Soaps
Sugar
Tires, bulk storage of
Tobacco, cigars, cigarettes and snuff
Upholstery and mattresses
Wax candles

Group S-2
Asbestos
Beverages up to and including 16-percent alcohol in metal, glass or ceramic containers
Cement in bags
Chalk and crayons
Dairy products in nonwaxed coated paper containers
Dry cell batteries
Electrical coils
Electrical motors
Empty cans
Food products
Foods in noncombustible containers
Fresh fruits and vegetables in nonplastic trays or containers
Frozen foods
Glass
Glass bottles, empty or filled with noncombustible liquids
Gypsum board
Inert pigments
Ivory
Meats
Metal cabinets
Metal desks with plastic tops and trim
Metal parts
Metals
Mirrors
Oil-filled and other types of distribution transformers
Parking garages, open or enclosed
Porcelain and pottery
Stoves
Talc and soapstones
Washers and dryers

Although the goods being stored in a Group S-2 occupancy must be noncombustible, the code permits a limited amount of combustibles in the packaging or support materials. Wood pallets, paper cartons, paper wrappings, plastic trim and film wrapping are permitted for such purposes.

Topic: Utility Uses
Reference: IBC 312.1
Category: Occupancy Classification
Subject: Group U Occupancies

Code Text: *Buildings and structures of an accessory character and miscellaneous structures not classified in any specific occupancy shall be constructed, equipped and maintained to conform to the requirements of the code commensurate with the fire and life hazard incidental to their occupancy.*

Discussion and Commentary: Those structures not ordinarily occupied by people are classified as Group U occupancies. The fire load in these structures varies considerably but is usually not excessive. Because these types of uses are not normally occupied, the concern for fire severity is not very great, and as a group they constitute a low hazard. Several of the structures regulated as Group U occupancies are never occupied, such as fences, towers, retaining walls and tanks.

Group U
Agricultural buildings
Aircraft hangars, accessory to 1- or 2-family dwelling
Barns
Carports
Communication equipment structures ≤ 1,500 sq ft
Fences > 6 feet in height
Grain silos, accessory to a residential occupancy
Livestock shelters
Private garages
Retaining walls
Sheds
Stables
Tanks
Towers

Private garages and carports classified as Group U occupancies are generally limited to 1,000 square feet and one story in height.

Topic: Methods of Compliance **Category:** Mixed Use and Occupancy
Reference: IBC 508.1 **Subject:** Mixed Occupancies

Code Text: *Each portion of a building shall be individually classified in accordance with Section 302.1. Where a building contains more than one occupancy group, the building or portion thereof shall comply with the applicable provisions of Sections 508.2, 508.3, 508.4 or a combination of these sections. (See the three exceptions.)*

Discussion and Commentary: It is not uncommon for two or more distinct occupancies to occur within a single structure. The code provides that such multiple-occupancy buildings be: 1) in compliance with the provisions for accessory occupancies, or 2) isolated from each other using fire-resistance-rated separation elements (fire barriers and/or horizontal assemblies), or 3) in lieu of a fire separation, regulated by the most restrictive height, area and fire protection provisions for the occupancy groups under consideration.

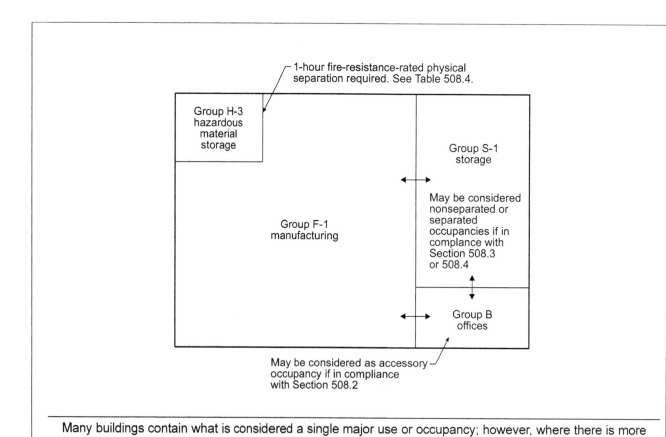

Many buildings contain what is considered a single major use or occupancy; however, where there is more than one distinct occupancy within a building, the building must be viewed as a mixed-occupancy structure and regulated accordingly.

Topic: Accessory Occupancies
Reference: IBC 508.2
Category: Mixed Use and Occupancy
Subject: Mixed Occupancies

Code Text: *Accessory occupancies are those occupancies that are ancillary to the main occupancy of the building or portion thereof. Aggregate accessory occupancies shall not occupy more than 10 percent of the building area of the floor area in which they are located and shall not exceed the tabular values for nonsprinklered buildings in Table 506.2 for each such accessory occupancy. No separation is required between accessory occupancies and the main occupancy.* (See the exceptions.)

Discussion and Commentary: Where two or more occupancies are located within a building, it is assumed that they pose different hazards, and as such, they must be isolated from each other using fire barriers and/or horizontal assemblies. Such walls and floor/ceiling assemblies are fire-resistance-rated elements that completely separate one occupancy from another. This provision acknowledges that an associated occupancy relatively small in floor area poses little added risk. Therefore, no fire-resistance-rated separation is required. Total accessory occupancies in a building continue to be limited to ten percent of the total building area.

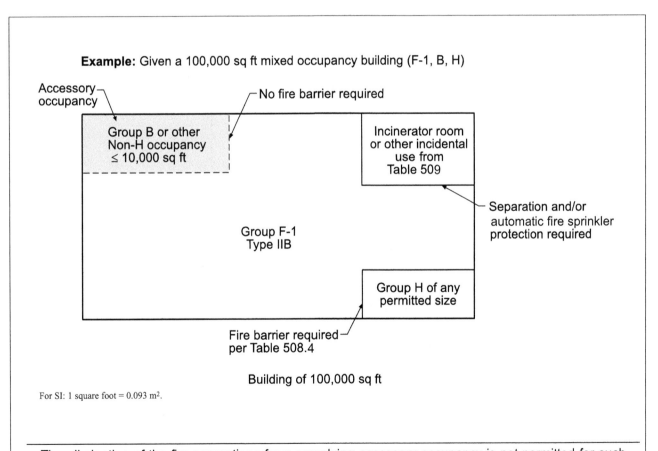

For SI: 1 square foot = 0.093 m².

The elimination of the fire separations for a complying accessory occupancy is not permitted for such areas classified as Group H hazardous occupancies. These types of uses pose unique hazards regardless of size and must be appropriately isolated from the remainder of the building.

Topic: Nonseparated Occupancies
Reference: IBC 508.3
Category: Mixed Use and Occupancy
Subject: Mixed Occupancies

Code Text: *Nonseparated occupancies shall be individually classified in accordance with Section 302.1. The requirements of this code shall apply to each portion of the building based on the occupancy classification of that space. In addition, the most restrictive provisions of Chapter 9 that apply to the nonseparated occupancies shall apply to the total nonseparated occupancy area... The allowable building area, height and number of stories of the building or portion thereof shall be based on the most restrictive allowances for the occupancy groups under consideration for the type of construction of the building in accordance with Section 503.1. No separation is required between nonseparated occupancies. (See the exceptions.)*

Discussion and Commentary: The criteria for nonseparated occupancies provide the designer one of several available options for addressing the relationship of multiple occupancies in the same building. Although no separation is required between the adjacent occupancies, the more restrictive provisions of height, number of stories, area and fire protection for the occupancies are applicable to the entire building.

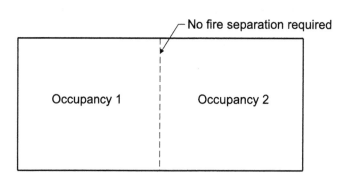

- Type of construction limited by:
    - Lesser height and number of stories limit of Occupancy 1 or 2
    - Lesser floor area limit of Occupancy 1 or 2

- Most restrictive fire-protection system requirements of Occupancy 1 and 2

In addition to the nonseparated occupancies method for eliminating any fire separations between differing occupancies, the code also provides for such elimination under the provisions for accessory occupancies and, to a considerable degree, separated occupancies.

Topic: Separated Occupancies
Reference: IBC 508.4, Table 508.4
Category: Mixed Use and Occupancy
Subject: Mixed Occupancies

Code Text: *Separated occupancies shall be individually classified in accordance with Section 302.1. Each separated space shall comply with this code based on the occupancy classification of that portion of the building. Individual occupancies shall be separated from adjacent occupancies in accordance with Table 508.4. Required separations shall be fire barriers constructed in accordance with Section 707 or horizontal assemblies constructed in accordance with Section 711, or both, so as to completely separate adjacent occupancies.*

Discussion and Commentary: One of the three methods for addressing multiple occupancies in a building includes the physical separation of each occupancy from the others with elements of fire-resistance-rated construction. The level of separation shown in the table typically equates to the dissimilarity of hazards between the two occupancies. Where fire-resistance-separations are required, their required ratings are often reduced in fully-sprinklered buildings.

TABLE 508.4
REQUIRED SEPARATION OF OCCUPANCIES (HOURS)

OCCUPANCY	A, E		I-1[a], I-3, I-4		I-2		R[a]		F-2, S-2[b], U		B[e], F-1, M, S-1		H-1		H-2		H-3, H-4		H-5	
	S	NS	S	NS	S	NS	S	NS	S	NS	S	NS	S	NS	S	NS	S	NS	S	NS
A, E	N	N	1	2	2	NP	1	2	N	1	1	2	NP	NP	3	4	2	3	2	NP
I-1[a], I-3, I-4	—	—	N	N	2	NP	1	NP	1	2	1	2	NP	NP	3	NP	2	NP	2	NP
I-2	—	—	—	—	N	N	2	NP	2	NP	2	NP	NP	NP	3	NP	2	NP	2	NP
R[a]	—	—	—	—	—	—	N	N	1[c]	2[c]	1	2	NP	NP	3	NP	2	NP	2	NP
F-2, S-2[b], U	—	—	—	—	—	—	—	—	N	N	1	2	NP	NP	3	4	2	3	2	NP
B[e], F-1, M, S-1	—	—	—	—	—	—	—	—	—	—	N	N	NP	NP	2	3	1	2	1	NP
H-1	—	—	—	—	—	—	—	—	—	—	—	—	N	NP	NP	NP	NP	NP	NP	NP
H-2	—	—	—	—	—	—	—	—	—	—	—	—	—	—	N	NP	1	NP	1	NP
H-3, H-4	—	—	—	—	—	—	—	—	—	—	—	—	—	—	—	—	1[d]	NP	1	NP
H-5	—	—	—	—	—	—	—	—	—	—	—	—	—	—	—	—	—	—	N	NP

S = Buildings equipped throughout with an automatic sprinkler system installed in accordance with Section 903.3.1.1.
NS = Buildings not equipped throughout with an automatic sprinkler system installed in accordance with Section 903.3.1.1. N = No separation requirement.
NP = Not permitted.
a. See Section 420.
b. The required separation from areas used only for private or pleasure vehicles shall be reduced by 1 hour but not to less than 1 hour.
c. See Section 406.3.2.
d. Separation is not required between occupancies of the same classification.
e. See Section 422.2 for ambulatory care facilities.
f. Occupancy separations that serve to define fire area limits established in Chapter 9 for requiring fire protection systems shall also comply with Section 707.3.10 and Table 707.3.10 in accordance with Section 901.7.

Although it is typical of Table 508.4 to provide for a fire separation between different occupancies, not all occupancy combinations require a separation. For example, no occupancy separation is mandated between a Group A-1 occupancy and the other Group A or Group E occupancies.

Topic: Separation and Protection
Reference: IBC 509, Table 509

Category: Incidental Uses
Subject: Incidental Uses

Code Text: *Incidental uses located within single occupancy or mixed occupancy buildings shall comply with the provisions of this section. Incidental uses are ancillary functions associated with a given occupancy that generally pose a greater level of risk to that occupancy and are limited to those uses listed in Table 509. The incidental uses listed in Table 509 shall be separated from the remainder of the building or equipped with an automatic sprinkler system, or both, in accordance with the provisions of that table.* See the exception for incidental use areas within dwelling units.

Discussion and Commentary: It is common to find uses that are typical of the general occupancy classification of the building, yet which create a hazard different from the other hazards found in the occupancy. An example would be a chemistry laboratory classroom in a high school building. The code addresses such conditions by requiring incidental uses to be separated from the remainder of the building with fire-resistance-rated construction, or to be protected with a fire-extinguishing system, or at times, both.

[F] TABLE 509
INCIDENTAL USES

ROOM OR AREA	SEPARATION AND/OR PROTECTION
Furnace room where any piece of equipment is over 400,000 Btu per hour input	1 hour or provide automatic sprinkler system
Rooms with boilers where the largest piece of equipment is over 15 psi and 10 horsepower	1 hour or provide automatic sprinkler system
Refrigerant machinery room	1 hour or provide automatic sprinkler system
Hydrogen fuel gas rooms, not classified as Group H	1 hour in Group B, F, M, S and U occupancies; 2 hours in Group A, E, I and R occupancies.
Incinerator rooms	2 hours and provide automatic sprinkler system
Paint shops, not classified as Group H, located in occupancies other than Group F	2 hours; or 1 hour and provide automatic sprinkler system
In Group E occupancies, laboratories and vocational shops not classified as Group H	1 hour or provide automatic sprinkler system
In Group I-2 occupancies, laboratories not classified as Group H	1 hour and provide automatic sprinkler system
In ambulatory care facilities, laboratories not classified as Group H	1 hour or provide automatic sprinkler system
Laundry rooms over 100 square feet	1 hour or provide automatic sprinkler system
In Group I-2, laundry rooms over 100 square feet	1 hour
Group I-3 cells and Group I-2 patient rooms equipped with padded surfaces	1 hour
In Group I-2, physical plant maintenance shops	1 hour
In ambulatory care facilities or Group I-2 occupancies, waste and linen collection rooms with containers that have an aggregate volume of 10 cubic feet or greater	1 hour
In other than ambulatory care facilities and Group I-2 occupancies, waste and linen collection rooms over 100 square feet	1 hour or provide automatic sprinkler system
In ambulatory care facilities or Group I-2 occupancies, storage rooms greater than 100 square feet	1 hour
Stationary storage battery systems having an energy capacity greater than the threshold quantity specified in Table 1206.2 of the *International Fire Code*	1 hour in Group B, F, M, S and U occupancies; 2 hours in Group A, E, I and R occupancies.
Electrical installations and transformers	See Sections 110.26 through 110.34 and Sections 450.8 through 450.48 of NFPA 70 for protection and separation requirements.

For SI: 1 square foot = 0.0929 m^2, 1 pound per square inch (psi) = 6.9 kPa, 1 British thermal unit (Btu) per hour = 0.293 watts, 1 horsepower = 746 watts, 1 gallon = 3.785 L, 1 cubic foot = 0.0283 m^3.

Where a fire-extinguishing system is used to provide protection for an incidental use area, the area must still be separated from the remainder of the building. The separation must be constructed such that smoke will be contained.

Study Session 7
IBC Chapter 3 and Sections 508 and 509

1. Which of the following is not one of the listed occupancy groups in the IBC?

    a. A-3 b. B-2

    c. S-2 d. R-4

    Reference _____

2. When a use does not match a specific occupancy group as described in the code, the use is placed in an occupancy group _____.

    a. it most nearly resembles

    b. as designated by the owner

    c. as designated by the architect

    d. as designated by the design professional in responsible charge

    Reference _____

3. Which of the following incidental use areas must always be separated from the main occupancy?

    a. waste and linen collection room in a Group I-2 occupancy containing bins able to hold 15 cubic feet of material

    b. a laundry room of 110 square feet in floor area

    c. a vocational shop in a group E occupancy

    d. a furnace room with one piece of equipment rated at over 400,000 Btu/h input

    Reference _____

4. What is the occupancy classification of a warehouse that contains food products stored on wood pallets?

    a. Group B   b. Group F

    c. Group S-1   d. Group S-2

    Reference _____

5. What is the occupancy classification of a horse barn?

    a. Group H-4   b. Group R-3

    c. Group S-2   d. Group U

    Reference _____

6. What is the occupancy classification of a hospital?

    a. Group H-1   b. Group H-2

    c. Group I-1   d. Group I-2

    Reference _____

7. What is the occupancy classification of a movie theater complex?

    a. Group A-1   b. Group A-2

    c. Group A-3   d. Group B

    Reference _____

8. What is the occupancy classification of a church?

    a. Group A-1   b. Group A-2

    c. Group A-3   d. Group R-2

    Reference _____

9. Utilizing the provisions for separated occupancies, what is the required fire-resistive separation between a Group R-1 and a Group I-1 located in a fully sprinklered building?

    a. 1 hour   b. 2 hours

    c. 3 hour   d. no rating required

    Reference _____

10. An elementary school is generally classified as what type of occupancy?

    a. Group A
    b. Group B
    c. Group E
    d. Group U

    Reference _____

11. What is the occupancy classification of a two-family dwelling designed and constructed under the provisions of the *International Building Code*?

    a. Group R-1
    b. Group R-2
    c. Group R-3
    d. Group R-4

    Reference _____

12. What is the primary difference between a Group I-1 occupancy and a Group I-2 occupancy?

    a. age of occupants
    b. level of security
    c. length of stay
    d. capability for self-preservation

    Reference _____

13. A structure used for the manufacture of highly toxic cleansers would most likely have an occupancy classification of _____.

    a. Group F-1
    b. Group F-2
    c. Group H-2
    d. Group H-4

    Reference _____

14. An 8-foot high fence surrounding an electronics warehouse would have an occupancy classification of _____.

    a. Group F-2
    b. Group R-3
    c. Group S-1
    d. Group U

    Reference _____

15. One of the primary differences between a Group R-1 occupancy and a Group R-2 occupancy is the _____.

    a. age of the occupants
    b. number of occupants
    c. number of stories above grade
    d. transient or nontransient nature of the occupants

    Reference _____

16. A convenience market with a motor vehicle fuel-dispensing facility is classified as a Group _____ occupancy.

    a. A-2   b. B
    c. H-4   d. M

    Reference_____

17. An airplane hangar accessory to a residence is considered a Group _____ occupancy.

    a. F-1   b. H-2
    c. S-2   d. U

    Reference_____

18. A building used for assembly purposes with an occupant load of less than 50 persons shall be considered a Group _____ occupancy.

    a. A-1   b. A-2
    c. B   d. M

    Reference_____

19. With conditions, an accessory occupancy is not required to be separated from the main occupancy by a fire barrier, provided the accessory occupancy occupies an area not more than _____ percent of the area of the story in which it is located.

    a. 10   b. 25
    c. 5   d. 20

    Reference_____

20. A day-care facility where supervision or personal care services are provided to 14 children, all above the age of $2^1/_2$ years, shall be classified as a Group _____ occupancy.

    a. A-3   b. E
    c. I-2   d. I-4

    Reference_____

21. A lumberyard is considered a Group _____ occupancy.

    a. B   b. H-2
    c. H-3   d. S-1

    Reference_____

22. An indoor sports arena should be classified as a Group _____ occupancy.

   a. A-3
   b. A-4
   c. A-5
   d. B

   Reference_____

23. A building that contains large quantities of highly explosive materials would be classified as a Group _____ occupancy

   a. H-1
   b. H-2
   c. S-1
   d. S-2

   Reference_____

24. A room that is intended to be occupied at different times for different purposes shall comply with _____.

   a. the most restrictive means of egress requirements
   b. the most restrictive fire protection requirements
   c. the requirements of the use having the highest occupant load
   d. all requirements that are applicable to each use

   Reference_____

25. A congregate living facility with primarily permanent residents and an occupant load of 12 persons would be classified as a Group _____ occupancy?

   a. R-1
   b. R-2
   c. R-3
   d. R-4

   Reference_____

Study Session

8

2018 IBC Chapters 6 and 12
Types of Construction and Interior Environment

OBJECTIVE: To gain an understanding of how a building is classified as a specific type of construction, based on the construction materials and the various building elements' resistance to fire; and the important issues concerning the interior environment, including light, ventilation, interior space dimensions, temperature control and access to unoccupied spaces.

REFERENCE: Chapters 6 and 12, 2018 *International Building Code*

KEY POINTS:
- What do the various types of construction indicate?
- How are the required fire-resistance ratings of building elements determined?
- What types of material are required to be used as building elements of a Type I or Type II building?
- How do the two different categories of Type I construction differ in fire protection? Type II construction?
- Which types of materials are required for use in the exterior walls of a Type III structure? For the interior building elements?
- What is another name for Type IV construction?
- Type V buildings may be constructed of which building materials?
- How does a Type VA building differ from a Type VB building?
- Which building elements are considered primary structural frame elements for the determination of required fire resistance?
- How must occupiable portions of buildings be ventilated? What special ventilation requirements apply to attics and under-floor spaces?
- If natural ventilation is utilized, how much openable area to the exterior must be provided?
- What is the minimum temperature capability required for heating systems serving interior spaces intended for human occupancy?
- What methods are available for providing adequate illumination to spaces intended for human occupancy?

KEY POINTS (Cont'd):

- In what type of building use is sound transmission regulated by the code? At what locations within the building is sound transmission required?
- What are the minimum required room widths of habitable spaces? Minimum required ceiling heights?
- What is the difference between "occupiable" and "habitable"?
- What is an efficiency dwelling unit? What are its unique requirements?
- What minimum size access opening is required for a crawl space? An attic?
- How must toilet and bathing room floors be covered for sanitation purposes? Walls adjacent to urinals and water closets? What type of building is exempt from the requirements?
- To what minimum height must showers and walls above bathtubs be finished with a smooth, nonabsorbent surface?

Topic: General Provisions
Reference: IBC 602.1
Category: Types of Construction
Subject: Construction Classification

Code Text: *Buildings and structures erected or to be erected, altered or extended in height or area shall be classified in one of the five construction types defined in Sections 602.2 through 602.5.*

Discussion and Commentary: There are two major groupings of "construction type" based on the materials of construction: noncombustible construction (Types I and II) and construction that may be either noncombustible or combustible (Types III, IV and V). These groupings are further divided into two major categories: protected, where the major building elements are protected with some recognized degree of fire resistance, and unprotected, where no fire resistance of the building elements is typically mandated. The "A" designation indicates a specified level of fire-resistance is required for the building elements. In other than Type I buildings, the "B" designation identifies buildings without the required level of fire-resistance for all of the building elements.

Noncombustible	Exterior and interior (bearing or nonbearing) walls, floors, roofs and structural elements are to be of noncombustible materials	I	A	B
		II	A	B
Combustible and/or noncombustible	Exterior walls are to be of noncombustible materials	III	A	B
		IV	HT	
		V	A	B

It is the intent of the *International Building Code* that each building be classified as a single type of construction. The construction materials and the degree to which such materials are protected determine the classification based on the criteria of Table 601 and Chapter 6.

Topic: Fire-Resistance Ratings
Reference: IBC 602.1, Table 601
Category: Types of Construction
Subject: Construction Classification

Code Text: *The building elements shall have a fire-resistance rating not less than that specified in Table 601.*

Discussion and Commentary: The building elements regulated by Table 601 for types of construction include: structural frame members such as columns, girders and trusses; bearing walls, both interior and exterior; floor construction, including support beams and joists; and roof construction, consisting of supporting beams, joists, rafters and other members. The required fire-resistance rating for each of these elements is based on the specific type of construction assigned to the building.

TABLE 601
FIRE-RESISTANCE RATING REQUIREMENTS FOR BUILDING ELEMENTS (HOURS)

BUILDING ELEMENT	TYPE I A	TYPE I B	TYPE II A	TYPE II B	TYPE III A	TYPE III B	TYPE IV HT	TYPE V A	TYPE V B
Primary structural frame[f] (see Section 202)	$3^{a,b}$	$2^{a,b}$	1^b	0	1^b	0	HT	1^b	0
Bearing walls Exterior[e,f] Interior	3 3^a	2 2^a	1 1	0 0	2 1	2 0	2 1/HT	1 1	0 0
Nonbearing walls and partitions Exterior	See Table 602								
Nonbearing walls and partitions Interior[d]	0	0	0	0	0	0	See Section 2304.11.2	0	0
Floor construction and associated secondary members (see Section 202)	2	2	1	0	1	0	HT	1	0
Roof construction and associated secondary members (see Section 202)	$1\frac{1}{2}^b$	$1^{b,c}$	$1^{b,c}$	0^c	$1^{b,c}$	0	HT	$1^{b,c}$	0

For SI: 1 foot = 304.8 mm.

a. Roof supports: Fire-resistance ratings of primary structural frame and bearing walls are permitted to be reduced by 1 hour where supporting a roof only.
b. Except in Group F-1, H, M and S-1 occupancies, fire protection of structural members in roof construction shall not be required, including protection of primary structural frame members, roof framing and decking where every part of the roof construction is 20 feet or more above any floor immediately below. Fire-retardant-treated wood members shall be allowed to be used for such unprotected members.
c. In all occupancies, heavy timber complying with Section 2304.11 shall be allowed where a 1-hour or less fire-resistance rating is required.
d. Not less than the fire-resistance rating required by other sections of this code.
e. Not less than the fire-resistance rating based on fire separation distance (see Table 602).
f. Not less than the fire-resistance rating as referenced in Section 704.10.

Where a structure is separated by one or more fire walls, the code treats those individual compartments created by the fire walls as separate buildings. Thus, each separate compartment would be considered a distinct building for the purpose of classification by type of construction.

Topic: Types I and II Construction
Reference: IBC 602.2
Category: Types of Construction
Subject: Construction Classification

Code Text: *Types I and II construction are those types of construction in which the building elements listed in Table 601 are of noncombustible materials, except as permitted in Section 603 and elsewhere in this code.*

Discussion and Commentary: Type I buildings are noncombustible, and the building elements are also provided with a mandated degree of fire resistance. This type of construction requires the highest level of fire protection specified in the code. Type II buildings are also of noncombustible construction; however, the level of fire resistance is usually less than that required for Type I structures. Buildings of Type II construction may have a limited degree of fire resistance (Type II-A) or no fire resistance whatsoever (Type II-B).

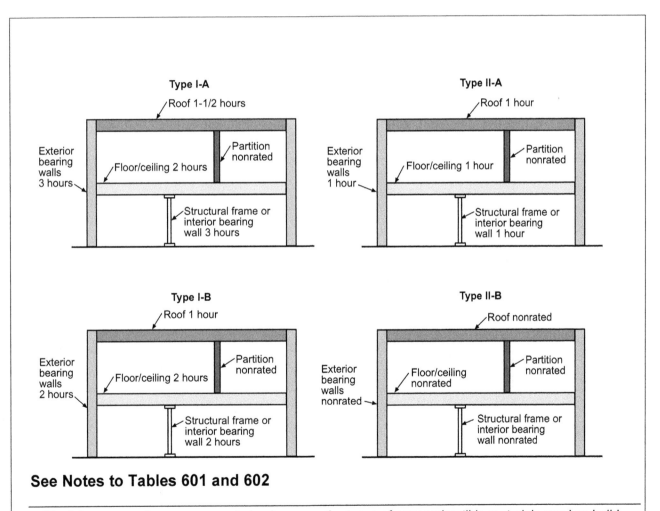

See Notes to Tables 601 and 602

Steel, iron, concrete, masonry and aluminum are the types of noncombustible materials used as building elements, or components of building elements, in Type I or II buildings. Section 703.5.2 also recognizes gypsum board as a noncombustible material. Typically, structures defined as high-rise buildings are of Type I construction.

Topic: Type III Construction
Reference: IBC 602.3

Category: Types of Construction
Subject: Construction Classification

Code Text: *Type III construction is that type of construction in which the exterior walls are of non-combustible materials and the interior building elements are of any material permitted by the code. Fire-retardant-treated wood framing and sheathing complying with Section 2303.2 shall be permitted within exterior wall assemblies of a 2-hour rating or less.*

Discussion and Commentary: Type III buildings are considered combustible buildings and, from a fire-resistive standpoint, are either protected or unprotected. This building type was developed out of the necessity to prevent conflagration in heavily built-up areas where buildings were erected side-by-side in congested downtown business districts. To limit the spread of fire from building to building, exterior walls were required to be of both noncombustible and fire-resistant construction.

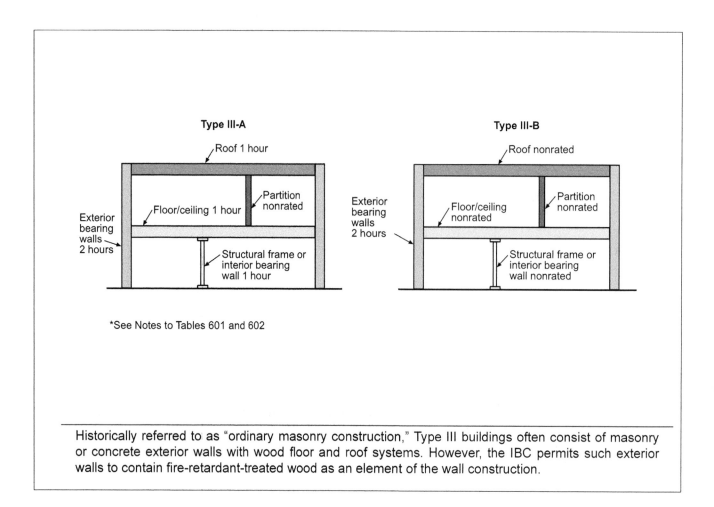

Historically referred to as "ordinary masonry construction," Type III buildings often consist of masonry or concrete exterior walls with wood floor and roof systems. However, the IBC permits such exterior walls to contain fire-retardant-treated wood as an element of the wall construction.

Topic: Type IV Construction
Reference: IBC 602.4

Category: Types of Construction
Subject: Construction Classification

Code Text: *Type IV construction is that type of construction in which the exterior walls are of noncombustible materials and the interior building elements are of solid wood, laminated wood, heavy timber (HT) or structural composite lumber (SCL) without concealed spaces. The minimum dimensions for permitted materials including solid timber, glued-laminated timber, structural composite lumber (SCL), and cross-laminated timber and details of Type IV construction shall comply with the provisions of this section and Section 2304.11. Exterior walls complying with Section 602.4.1 or 602.4.2 shall be permitted. Interior walls and partitions not less than 1-hour fire-resistance rating or heavy timber complying with Section 2304.11.2.2 shall be permitted.*

Discussion and Commentary: Referred to as heavy-timber, buildings of Type IV construction are essentially Type III buildings with an interior of large timber members. In order to conform to Type IV construction, building members must be of substantial thickness. Given the characteristics of massive wood members, there is little chance for sudden structural collapse during or after a fire. The materials for interior construction can be solid wood, laminated wood, heavy timber or structural composite lumber (SCL) provided they meet the dimension requirements and have no concealed spaces. Cross-laminated timber and fire-retardant-treated wood may be used in exterior walls when the wall assembly has a 2-hour rating or less.

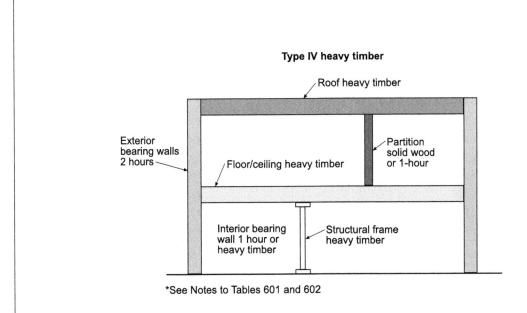

In accordance with Section 602.4, Table 601 and its Note d, modern-day Type IV buildings can include both heavy-timber and one-hour fire-resistance-rated construction. Though they are not considered equal, both methods of construction tend to provide equivalent fire resistance.

Topic: Type V Construction
Reference: IBC 602.5
Category: Types of Construction
Subject: Construction Classification

Code Text: *Type V construction is that type of construction in which the structural elements, exterior walls and interior walls are of any materials permitted by this code.*

Discussion and Commentary: Type V buildings are essentially composed of construction systems that will not fit into any of the other higher types of construction specified by the IBC. Although the construction normally considered Type V is the conventional light-frame wood building, any combination of approved materials can be considered Type V construction. Section 602.1.1 indicates that a building is not required to conform to the details of a type of construction higher than the type that meets the minimum requirements based on occupancy, even though certain features of such a building actually conform to a higher construction type.

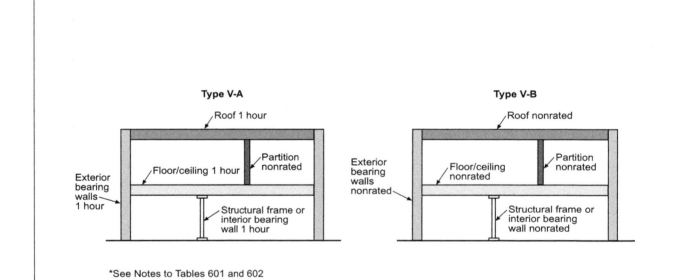

In the design and review of a building for type of construction requirements, it is wise to first determine if the structure can be built as a Type VB building, based on occupancy, location on property, building height and building floor area. If so, any other construction type is also permitted.

Topic: Primary Structural Frame
Reference: IBC 202, Table 601
Category: Types of Construction
Subject: Construction Classification

Code Text: *The primary structural frame shall include all of the following structural members: 1. the columns; 2. structural members having direct connections to the columns, including girders, beams, trusses and spandrels; 3. members of the floor construction and roof construction having direct connections to the columns; and 4. bracing members that are essential to the vertical stability of the primary structural frame under gravity loading shall be considered part of the primary structural frame whether or not the bracing member carries gravity loads.*

Discussion and Commentary: To maintain stability of the building as a whole, the major structural elements are regulated for endurance when subjected to a fire. In addition to the columns, beams and girders, both interior bearing walls and exterior bearing walls are regulated to a level of fire resistance equal to or greater than that of other structural elements. Secondary members, such as floor joists, roof joists or rafters are protected within the rated floor-ceiling or roof-ceiling assemblies.

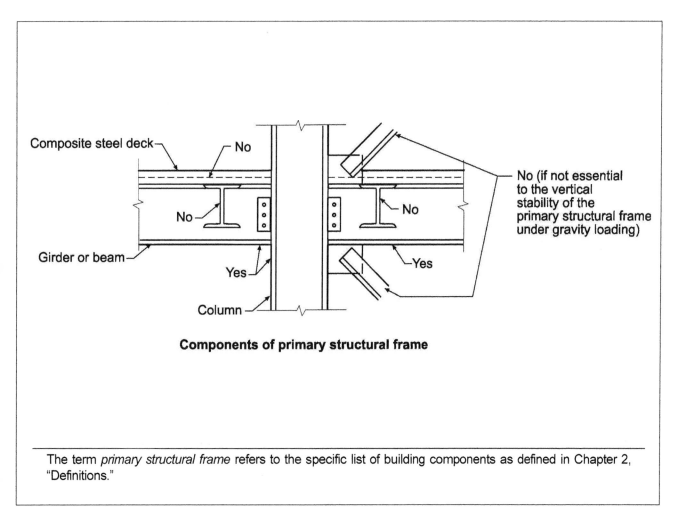

Components of primary structural frame

The term *primary structural frame* refers to the specific list of building components as defined in Chapter 2, "Definitions."

Topic: Natural Ventilation
Reference: IBC 1202.1, 1202.5
Category: Interior Environment
Subject: Ventilation

Code Text: *Buildings shall be provided with natural ventilation in accordance with Section 1202.5 or mechanical ventilation in accordance with the* International Mechanical Code. *Natural ventilation of an occupied space shall be through windows, doors, louvers or other openings to the outdoors. . . The openable area of the openings to the outdoors shall be not less than 4 percent of the floor area being ventilated.*

Discussion and Commentary: To obtain a minimum level of environmental comfort, as well as to maintain sanitary conditions, some form of ventilation must be provided to those portions of a building that are normally occupied. To provide the necessary natural ventilation to a 100-square-foot occupiable room, multiply the room area by 4 percent (.04) to obtain the minimum required amount of 4 square feet. A window with at least 4 square feet of openable area would be one method of complying with this requirement. If natural ventilation is unavailable, the *International Mechanical Code* must be utilized to provide adequate mechanical ventilation.

For dwelling units, if a blower door test as required by the *International Energy Conservation Code* determines that the air infiltration rate is less than 5 air changes per hour at the prescribed pressure, mechanical ventilation must be installed in accordance with the *International Mechanical Code*, whether or not adequate openings are provided for natural ventilation.

Topic: Mechanical Ventilation
Reference: IBC 1202.1
Category: Interior Environment
Subject: Ventilation

Code Text: *Where the air infiltration rate in a dwelling unit is less than 5 air changes per hour where tested with a blower door at a pressure 0.2 inch w.c. (50 Pa) in accordance with Section 402.4.1.2 of the* International Energy Conservation Code—Residential Provisions, *the dwelling unit shall be ventilated by mechanical means in accordance with Section 403 of the* International Mechanical Code.

Discussion and Commentary: With a heightened focus on energy efficiency, residential construction increasingly relies on insulation, air barriers and sealants to provide a tighter thermal envelope, which significantly reduces natural infiltration of outside air. The *International Energy Conservation Code* limits air leakage rates based on climate zone and requires a blower door test on all residential buildings to verify compliance with the air leakage provisions. Such tight construction under closed-house conditions may contribute to inadequate fresh air and poor indoor air quality. Therefore, when a blower door test is conducted under the prescribed conditions and the resulting air leakage rate is less than 5 ACH, the IBC requires mechanical ventilation to supply outdoor air to the dwelling unit. In this case, natural ventilation provided by openable windows does not satisfy the ventilation requirements. For Group I-2 occupancies and ambulatory care facilities, mechanical ventilation must be provided meeting the requirements of ASHRAE 170 as referenced in Section 407 of the IMC.

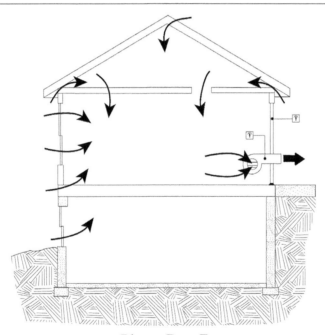

Blower Door Test

Mechanical ventilation for dwelling units must be designed and installed to provide the required outdoor airflow rate in accordance with the *International Mechanical Code*. A minimum rate of 0.35 ACH and not less than 15 cfm per person is required. The occupant load for purposes of ventilation is based on the number of bedrooms—two people for the first bedroom and one person for each additional bedroom.

Topic: Attic Spaces
Reference: IBC 1202.2
Category: Interior Environment
Subject: Ventilation

Code Text: *Enclosed attics and enclosed rafter spaces formed where ceilings are applied directly to the underside of roof framing members shall have cross ventilation for each separate space by ventilation openings protected against the entrance of rain and snow. Blocking and bridging shall be arranged so as not to interfere with the movement of air. An airspace of not less than 1 inch (25 mm) shall be provided between the insulation and the roof sheathing. The net free ventilating area shall not be less than $^1/_{150}$th of the area of the space ventilated.* See the exceptions for reducing the ratio to 1/300 based on the distribution of vents or the application of a vapor barrier.

Discussion and Commentary: Attic ventilation serves to prevent moisture build-up and condensation within attic spaces. Historically the ventilation rate of 1 square foot of free ventilating area for every 150 square feet of attic space (1/150) has been considered the general requirement with exceptions permitting a reduction to 1/300. The first exception recognizes designs that distribute the vents to help promote airflow through the attic. The second exception requires a vapor barrier to be installed on the ceiling of the living space below the attic to reduce the amount of water vapor passing from the conditioned space into the unconditioned attic space.

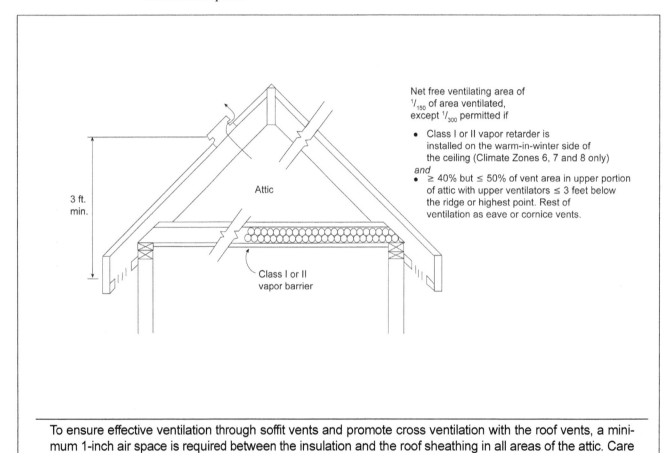

To ensure effective ventilation through soffit vents and promote cross ventilation with the roof vents, a minimum 1-inch air space is required between the insulation and the roof sheathing in all areas of the attic. Care must be taken to avoid obstruction of air flow to prevent condensation in the attic area.

Topic: Equipment and Systems
Reference: IBC 1203.1
Category: Interior Environment
Subject: Temperature Control

Code Text: *Interior spaces intended for human occupancy shall be provided with active or passive space-heating systems capable of maintaining a minimum indoor temperature of 68° F (20° C) at a point 3 feet (914 mm) above the floor on the design heating day.* See the exception for interior spaces where the primary purpose is not associated with human comfort.

Discussion and Commentary: For those interior spaces where human comfort is of primary concern, the IBC requires that a minimum room temperature be achievable. Although the code does not require this temperature be constantly provided, it does mandate that such interior spaces be served by equipment or systems having the capability of maintaining the desired temperature.

Interior spaces where the primary purpose is not associated with human comfort—such as warehouses, factories, storage areas and garages—do not need to comply with these provisions.

Topic: Natural Light
Category: Interior Environment
Reference: IBC 1204.1, 1204.2
Subject: Lighting

Code Text: *Every space intended for human occupancy shall be provided with natural light by means of exterior glazed openings in accordance with Section 1204.2 or shall be provided with artificial light in accordance with Section 1204.3. . . The minimum net glazed area shall not be less than 8 percent of the floor area of the room served.*

Discussion and Commentary: As with ventilation, adequate illumination is necessary to obtain a minimum level of environmental comfort. A minimum amount of illumination must be provided if the area is to be used for human occupancy. Artificial lighting is acceptable if it complies with Section 1204.3, as this would provide for illumination at any time of the day or night.

To provide the required illumination through the use of natural lighting for a 100-square-foot room intended for human occupancy, multiply the room area by 8 percent (.08) in order to obtain the minimum required amount of 8 square feet. A window with at least 8 square feet of glass (glazed) area would be one method of complying with the requirement. Typically, it is assumed that half of this window will open, thereby providing the required 4 square feet (4 percent) of natural ventilation.

Topic: Minimum Room Widths
Reference: IBC 1207.1
Category: Interior Environment
Subject: Interior Space Dimensions

Code Text: *Habitable spaces, other than a kitchen, shall not be less than 7 feet (2134 mm) in any plan dimension. Kitchens shall have a clear passageway of not less than 3 feet (914 mm) between counter fronts and appliances or counter fronts and walls.*

Discussion and Commentary: To maintain a minimum level of comfort, this provision specifies the minimum horizontal dimension required for all habitable spaces. Any room that functions as a bedroom, living room, dining room or other similar habitable room must comply with this code section. In addition, the code sets minimum area requirements for all habitable spaces in dwelling units except kitchens.

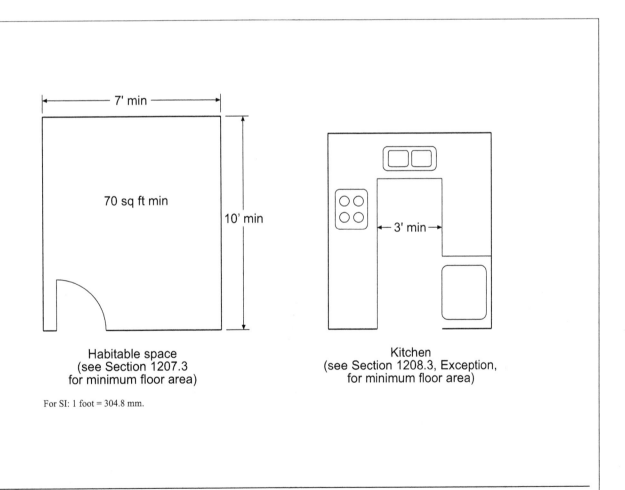

Habitable space
(see Section 1207.3
for minimum floor area)

Kitchen
(see Section 1208.3, Exception,
for minimum floor area)

For SI: 1 foot = 304.8 mm.

Although kitchens are exempt from the 7-foot dimension, they still must maintain a minimum amount of space in order to be functional. The 3-foot minimum dimension allows for cabinets and drawers to open, as well as providing for the use of appliances and the passage of occupants.

Topic: Minimum Ceiling Heights
Reference: IBC 1207.2
Category: Interior Environment
Subject: Interior Space Dimensions

Code Text: *Occupiable spaces, habitable spaces and corridors shall have a ceiling height of not less than 7 feet 6 inches (2286 mm) above the finished floor. Bathrooms, toilet rooms, kitchens, storage rooms and laundry rooms shall have a ceiling height of not less than 7 feet (2134 mm) above the finished floor. See the exceptions for 1) one- and two-family dwellings, 2) rooms with sloped ceilings, 3) mezzanines and 4) corridors within a dwelling or sleeping unit.*

Discussion and Commentary: Ceiling height is one of the variables that affect the circulation of air in a space. Additionally, there is a psychological need for spaciousness in a living space. Because less time is spent in storage rooms, laundry rooms and bathrooms, a lesser ceiling height is acceptable. The code also provides for sloped ceilings and for various projections, such as beams, when they meet certain criteria.

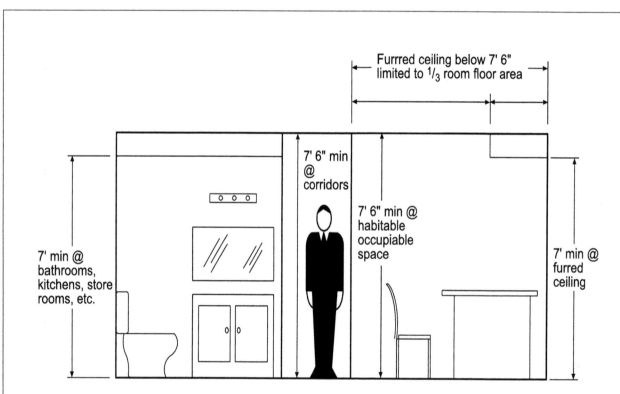

For SI: 1 inch = 25.4 mm, 1 foot = 304.8 mm.

It is important to distinguish between "occupiable spaces" and "habitable spaces" when dealing with interior spaces. Section 202 in the IBC contains the definitions of these two terms as well as others important to the enforcement of this code.

Topic: Room Area
Reference: IBC 1207.3

Category: Interior Environment
Subject: Interior Space Dimensions

Code Text: *Every dwelling unit shall have not less than one room that shall have not less than 120 square feet (13.9 m²) of net floor area. Other habitable rooms shall have a net floor area of not less than 70 square feet (6.5 m²). See the exception for kitchens.*

Discussion and Commentary: The provisions regulating minimum room area apply only to dwelling units. These minimum dimensions reflect the psychological requirements of light and ventilation and also preserve the individual's perception of space and the elements necessary for a psychological sense of well-being. The code does not regulate the minimum room sizes in other than residential occupancies.

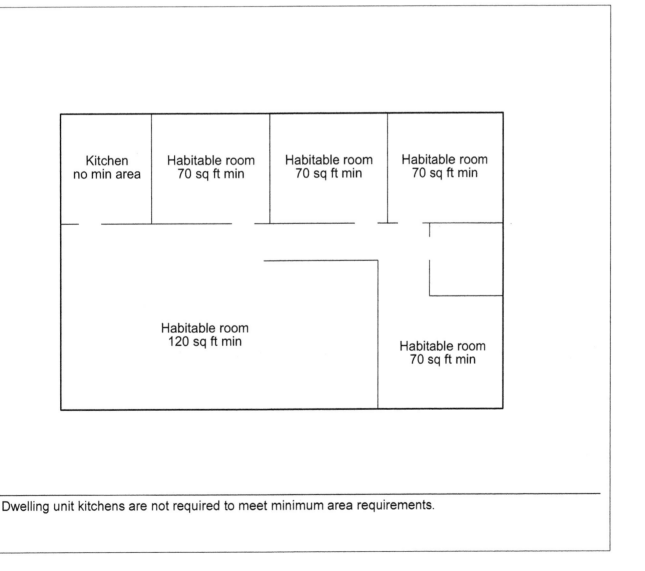

Dwelling unit kitchens are not required to meet minimum area requirements.

Topic: Crawl Spaces and Attic Spaces
Reference: IBC 1208.1, 1208.2
Category: Interior Environment
Subject: Access to Unoccupied Spaces

Code Text: *Crawl spaces shall be provided with not fewer than one access opening that shall be not less than 18 inches by 24 inches (457 mm by 610 mm). An opening not less than 20 inches by 30 inches (559 mm by 762 mm) shall be provided to any attic area having a clear height of over 30 inches (762 mm). Clear headroom of not less than 30 inches (762 mm) shall be provided in the attic space at or above the access opening.*

Discussion and Commentary: Plumbing piping, mechanical equipment and wiring installations often pass through or are contained in crawl spaces. Inspections, maintenance and repairs cannot be carried out without access to such crawl spaces. Attic access is also mandated for similar reasons. Although uncommon, access to the attic for fire department purposes can also be accomplished through such openings. The required openings are a convenient and nondestructive means for any user to access such concealed spaces.

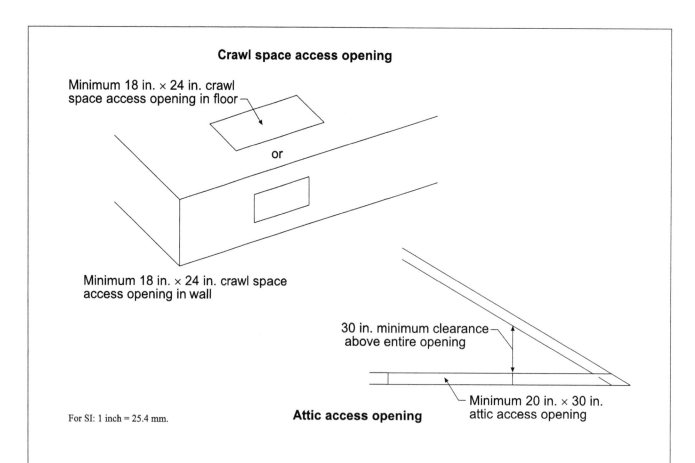

Although there is no definitive description of crawl space in the IBC, this does not typically present a problem in making a determination based on the use of the space, its height and means of access. Access to the attic is only required when the attic space has a clear height greater than 30 inches, measured from the top of the ceiling joists (or top of floor sheathing, if present) to the underside of the roof rafters.

Topic: Finish Materials
Reference: IBC 1209.2.1, 1209.2.2

Category: Interior Environment
Subject: Toilet and Bathroom Requirements

Code Text: *In other than dwelling units, toilet, bathing and shower room floor finish materials shall have a smooth, hard, nonabsorbent surface. The intersections of such floors with walls shall have a smooth, hard, nonabsorbent vertical base that extends upward onto the walls not less than 4 inches (102 mm). Walls and partitions within 2 feet (610 mm) of service sinks, urinals and water closets shall have a smooth, hard, nonabsorbent surface, to a height of not less than 4 feet (1219 mm) above the floor, and except for structural elements, the materials used in such walls shall be of a type that is not adversely affected by moisture. See the exceptions for dwelling units, sleeping units and toilet rooms that are not accessible to the public and have only one water closet.*

Discussion and Commentary: Smooth, hard, nonabsorbent surfaces in the prescribed areas of public restrooms are necessary for effective cleaning and maintaining sanitary conditions. Ceramic tile is the most common material used for satisfying these requirements, but any durable material that provides satisfactory resistance to moisture and is easy to clean is acceptable.

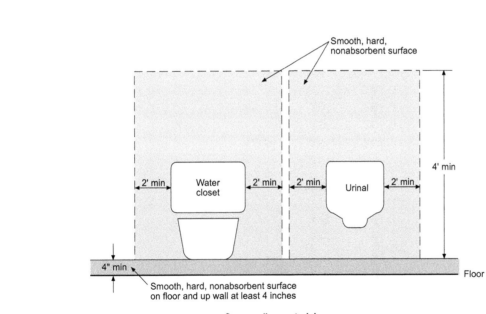

Surrounding materials

For SI: 1 inch = 25.4 mm, 1 foot = 304.8 mm.

Shower compartment walls also require smooth, nonabsorbent surfaces to a height of 72 inches above the drain inlet. This requirement applies to bathtubs with shower heads.

Topic: Urinal Partitions
Reference: IBC 1209.3.2
Category: Interior Environment
Subject: Toilet and Bathroom Requirements

Code Text: *Each urinal utilized by the public or employees shall occupy a separate area with walls or partitions to provide privacy. The walls or partitions shall begin at a height not more than 12 inches (305 mm) from and extend not less than 60 inches (1524 mm) above the finished floor surface. The walls or partitions shall extend from the wall surface at each side of the urinal not less than 18 inches (457 mm) or to a point not less than 6 inches (152 mm) beyond the outermost front lip of the urinal measured from the finished backwall surface, whichever is greater.* See the exceptions for single occupancy, family use and child day-care toilet rooms.

Discussion and Commentary: As with separate compartments for water closets, urinal partitions provide privacy to users of public restrooms. The code sets minimum dimensions to provide an adequate privacy screen between urinals. Privacy partitions are also required for a single urinal. The exceptions recognize that single user bathrooms, including family or assisted-use facilities, with a privacy lock on the door afford the same level of privacy. In child day-care bathrooms, having one urinal without partitions is necessary to provide assistance to children with special needs.

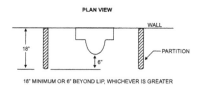

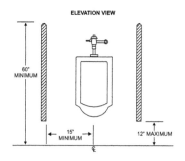

The provision for a minimum dimension of 15 inches from the centerline of the urinal to the face of the urinal partition comes from the *International Plumbing Code*.

Quiz

Study Session 8
IBC Chapters 6 and 12

1. Generally, the building elements in Types I and II construction must be _____.

    a. combustible
    b. fire-resistive
    c. fire-retardant
    d. noncombustible

    Reference _____

2. In most cases, exterior wall materials for buildings of Type III construction must be _____.

    a. steel
    b. masonry
    c. concrete
    d. noncombustible

    Reference _____

3. What is the minimum required size of a solid sawn beam supporting floor framing for consideration as Type IV, Heavy Timber construction?

    a. 4 inches by 6 inches
    b. 4 inches by 8 inches
    c. 6 inches by 8 inches
    d. 6 inches by 10 inches

    Reference _____

4. A Type V building is permitted to be constructed of _____.

    a. only fire-resistive materials
    b. only noncombustible materials
    c. only steel or masonry materials
    d. any materials permitted by the code

    Reference _____

5. According to Table 601, the minimum fire-resistance rating of the primary structural frame for a building of Type IIB construction shall be _____ hour(s).

   a. 0
   b. 1
   c. 2
   d. 3

   Reference _____

6. Habitable spaces, other than a kitchen, shall have a minimum dimension in any direction of _____ feet.

   a. 5
   b. 7
   c. 10
   d. 15

   Reference _____

7. Every dwelling unit shall have at least one room that is not less than _____ square feet.

   a. 70
   b. 100
   c. 120
   d. 150

   Reference _____

8. An access opening is required into any attic having a clear height exceeding _____ inches.

   a. 20
   b. 24
   c. 30
   d. 36

   Reference _____

9. Unless provided with complying artificial light, a space intended for human occupancy shall be provided with natural light by exterior glazed openings with a net glazed area not less than _____ percent of the floor area of the room served.

   a. 5
   b. 8
   c. 10
   d. 12

   Reference _____

10. Where required natural ventilation is provided by exterior openings, the minimum openable area to the outdoors shall be _____ percent of the space being ventilated.

    a. 2
    b. 4
    c. 8
    d. 10

    Reference _____

11. A space in a building used for living, sleeping, eating or cooking is considered a(n) _____.

    a. dwelling unit
    b. livable space
    c. habitable space
    d. occupiable space

    Reference _____

12. Generally, a room or enclosed space designed for human occupancy in which individuals congregate for amusement, education, labor or similar purposes is considered a(n) _____.

    a. dwelling unit
    b. workable space
    c. habitable space
    d. occupiable space

    Reference _____

13. Which of the following would be considered a habitable space?

    a. closet
    b. kitchen
    c. utility room
    d. bathroom

    Reference _____

14. Which of the following would typically not be considered occupiable space?

    a. church choir area
    b. Group S-2 warehouse
    c. 100,000-square-foot office building
    d. mechanical equipment room

    Reference _____

15. Which of the following rooms would not be permitted to have a ceiling height of 7 feet 0 inches throughout the room?

    a. kitchen
    b. bedroom
    c. bathroom
    d. laundry room

    Reference _____

16. An efficiency dwelling unit requires a living room with a floor area of not less than _____ square feet.

    a. 70
    b. 100
    c. 120
    d. 220

    Reference _____

17. Generally, habitable spaces are required to have a heating system capable of maintaining a minimum indoor temperature of _____ degrees Fahrenheit.

    a. 65
    b. 68
    c. 70
    d. 72

    Reference _____

18. In public restrooms, walls within 2 feet of a water closet must have a smooth, nonabsorbent surface to a point at least _____ inches above the floor.

    a. 6
    b. 24
    c. 48
    d. 60

    Reference _____

19. Smooth, nonabsorbent surfaces must be placed to a minimum height of _____ inches above the drain inlet in shower compartments and bathtubs with shower heads.

    a. 68
    b. 70
    c. 72
    d. 78

    Reference _____

20. Required urinal partitions must extend not less than _____ inches above the finished floor surface.

    a. 60   b. 48
    c. 36   d. 72

    Reference_____

21. Walls separating dwelling units must have a sound transmission class of not less than _____ for airborne noise.

    a. 50   b. 25
    c. 100 d. 75

    Reference_____

22. Where artificial light is provided in lieu of natural light, the code requires a minimum average illumination of _____ footcandle(s) over the area of the room at a height 30 inches above the floor level.

    a. 20   b. 40
    c. 1   d. 10

    Reference_____

23. A minimum of _____ inches in clear headroom in the attic space shall be provided at or above the access opening.

    a. 18   b. 20
    c. 24   d. 30

    Reference_____

24. An access opening of at least _____ shall be provided for all crawl spaces.

    a. 16 inches by 24 inches   b. 18 inches by 24 inches
    c. 22 inches by 24 inches   d. 22 inches by 30 inches

    Reference_____

25. Dwelling units require mechanical ventilation when the air infiltration rate is less than 5 air changes per hour based on _____ .

    a. the results of a blower door test
    b. closed house conditions
    c. prescriptive tables of the *International Energy Conservation Code*
    d. the methods prescribed in ASHRAE 62.1

    Reference_____

Study Session

9

2018 IZC Chapters 1 and 3 through 7
Scope and Administration and Use Districts

OBJECTIVE: To gain an understanding of the administrative provisions and use districts set forth in the *International Zoning Code*, including the scope and purpose of the code; duties of the zoning code official, planning commission, board of adjustment and hearing officer; permits and approvals; and the definitions and bulk regulations of the various zoning districts.

REFERENCE: Chapters 1 and 3 through 7, 2018 *International Zoning Code*

KEY POINTS:
- What is the intent and purpose of the *International Zoning Code*?
- What is the scope of the *International Zoning Code*?
- How are existing buildings to be addressed?
- How are moved and temporary buildings to be regulated?
- What are the duties and powers of the zoning code official in regard to the application and interpretation of the code? How are deputies appointed?
- What degree of liability does the zoning code official and other employees have in regard to performance of their duties?
- What are the duties of the planning commission?
- What is involved in the creation of a comprehensive plan?
- What are the duties of the board of adjustment?
- What is a variance? Under what conditions may a variance be granted?
- What are the duties of the hearing examiner?
- What is the procedure for a public hearing? For appeals to a previous decision?
- How long are permits valid?
- How are zoning districts classified?
- When territory is annexed, what use district is it to be initially classified as?
- What is a conditional use? Why is it necessary?

KEY POINTS (Cont'd):

- What are the four major zoning districts? What general criteria are regulated for each of the zoning districts as bulk regulations?
- What three types of agricultural zones are designated?
- How many residential zones are defined? What distinguishes R-1 zones from R-2 or R-3 zones?
- What are the two general types of commercial zones? How do the two classifications differ?
- What types of uses are permitted in FI zones?

Topic: Intent
Reference: IZC 101.2
Category: Scope and Administration
Subject: General Requirements

Code Text: *The purpose of this code is to safeguard the health, property and public welfare by controlling the design, location, use or occupancy of all buildings and structures through the regulated and orderly development of land and land uses within this jurisdiction.*

Discussion and Commentary: Although the purpose of the *International Zoning Code* is similar to the purpose of the *International Building Code*, the zoning code primarily regulates the use and development of land, whereas the building code regulates the use and construction of buildings.

IZC and IBC

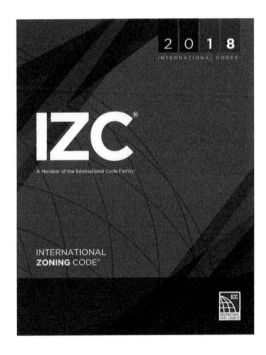
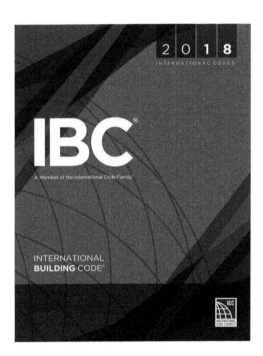

It is important to understand that an R-1 use district in the zoning code (IZC) allows single-family uses because it is a designation of land use. The same classification (R-1) in the building code (IBC) pertains to hotels, motels and similar occupancies because it is a designation of *building* use.

Topic: Scope
Reference: IZC 101.3

Category: Scope and Administration
Subject: General Requirements

Code Text: *The provisions of this code shall apply to the construction, addition, alteration, moving, repair and use of any building, structure, parcel of land or sign within a jurisdiction, except work located primarily in a public way, public utility towers and poles, and public utilities unless specifically mentioned in this code.*

Discussion and Commentary: The *International Zoning Code* is intended to regulate, with some exceptions, the broad spectrum of land use activities associated with parcels of land, buildings, structures and signs. General provisions allow for a comprehensive overview of regulations; however, where more specific circumstances exist, any applicable specific requirements will take precedence.

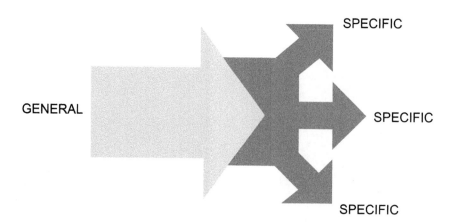

The *International Zoning Code* is intended to benefit the public as a whole and not any specific person or class of persons. Unintentional breaches of the obligations imposed on the jurisdiction are not to be enforceable in tort.

Topic: General Provisions	Category: Scope and Administration
Reference: IZC 102.1	Subject: Existing Buildings and Uses

Code Text: *Lawfully established buildings and uses in existence at the time of the adoption of this code shall be permitted to have their existing use or occupancy continued, provided such continued use is not dangerous to life.*

Discussion and Commentary: Typically, an existing building is exempt or grandfathered if, when initially established, it complied with all jurisdictional regulations. As long as the building or structure is properly maintained, it is permissible for the existing use to be continued.

If the existing building or structure presents a hazard that is dangerous to life, the zoning code official is authorized to take action to eliminate the hazard.

Study Session 9

Topic: Moved and Temporary Buildings
Reference: IZC 102.4
Category: Scope and Administration
Subject: Existing Buildings and Uses

Code Text: *Buildings or structures moved into or within the jurisdiction shall comply with the provisions of this code for new buildings and structures. Temporary buildings, structures and uses such as reviewing stands and other miscellaneous structures, sheds, canopies or fences used for the protection of the public shall be permitted to be erected, provided a special approval is received from the code official for a limited period of time. Temporary buildings or structures shall be completely removed upon the expiration of the time limit stated in the permit.*

Discussion and Commentary: Consistent with similar provisions in the *International Building Code*, a building or structure moved into the jurisdiction must comply with the jurisdiction's current zoning laws for that use district as if it were being newly constructed. The code official is authorized to allow temporary structures with certain stipulations pertaining to use and length of service.

Once the time period for temporary use expires as stated on the permit, all structures must be completely removed from the site. Tents and enclosures used at circuses, carnivals and fairs, as well as construction and sales trailers, are typical examples of temporary structures.

Topic: Establishment of the Commission
Reference: IZC 103.2

Category: Scope and Administration
Subject: Planning Commission

Code Text: *The establishment of the (planning) commission shall be in accordance with the policies and procedures as set forth in state law. The commission shall consist of the number of members as specified in state law.*

Discussion and Commentary: The planning commission is an advisory body that creates and develops a comprehensive plan, zoning code and official zoning map. These documents are then brought before the legislative body for adoption. The legislative body can accept, reject or revise the recommendations of the planning commission. The commission also can recommend amendments to the previously adopted regulations.

Duties of the Planning Commission:

Create and recommend a comprehensive plan for physical development of the jurisdiction

Develop and recommend a zoning code in accordance with the comprehensive plan

Develop and certify regulations governing the division of land

Review conditional-use permits

Adopt an official zoning map for the jurisdiction

The comprehensive plan is an important document for jurisdictions because it contains official maps. It addresses such issues as growth and land use, commercial/industrial areas, transportation and utilities, community facilities, housing, and environmental and geological/natural hazards.

Study Session 9

Topic: General Provisions
Reference: IZC 104.1
Category: Scope and Administration
Subject: Duties and Powers of the Code Council

Code Text: *This section establishes the duties and responsibilities for the zoning code official and other officials and agencies, with respect to the administration of this code. The zoning code official and/or designee shall be referred to hereafter as "the code official."*

Discussion and Commentary: It is important that the code official be knowledgeable to the point of being able to rule on those issues that may not be clearly addressed in the zoning code. The code official is responsible for the interpretation and application of the zoning code, and such interpretations should always be based on the scope, purpose and intent of the code as established in Sections 101.2 and 101.3.

The zoning code official is responsible for

- **Reviews and approvals**
- **Assisting with the development and implementation of the comprehensive plan**

    Administrative reviews of building permits, site plans, conditional-use permits and variances

    Processing amendments or changes to the comprehensive plan or map

In order to carry out the duties and responsibilities set forth in the IZC, the code official may deputize other employees of the jurisdiction. The authority of the code official is granted to such deputies to the extent permitted by the governing agency.

Topic: Liability	Category: Scope and Administration
Reference: IZC 104.7	Subject: Duties and Powers of the Code Official

Code Text: *The code official, or designee, charged with the enforcement of this code, acting in good faith and without malice in the discharge of the duties described in this code, shall not be personally civilly or criminally liable for any damage that may accrue to persons or property as a result of an act or by reason of an act or omission in the discharge of such duties. A suit brought against the code official . . . shall be defended by the jurisdiction until final termination of such proceedings . . .*

Discussion and Commentary: This important section allows the code official, or designee, to conduct their duties with the reasonable expectation that legal action against them will not be initiated as long as they are performing their assigned duties in good faith and without malice. In the event action is brought against the employee, the jurisdiction must absorb the costs to defend the employee. However, there seems to be an increasing trend in the courts to find civil officers personably liable for careless acts.

Case law regarding tort liability of code officials is in a state of flux, and old doctrines may not be applicable. Therefore, the legal officer of the jurisdiction should always be consulted when there is any question about liability.

Topic: Establishment of the Board
Reference: IZC 106.2
Category: Scope and Administration
Subject: Board of Adjustment

Code Text: *The establishment of the board* (of adjustment) *shall be in accordance with the procedures and policies as set forth in state law. The board shall consist of the number of members as specified in state law.*

Discussion and Commentary: The board of adjustment has great authority and power in deciding on matters relating to the administration and, with some limitations, variances of the zoning code, including matters brought before it by the zoning code official and the public. The board must abide by the spirit and intent of the zoning code provisions when considering variances, interpreting code language and applying specific requirements.

VARIANCE APPLICATION

Owner: _____

Address: _____

City: _____ State: _____ Zip: _____

Phone: _____ Fax: _____ Email: _____

General location and address of property: _____

Legal Description/ Parcel Number: _____

Contact Person: _____

Phone: _____ Fax: _____ Email: _____

Address: _____

City: _____ State: _____ Zip: _____

HEREBY REQUEST that this property be granted variance for:
- ☐ Lot Area Requirements ☐ Lot Coverage
- ☐ Pools ☐ Parking
- ☐ Fence/Walls ☐ Setbacks
- ☐ Height ☐ Signs
- ☐ Landscaping ☐ Other: _____

Specific Zoning Ordinance citation where the current standard may be found (Article, section number, page number, etc.) and seeking relief from: _____

Applicant would like staff comments returned by: (please check all that apply)

E-Mail ☐ _____ Fax ☐ _____ U.S. Postal ☐

Property Owner Signature: _____ Date: _____

Date Property Posted: _____
Date Public Notice Published: _____
Notification of Hearing to Applicant: _____
Hearing Date: _____ ☐ Granted ☐ Denied
Appeal: ☐ Yes ☐ No

Submittals Shall Include the Following:
- ☐ Plot Plan/Site Plan
- ☐ Narrative
- ☐ Pictures or illustrations demonstrating hardship
- ☐ *Fees: $136 + $300 Posting + $60 Advertising*

R/7/04

Typically, no variance can be granted to any applicant unless hardship can be demonstrated. Further, the applicant cannot have created a self-imposed hardship.

Topic: Duties and Powers
Reference: IZC 107.3
Category: Scope and Administration
Subject: Hearing Examiner

Code Text: *The (hearing) examiner shall hear and consider all applications for discretionary land rezones and use decisions as authorized by the legislative body by resolution. Such considerations shall be set for public hearing. The examiner shall be bound by the same standards of conduct as the commission and board, with respect to the administration of this code.*

Discussion and Commentary: The hearing examiner is a neutral party who conducts quasi-judicial proceedings regarding rezoning and land use. This individual must issue decisions and recommendations within 10 working days after the hearing. All notices and decisions shall be in writing and given to the zoning code official for distribution as required.

The hearing examiner is appointed and approved by the legislative body of the jurisdiction, and all meetings and documents must be open to the public.

Topic: Expiration or Cancellation **Category:** Scope and Administration
Reference: IZC 110.2 **Subject:** Permits and Approvals

Code Text: *Each license, permit or approval issued shall expire after 180 days if no work is undertaken or such use or activity is not established, unless a different time of issuance of the license or permit is allowed in this code, or unless an extension is granted by the issuing agency prior to expiration.*

Discussion and Commentary: As specified in the *International Building Code,* permits issued under the *International Zoning Code* have a limited life span unless they are acted on within a specified time period or where they are properly extended by those having the authority to do so.

Zoning permit application

Owner's Name _____
Address _____
Owner's Phone _____
Builder's Name _____
Address _____
Builder's Phone _____

Description of Building/Type of Construction

Permit For _____
Address _____
Lot Number _____ Subdivision _____
Parcel Number _____
Section_____ Town_____ Range_____ Zone_____
Type of Occupancy_____ Public Road Frontage _____
Size of Lot _____ Size of Building _____
Number of Stories_____ Square Feet_____
Fees_____ Plans Received_____

**Deeds and/or subdivision restrictions may be violated.
It is your responsibility for their compliance.**

Signature of Applicant_____ Date_____
Zoning Approved By_____ Date_____

Location of building must be staked out for approval.

A permit or license can be cancelled or revoked if the terms or conditions of issuance are not fully in compliance. Any cancellation or revocation can be appealed to the appropriate board or commission.

Topic: Classification
Reference: IZC 301.1

Category: Use Districts
Subject: District Classifications

Code Text: *In order to classify, regulate and restrict the locations of uses and locations of buildings designated for specific areas; and to regulate and determine the areas of yards, courts and other open spaces within or surrounding such buildings, property is hereby classified into districts as prescribed in this chapter.*

Discussion and Commentary: In the *International Zoning Code* there are four primary Use Districts (also identified as Zoning Districts). Each one of these districts is further classified into Divisions that set forth specific uses that can be established in each area. Each district, or zone, has specific requirements for minimum lot widths, depths and areas, as well as minimum setback requirements. Per the IZC, any territory annexed into the jurisdiction will automatically be classified as an R, Division 1a residential district and must comply with all applicable regulations.

The Primary Use Districts

Agricultural (A) Zone	**(3 Divisions)**
Residential (R) Zone	**(3 Divisions)**
Commercial (C) Zone	**(4 Divisions)**
Commercial/Residential (CR) Zone	**(2 Divisions)**
Factory/Industrial (FI) Zone	**(3 Divisions)**

Many definitions such as Building Line, Setback, Yard, Structure, Building and Use are found in Chapter 2 of the IZC and should be referred to as necessary.

Topic: General Provisions
Reference: IZC 305.1
Category: Use Districts
Subject: Conditional Uses

Code Text: *In addition to those uses specifically classified and permitted in each district, there are certain additional uses which it may be necessary to allow because of the unusual characteristics of the service they provide the public. These conditional uses require particular considerations as to their proper location to adjacent, established or intended uses, or to the planned growth of the community. The conditions controlling the locations and operation of special uses are established by the applicable sections of this code.*

Discussion and Commentary: A conditional use is that type of use not specifically permitted in a designated use district but considered harmonious or compatible with neighboring uses through the application and maintenance of qualifying conditions. Such criteria may include uses that provide a public benefit, with conditions qualifying noise restrictions, limited hours of operation, traffic control and visual impacts.

In residential districts, examples of conditional uses are places of worship, parking lots, bed and breakfast establishments, cemeteries, mausoleums and day-care centers.

Topic: A Zones
Reference: IZC 401.1

Category: Use Districts
Subject: Agricultural Zones

Code Text: *Allowable agricultural (A) zone uses shall be: A-1, any designated open space as set forth in this code; A-2, any agricultural use, including, but not limited to, dwellings, maintenance/ storage buildings and other such uses necessary for the principal use; and A-3, any public park land or other similar recreational use, including, but not limited to, amusement rides, office buildings, retail buildings and dwellings necessary for the maintenance of the principal use.*

Discussion and Commentary: The agricultural aspects consistent with an "A-zone" designation typically provide for open spaces with limited buildings or structures on the site. In addition to those farming and ranching uses expected in an agricultural zone, park and recreation areas are also permitted. Dwellings, office buildings and retail sales buildings are allowed, but only as accessory elements to the major permitted use.

TABLE 402.1
AGRICULTURAL (A) ZONE BULK REGULATIONS
(in feet, unless noted otherwise)

ZONE DIVISION	MINIMUM LOT AREA (acres)	MAXIMUM DENSITY (units/acre)	LOT DIMENSIONS		SETBACK REQUIREMENTS			MAXIMUM BUILDING HEIGHT[b]
			Minimum lot width	Minimum lot depth	Minimum front yard	Minimum side yard	Minimum rear yard	
1	20	1 dwelling unit/20 acres	600	600	30	15	60	35
2	10	1 dwelling unit/10 acres	400	400	30	15	60	35
3	5	1 dwelling unit/5 acres	250	250	30	15	60	35

For SI: 1 foot = 304.8 mm, 1 acre = 4047 m^2.
a. Open spaces and parks can be of a reduced size, if approved.
b. Access storage structures, windmills and similar structures shall be permitted to exceed the maximum height when approved by the code official.

A unique use permitted in an A-3 zone is that of an amusement park, including amusement rides and other support facilities associated with the amusement use.

Study Session 9

Topic: R Zones
Reference: IZC 501.1
Category: Use Districts
Subject: Residential Zones

Code Text: *Allowable residential (R) zone uses shall be: R-1, single-family dwellings, public owned and operated parks, recreation centers, swimming pools and playgrounds, police and fire department stations, public and governmental services, public libraries, schools and colleges (excluding colleges or trade schools operated for profit), public parking lots, private garages, buildings accessory to the above permitted uses (including private garages and accessory living quarters), and temporary buildings; R-2, any use permitted in R, Division 1 zones and two-family dwellings; and R-3, all uses permitted in R, Division 2 zones, multiple-unit dwellings, such as apartment houses, boarding houses, condominiums and congregate residences.*

Discussion and Commentary: As expected, the most common uses permitted in an R-zone are single-family dwellings. In addition, many of the necessary governmental support facilities are also included.

TABLE 502.1
RESIDENTIAL (R) ZONE BULK REGULATIONS
(in feet, unless noted otherwise)

DIVISION		MINIMUM LOT AREA/SITE (square feet)	MAXIMUM DENSITY (dwelling unit/acre)	LOT DIMENSIONS		SETBACK REQUIREMENTS			MAXIMUM BUILDING HEIGHT[a]
				Minimum lot width	Minimum lot depth	Minimum front yard	Minimum side yard	Minimum rear yard	
1	a	35,000	1	125	150	25	10	30	35
	b	20,000	2	100	125	20	10	25	35
	c	10,000	4	75	100	20	5	25	35
	d	6,000	6	60	90	15	5	20	35
2	a	10,000	4	60	70	20	5	20	35
	b	6,000	6	60	70	15	5	20	35
3	a	6,000	8	60	70	15	5	20	35
	b	6,000	12	60	70	15	5	20	35

For SI: 1 foot = 304.8 mm, 1 square foot = 0.0929 m^2, 1 acre = 4047 m^2.

a. Accessory towers, satellite dishes and similar structures shall be permitted to exceed the maximum height when approved by the code official.

The residential zones are more inclusive as they progress from Division 1 to Division 3. An R-2 zone includes all uses permitted in an R-1 zone, plus two-family dwellings. The R-3 zone allows for all of these accumulated uses, as well as larger multiple family buildings.

Topic: C and CR Zones
Reference: IZC 601.1
Category: Use Districts
Subject: Commercial Zones

Code Text: *Allowable commercial (C) zone and commercial/residential (CR) zone uses shall be: C-1, minor automotive repair . . . public utility stations and restaurants; C-2, any uses permitted in C, Division 1 zone, and light commercial (excluding wholesale sales) . . . schools and colleges operated for profit (including commercial, vocational and trade schools); C-3, any uses permitted in C, Division 2 zones and amusement centers . . . indoor theaters and self-storage warehouses; and C-4, any uses permitted in C, Division 3 zones and major automotive repair . . . and wood products manufacture and finishing; CR-1, any use permitted in a C, Division 1 zone and residential use permitted, except in the story or basement abutting street grade; and CR-2, any use permitted in a C, Division 2 zone and residential use permitted, except in the story or basement abutting street grade.*

Discussion and Commentary: Uses that are not of a residential character would be considered for inclusion in one or more of the C zones. Where residential uses are included, a CR-1 or CR-2 designation is necessary.

TABLE 602.1
COMMERCIAL (C) AND COMMERCIAL/RESIDENTIAL (CR) ZONES BULK REGULATIONS
(in feet, unless noted otherwise)

DIVISION	MINIMUM LOT AREA (square feet)	MAXIMUM DENSITY (units/acre)	LOT DIMENSIONS		SETBACK REQUIREMENTS			MAXIMUM BUILDING HEIGHT[a]
			Minimum lot width	Minimum lot depth	Minimum front yard	Minimum side yard	Minimum rear yard	
1	6,000	12	30	70	0	0	0	30
2	Not Applicable	Not Applicable	30	70	0	0	0	40
3	Not Applicable	Not Applicable	75	100	0	0	0	50
4	Not Applicable	Not Applicable	75	100	0	0	0	50

For SI: 1 foot = 304.8 mm, 1 square foot = 0.0929 m^2, 1 acre = 4047 m^2.
a. Accessory towers, satellite disks and similar structures shall be permitted to exceed the listed heights when approved by the code official.

The various uses designated for C or CR zones are additive in nature, similar to the methodology for R zones. As such, the C-1 zone is considered the most restrictive in terms of allowable uses, whereas the C-4 zone permits the greatest variety of commercial uses.

Study Session 9

Topic: FI Zones
Reference: IZC 701.1

Category: Use Districts
Subject: Factory and Industrial Zones

Code Text: *Allowable factory/industrial (FI) zone uses shall be: FI-1, any light-manufacturing or industrial use, such as warehouses, research or testing laboratories, product distribution centers, woodworking shops, auto body shops, furniture assembly, dry cleaning plants, places of religious worship, public and governmental services, machine shops and boat building storage yards; FI-2, any use permitted in the FI, Division 1 zone and stadiums and arenas, indoor swap meets, breweries, liquid fertilizer manufacturing, carpet manufacturing, monument works and a regional recycling center; and FI-3, any use permitted in the FI, Division 2 zone and auto-dismantling yards, alcohol manufacturing, cotton gins, paper manufacturing, quarries, salt works, petroleum refining and other similar uses.*

Discussion and Commentary: Although the majority of uses permitted in an FI zone are reflective of the zone's title (Factory/Industrial), there are several unique allowances, including arenas and stadiums, worship facilities and governmental service buildings.

TABLE 702.1
FACTORY/INDUSTRIAL (FI) ZONE BULK REGULATIONS
(in feet, unless noted otherwise)

DIVISION	MINIMUM LOT AREA (square feet)	MAXIMUM DENSITY (units/acre)	LOT DIMENSIONS		SETBACK REQUIREMENTS			MAXIMUM BUILDING HEIGHT[a]
			Minimum lot width	Minimum lot depth	Minimum front yard	Minimum side yard	Minimum rear yard	
1	Not Applicable	Not Applicable	50	75	0	0	0	60
2	Not Applicable	Not Applicable	75	100	0	0	0	80
3	Not Applicable	Not Applicable	100	150	0	0	0	80

For SI: 1 foot = 304.8 mm, 1 square foot = 0.0929 m², 1 acre = 4047 m².
a. Accessory towers, satellite dishes and similar structures shall be permitted to exceed the maximum height when approved by the code official.

Although many uses are limited to a single-use district, some are permitted in multiple zones. For example, places of religious worship are selectively allowed in C, CR and FI zones.

Study Session 9
IZC Chapters 1 and 3 through 7

1. If any portion of the code is held to be invalid, the remaining portions _____.

    a. are also considered invalid

    b. are not affected

    c. must undergo a legal review

    d. require a restart of the adoption process

    Reference _____

2. Unless an extension is granted, a permit expires after _____ if no work is undertaken.

    a. 30 days

    b. 120 days

    c. 180 days

    d. one year

    Reference _____

3. Where there is a conflict between a general requirement and a specific requirement, the _____ requirement shall be applicable.

    a. general

    b. specific

    c. most current

    d. more restrictive

    Reference _____

Study Session 9

4. Buildings and uses lawfully established and in existence at the time of adoption of the code may continue that use, provided such condition is _____.
   a. not dangerous to life
   b. not in violation of the zoning code
   c. compatible with the neighborhood
   d. not objected to by any adjacent property owners

   Reference _____

5. Who shall make interpretations of the *International Zoning Code*?
   a. the code official
   b. the board of appeals
   c. the planning director
   d. the planning commission

   Reference _____

6. The official charged with the enforcement of the IZC, acting in good faith and _____, shall not be personally liable for any damage that may accrue to persons or property as a result of an act or by reason of an act or omission in the discharge of such duties.
   a. an efficient manner
   b. with full authority
   c. without malice
   d. within the limits set by law

   Reference _____

7. Which of the following elements is not required to be in the comprehensive plan?
   a. official maps
   b. community facilities
   c. historical landmarks
   d. commercial and industrial uses

   Reference _____

8. The terms for members of the board of adjustment shall be _____.
   a. limited to two years
   b. established by the jurisdiction
   c. as set forth in state law
   d. determined by the code official

   Reference _____

9. The zoning board of adjustment is not permitted to grant a variance to _____.
    a. establish a prohibited use in a zoning district
    b. increase the allowable number of signs on a property
    c. reduce setbacks from property lines
    d. reduce the minimum lot area

    Reference _____

10. When an application for a discretionary land re-zone is heard by a hearing examiner, how many working days does the hearing examiner have to make a decision?
    a. 5
    b. 10
    c. 15
    d. As determined by the adopting ordinance of the jurisdiction

    Reference _____

11. When appealing an action related to the IZC, an appeal must be filed within how many working days after the cause arises?
    a. 5
    b. 10
    c. 15
    d. As determined by the adopting ordinance of the jurisdiction

    Reference _____

12. A boarding house is defined as a dwelling containing a single dwelling unit and not more than _____ sleeping units.
    a. 2
    b. 6
    c. 10
    d. 12

    Reference _____

13. The lowest point of elevation of the existing surface of the ground, limited to the area between the building and a line 5 feet from the building, is known as the _____.
    a. grade
    b. grade plane
    c. ground level
    d. building elevation

    Reference _____

14. According to the IZC, which of the following rooms is not considered "habitable space?"

    a. kitchen
    b. bathroom
    c. bedroom
    d. living room

    Reference _____

15. Minimum setback requirements (front, side, rear) for a future funeral home in a Division 1 commercial zone are _____ feet.

    a. 0, 0, 0
    b. 10, 5, 5
    c. 20, 5, 10
    d. 20, 10, 30

    Reference_____

16. Property annexed into the jurisdiction will automatically, upon annexation, be classified as a(n) _____ district.

    a. A-1
    b. FI-3
    c. CR-2
    d. R-1a

    Reference_____

17. A public park is permitted in a(n) _____ zoning district.

    a. R-1
    b. C-1
    c. FI-2
    d. CR-2

    Reference _____

18. An _____ zone is acceptable for a lot containing a house and a family farm.

    a. A-1
    b. A-2
    c. R-1
    d. R-3

    Reference_____

19. Amusement rides are permitted in a(n) _____ zoning district.

    a. A-2
    b. A-3
    c. C-1
    d. C-2

    Reference_____

20. The minimum required lot width in an R-1a zone is _____ feet.
    a. 60   b. 75
    c. 100   d. 125

    Reference_____

21. The minimum required lot area in a C-1 zone is _____ square feet.
    a. 2,000   b. 3,000
    c. 6,000   d. 8,000

    Reference_____

22. The maximum permitted building height in an R-3b zone is _____.
    a. 30 feet   b. 35 feet
    c. 75 feet   d. unlimited

    Reference_____

23. The minimum required rear yard setback in an R-2a zone is _____ feet.
    a. 30   b. 25
    c. 20   d. 15

    Reference_____

24. Auto body shops are permitted in which one of the following zoning districts?
    a. A-3   b. C-2
    c. CR-1   d. FI-1

    Reference_____

25. Which of the following would not be permitted in an R-2 zoning district?
    a. public parking lot   b. boarding house
    c. two-family dwelling   d. recreation center

    Reference_____

Study Session 9

Study Session

10

2018 IZC Chapters 8, 9, 11, 12 and 13

General Provisions, Special Regulations, Nonconforming Structures and Uses, Conditional Uses and Planned Unit Developments

OBJECTIVE: To gain an understanding of the general and special provisions of the 2009 *International Zoning Code*, including the regulation of off-street parking, landscape and grading, fences, accessory buildings, home occupations, nonconforming structures, conditional uses and planned unit developments.

REFERENCE: Chapters 8, 9, 11, 12 and 13, 2018 *International Zoning Code*

KEY POINTS:
- How are off-street parking requirements established? What is the minimum required number of spaces? What are the minimum parking stall dimensions?
- How are driveways and stall access regulated? What type of screening is required at parking lots?
- What is the maximum ratio of compact vehicle stalls to standard vehicle stalls?
- What is the maximum fence height permitted in the front yard? A side yard? The rear yard?
- What is the minimum distance required between an accessory building and the main building?
- What conditions apply specifically to the location of private garages?
- What projections are allowed in the various yards? What special projections are permitted in the front yard? In the rear yard?
- Where is landscaping required and when must it be completed?
- In which use districts must loading spaces be provided? What are the minimum dimensions for a loading zone?
- What type of passageways must be provided for building access? How is the passageway to be sized?
- What are the general requirements for home occupations? What special conditions are applicable?
- What type of permit is required for an adult-use business? What are the restrictions regarding their location?

KEY POINTS (Cont'd):

- Adult-use businesses are limited to what zoning district?
- When must a nonconforming structure or use come into compliance?
- What two conditions provide for a discontinuance of a nonconforming use?
- What procedures must be followed to request a conditional use?
- What evidence must be presented for authorization of a conditional use?
- Under what conditions may a conditional use permit expire or be revoked?
- What criteria must be met for the approval of a conditional use?
- What is the intent of a Planned Unit Development (PUD)? What conditions must be considered in the approval of a PUD?

Topic: General Requirements
Reference: IZC 801.1

Category: General Provisions
Subject: Off-Street Parking

Code Text: *Off-street parking shall be provided in compliance with this chapter where any building is erected, altered, enlarged, converted or increased in size or capacity.*

Discussion and Commentary: Multiple requirements are set forth regarding off-street parking areas. Section 801.2 and Table 801.2.1 establish the required number of spaces based on the use of the property. Section 801.3 establishes parking stall dimensions, as well as several exceptions, and the remaining provisions address other details such as driveway slopes, stall access, compact-to-standard stall ratios, screening, striping and lighting.

TABLE 801.2.1
OFF-STREET PARKING SCHEDULE

USE	NUMBER OF PARKING SPACES REQUIRED
Assembly	1 per 300 gross square feet
Dwelling unit	2 per dwelling unit
Health club	1 per 100 gross square feet
Hotel/motel	1 per sleeping unit plus 1 per 500 square feet of common area
Industry	1 per 500 square feet
Medical office	1 per 200 gross square feet
Office	1 per 300 gross square feet
Restaurant	1 per 100 gross square feet
Retail	1 per 200 gross square feet
School	1 per 3.5 seats in assembly rooms plus 1 per faculty member
Warehouse	1 per 500 gross square feet

For SI: 1 square foot = 0.0929 m^2.

Because parking occurs in just about every zoning district, all parking requirements are placed in Chapter 8 rather than located in each specific use-district chapter.

Topic: Location and Separation
Reference: IZC 803.1, 803.2
Category: General Provisions
Subject: Location of Accessory Buildings

Code Text: *Accessory buildings shall occupy the same lot as the main use or building. Accessory buildings shall be separated from the main building by 10 feet (3048 mm).*

Discussion and Commentary: Typically, every lot will have a principal or main building, such as a house or office building. (See definition of "Building, Main" in Chapter 2.) Any detached secondary building such as a garage, carport or storage shed would be classified as an accessory building (See definition of "Accessory Use"). The *International Zoning Code* prescribes a separation distance between the primary building and the accessory building.

The *International Building Code* regulates conditions where two or more structures are located on the same lot, but typically there is no minimum separation distance required between buildings. However, where the exterior walls of adjacent buildings are located in close proximity to each other, some degree of fire-resistance is often mandated for the opposing walls.

Topic: Eaves, Cornices and Chimneys
Reference: IZC 804.1

Category: General Provisions
Subject: Allowable Projections into Yards

Code Text: *Eaves, cornices or other similar architectural features shall be permitted to project into a required yard no more than 12 inches (305 mm). Chimneys shall be permitted to project no more than 2 feet (610 mm), provided the width of any side yard is not reduced to less than 30 inches (762 mm).*

Discussion and Commentary: The IZC establishes specific minimum yard dimensions that must be adhered to in the various zoning districts; however, Section 804 allows certain exceptions that permit several architectural elements of a building to minimally encroach into these required yards.

Without the allowances for projections into a required yard, the general limitations would effectively prohibit roof overhangs, bay or bow windows, and other features that enhance a building's appearance at those exterior walls located directly on a setback line.

Study Session 10

Topic: General Requirements
Reference: IZC 805.1

Category: General Provisions
Subject: Landscaping Requirements

Code Text: *Landscaping is required for all new buildings and additions over 500 square feet (46.5 m^2) as defined in this section. Said landscaping shall be completed within 1 year from the date of occupancy of the building.*

Discussion and Commentary: Landscaping is defined as "the finishing and adornment of unpaved yard areas." It may include naturally growing elements such as grass, trees, shrubs and flowers, as well as decorative elements such as logs, pavers, rocks, fountains and water features. In some colder climates it may not be possible to install landscaping if the building is going to be occupied in the winter season. The provisions allow the required landscaping to be completed over a one-year period of occupancy, which should give the owner sufficient time to achieve compliance.

Section 805.4 requires all landscaping to be properly maintained once installed. This would include the mowing and irrigation of sodded areas, as well as the immediate replacement of dead or dying grass, plants and trees. Although there is a definition of "Landscaping" in Chapter 2, there is no mention as to the extent of landscaping that would be required for compliance purposes.

Topic: Entrances and Building Separation **Category:** General Provisions
Reference: IZC 807.1, 807.2 **Subject:** Passageways

Code Text: *There shall be a passageway leading from the public way to the exterior entrance of each dwelling unit in every residential building of not less than 10 feet (3048 mm) in width. The passageway shall be increased by 2 feet (610 mm) for each story over two. There shall be not less than 10 feet (3048 mm) of clear space between every main building and accessory building on a lot. There shall be not less than 20 feet (6096 mm) of clear space between every residential building and another main building on the same lot.*

Discussion and Commentary: Adequate access must be provided to the exterior entrance of residential units. In addition, open space is required between every building located on the lot. Greater livability is a fundamental benefit of such access and open space. In addition, fire safety and fire department/emergency responder access is enhanced.

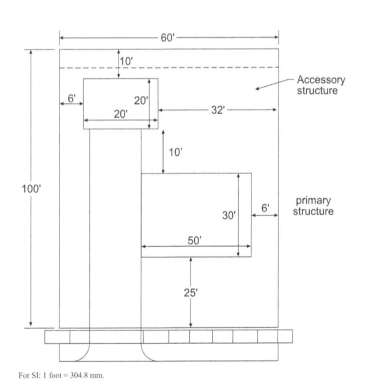

For SI: 1 foot = 304.8 mm.

Although the IBC may allow buildings to be located in closer proximity to each other through the use of fire-rated construction, the minimum separations set forth in the IZC must still be maintained.

Topic: General Requirements
Reference: IZC 901.1
Category: Special Regulations
Subject: Home Occupations

Code Text: *Home occupations shall be permitted in all zones, provided the home occupation is clearly and obviously subordinate to the main use or dwelling unit for residential purposes. Home occupations shall be conducted wholly within the primary structure on the premises.*

Discussion and Commentary: A zoning code establishes different zoning districts in order to provide orderly regulation of related uses. Many homeowners, however, have small, inconspicuous businesses in their homes that do not interfere with the surrounding neighborhood. When complying with the limitations set by the code, the home occupation is considered compatible with the principal uses of the zoning district, and business-related activities such as deliveries, customer arrival and departure, and storage of inventory do not adversely impact the district.

Some Typical Examples of Permitted Home Occupations

Artisans	Computer Design Services
Home Crafters	Cleaning Services
Mail Order Business	Accounting
Minor Repair Shops	Internet Consulting
Tailors/Seamstresses	Babysitting
Music Instructors	Composers
Food and Beverage Preparation (Without Consumption)	Teaching or Tutoring

A home occupancy is considered "the partial use of a dwelling unit for commercial or nonresidential uses by a resident thereof, which is subordinate and incidental to the use of the dwelling for residential purposes."

Topic: General Requirements
Reference: IZC 902.1

Category: Special Regulations
Subject: Adult Uses

Code Text: *A conditional-use permit shall be obtained for all adult-use businesses.*

Discussion and Commentary: Although the IZC makes no attempt to define an "adult use," it does establish specific restrictions as to its location. Most adult uses are generically defined as a use that customarily prohibits minors. This category could range from stereotypical adult book and video stores to massage parlors, adult tanning spas and erotic dance establishments.

One Definition of an Adult Use:

Adult uses include adult bookstores, adult motion picture theaters, adult mini-motion picture theaters, adult massage parlors, adult steam room/bath-house/sauna facilities, adult companionship establishments, adult rap/conversation parlors, adult health/sports clubs, adult cabarets, adult novelty businesses, adult motion picture arcades, adult modeling studios, adult hotels/motels, adult body painting studios:, and other premises, enterprises, establishments, businesses or places open to some or all members of the public at or in which there is an emphasis on the presentation, display, depiction or description of "specified sexual activities" or "specified anatomical areas," which are capable of being seen by members of the public.

Many courts have deemed adult uses, with some exceptions, to be considered constitutionally protected speech and, as such, a jurisdiction must proceed cautiously when considering approval or refusal of such a use.

Study Session 10

Topic: Vacancy or Damage
Reference: IZC 1102

Category: Nonconforming Structures and Uses
Subject: Discontinuance

Code Text: *Any lot or structure, or portion thereof, occupied by a nonconforming use, which is or hereafter becomes vacant and remains unoccupied by a nonconforming use for a period of 6 months shall not thereafter be occupied, except by a use that conforms to this code. If any nonconforming structure or use is, by any cause, damaged to the extent of 50 percent of its value as determined by the code official, it shall not thereafter be reconstructed as such.*

Discussion and Commentary: The intent of the IZC is to allow existing buildings to remain unless they reach an extreme point of deterioration or become abandoned for a certain period of time. Once they reach a pre-established threshold, they must comply with the current zoning regulations in effect. If additional construction takes place, it must also comply with the current building codes in effect.

Where damage to a nonconforming structure totals at least 50 percent of its value, the structure cannot be reconstructed and continue to house the nonconforming use. The code official must make the determination as to the value of the structure and the amount of damage that occurred.

Topic: Conditional-Use Permit
Reference: IZC 1201.1
Category: Conditional Uses
Subject: General Requirements

Code Text: *A conditional-use permit shall be obtained for certain uses, which would become harmonious or compatible with neighboring uses through the application and maintenance of qualifying conditions and located in specific locations within a zone, but shall not be allowed under the general conditions of the zone as stated in this code.*

Discussion and Commentary: Uses such as places of worship, day-care centers and parking lots are typical examples of when a conditional-use permit might be necessary. Most of these types of uses are not generally considered detrimental to a neighborhood, provided certain criteria for noise, traffic, hours of operation, overall compatibility and similar issues are addressed prior to allowing the use to be approved.

If a building permit has been issued for the conditional use, and the permit is abandoned for a period of one year, it cannot be reestablished unless authorized by the planning commission or other appropriate legislative body.

Study Session 10

Topic: Intent
Reference: IZC 1301.2
Category: Planned Unit Development
Subject: General Requirements

Code Text: *These regulations are to encourage and provide means for effecting desirable and quality development by permitting greater flexibility and design freedom than that permitted under the basic district regulations, and to accomplish a well-balanced, aesthetically satisfying city and economically desirable development of building sites within a planned unit development.*

Discussion and Commentary: In essence, a planned unit development (PUD) is intended to relax many of the strict requirements in the zoning code as long as the purpose, spirit and intent of the zoning code is adhered to, and provided the development is not found to be harmful, hazardous or offensive to the environment, property values or characteristics of the neighborhood or community.

Section 1302

Conditions to Be Considered in a Planned Unit Development

- Area
- Uses
- Ownership
- Design
- Land Density
- Building Arrangement
- Specific Lot Regulations
- Landscaping
- Signs
- Desirability

The flexibility allowed by a planned unit development often accrues in the form of relief from compliance with conventional zoning ordinance site and design requirements. Ideally, this flexibility results in a development that is better planned, contains more amenities and is more desirable than one produced in accordance with typical zoning ordinance and subdivision controls.

Quiz

Study Session 10
IZC Chapters 8, 9, 11, 12 and 13

1. The minimum number of parking spaces required for a 5,000-square-foot health club is _____ spaces.

    a. 30   b. 50
    c. 500   d. 550

    Reference _____

2. The minimum number of parking spaces required for a building housing a 3,000-square-foot office and a 30,000-square-foot warehouse is _____ spaces.

    a. 10   b. 60
    c. 70   d. 75

    Reference _____

3. Accessible parking spaces shall be provided in accordance with the _____.

    a. zoning code   b. building code
    c. comprehensive plan   d. planning commission requirements

    Reference _____

4. The minimum required width of a parallel parking stall is _____ feet.

    a. 8   b. 9
    c. 10   d. 20

    Reference _____

5. For accessing a parking facility, the minimum required width of a commercial driveway with a two-way entrance or exit is _____ feet.

    a. 9   b. 10

    c. 12   d. 24

Reference _____

6. The maximum fence height permitted in a required side yard located along a street is _____ feet.

    a. 3.5   b. 5.5

    c. 6   d. 6.5

Reference _____

7. An accessory building used as a private garage shall be separated from the main building by a minimum of _____ feet.

    a. 5   b. 10

    c. 15   d. 50

Reference _____

8. Windows shall be permitted to project into a required rear yard a maximum of _____ inches.

    a. 6   b. 12

    c. 18   d. 24

Reference _____

9. Landscaping required for all new buildings must be completed within _____ of occupancy of the building.

    a. 30 days   b. 180 days

    c. 1 year   d. 2 years

Reference _____

10. Loading spaces shall be provided on the same lot for buildings located in the _____ or _____ zones.
    a. A, FI
    b. CR, R
    c. A, C
    d. C, FI

    Reference _____

11. Which of the following is not a condition of a home occupation?
    a. no exterior display or storage of goods
    b. inventory area limited to 25 percent of area assigned to home occupation
    c. no more than one patron vehicle on the property at one time
    d. shall not exceed 15 percent of the floor area of the primary structure

    Reference _____

12. An adult use is only permitted in a(n) _____ zoning district.
    a. C-1
    b. C-2
    c. CR-1
    d. FI

    Reference _____

13. Generally, a lot or structure occupied by a nonconforming use that has been vacant for _____ must come into compliance with current zoning code before the structure can be occupied.
    a. 30 days
    b. 60 days
    c. 6 months
    d. 12 months

    Reference _____

14. If a nonconforming structure is damaged beyond _____ percent of its value, reconstruction requires compliance with the current zoning code.
    a. 10
    b. 25
    c. 33
    d. 50

    Reference _____

15. Which of the following would not be allowed to occur on a nonconforming structure?
    a. repairs
    b. maintenance
    c. additional floor area
    d. structural alterations

    Reference_____

16. All conditional-use permit applications must be submitted to the _____.
    a. code official
    b. clerk's office
    c. board of appeals
    d. planning commission

    Reference_____

17. After the completion of a public hearing regarding a conditional use, the commission shall enter a decision within _____.
    a. 5 working days
    b. 10 working days
    c. 30 working days
    d. a time limit as required by law

    Reference_____

18. An amendment to an approved conditional use shall be submitted to the _____, accompanied by supporting information.
    a. code official
    b. board of appeals
    c. attorney for the jurisdiction
    d. chairperson of the planning commission

    Reference_____

19. Which of the following is not a condition for approval of a conditional use?
    a. will not create undue traffic congestion
    b. will not adversely affect adjacent properties
    c. will not cause a financial burden on the jurisdiction
    d. will not adversely affect the public health, safety and welfare

    Reference_____

20. A conditional-use permit shall expire when such permit is abandoned or discontinued for a period of _____.
    a. 1 year
    b. 60 working days
    c. 60 calendar days
    d. 180 calendar days

    Reference_____

21. Planned unit developments are permitted in which of the following zoning districts?
    a. R only
    b. C and R only
    c. A, R and CR only
    d. all zoning districts

    Reference_____

22. Landscaping and screening requirements for planned unit developments must be approved by the _____.
    a. code official
    b. board of appeals
    c. hearing officer
    d. planning commission

    Reference_____

23. The density of the land use in a planned unit development shall be no more than _____ percent higher than allowed in that particular zoning district.
    a. 2
    b. 5
    c. 10
    d. 15

    Reference_____

24. The intent of a planned unit development is to _____.
    a. establish strict guidelines for each zoning district
    b. permit latitude in the development of a building site
    c. encourage higher densities in residential zoning districts
    d. permit uses not normally allowed in certain zoning districts

    Reference_____

25. Which of the following is not specified as a required contribution in obtaining a planned unit development approval?

     a. installation of traffic safety devices

     b. contributions for school athletic programs

     c. dedication of land for public school purposes

     d. dedication of land for public road right-of-way purposes

Reference_____

Study Session 11

2018 IZC Chapter 10
Signs

OBJECTIVE: To gain an understanding of the various sign provisions of the 2018 *International Zoning Code,* including general provisions, exempt and prohibited signs, permits and specific sign requirements.

REFERENCE: Chapter 10, 2018 *International Zoning Code*

KEY POINTS:
- What is the purpose of Chapter 10 of the IZC?
- What are the different types of animated signs? What is a free-standing sign?
- A projecting sign extends at least how far from a building face?
- What are the general sign types?
- How is the area of a sign to be computed?
- To which codes must all signs comply? How are signs in rights-of-ways handled? Signs projecting over public ways?
- What is the procedure for addressing dangerous signs?
- How is obsolete sign copy to be regulated?
- What are the limitations for the continued use of a nonconforming sign?
- What signs are considered exempt from the IZC?
- What types of signs are prohibited by the IZC?
- When are permits required for signs?
- What information is necessary to apply for a sign permit?
- When are the permits required for changes to signs?
- What three types of identification signs are regulated by the IZC? What six types of temporary signs?
- What specific requirements apply to canopy and marquee signs? Awning signs? Projecting signs?
- How are roof signs and window signs to be regulated?
- When is a master sign plan required? What items must be addressed by a master sign plan?

Topic: Safety and Orderly Development	**Category:** Sign Regulations
Reference: IZC 1001.1	**Subject:** Purpose

Code Text: *The purpose of this chapter is to protect the safety and orderly development of the community through the regulation of signs and sign structures.*

Discussion and Commentary: More and more communities are regulating the types, aesthetics and sizes of signs in order to reduce visual pollution. There is a fine line between allowing a business to advertise in order to produce revenue, some of which may go back to the jurisdiction in the form of taxes, and allowing signs to dominate the street scape. Traffic safety issues may also arise with signs that block motorists' vision at intersections, or entrances and exits of businesses.

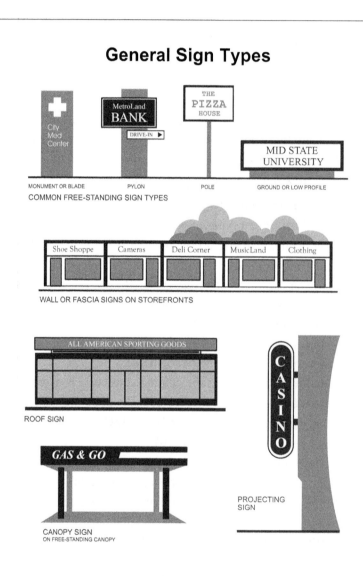

Section 1002 has many definitions of various types of signs, but many signs defy categorization. After making an interpretation, the zoning code official may, in some instances, need to take the proposed sign to an advisory board for a final decision on its classification.

Topic: Sign Types and Area Computation
Reference: IZC 1003.1
Category: Sign Regulations
Subject: General Signs Types

Code Text: *Sign types and the computation of sign area shall be as depicted in Figures 1003.1(1) through 1003.1(4).*

Discussion and Commentary: These provisions attempt to categorize many of the most common signs that are encountered. Along with the general classifications, more specific details are provided, such as signs on a flat roof versus signs on a sloped roof, and the various methods for computing actual sign area.

METROLAND BANK
Drive-In Branch ◀ COMPUTE AREA AROUND COPY ELEMENTS ONLY.

COMPUTE AREA INSIDE DEFINED BORDER OR INSIDE CONTRASTING COLOR AREA. ▶

METROLAND BANK
Drive-In Branch

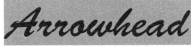

COMPUTE SUM OF AREAS OF INDIVIDUAL ELEMENTS ON WALL OR STRUCTURE.

PARKING ▶

IN COMPUTING AREA FOR UPPER- AND LOWER-CASE LETTERING, INCLUDE ASCENDERS OR DESCENDERS, BUT NOT BOTH. CALCULATE SUPER ASCENDERS SEPARATELY AS INDICATED.

Some businesses are identifiable purely by their roof based on color or geometrical shape. Typically, such identification would not be classified as a "sign," based on the definition in Chapter 2 of the IZC.

Topic: Conformance to Codes
Reference: IZC 1004.1
Category: Sign Regulations
Subject: General Provisions

Code Text: *Any sign hereafter erected shall conform to the provisions of this ordinance and the provisions of the* International Building Code *and any other ordinance or regulation within this jurisdiction.*

Discussion and Commentary: Not only do signs need to meet the requirements of the IZC for height, size and location; they must also meet the structural requirements in the building code (IBC), as signs are subject to wind and/or seismic loads similar to those imposed on other structures. In addition, many signs are constructed with electrical components that need to comply with the applicable codes.

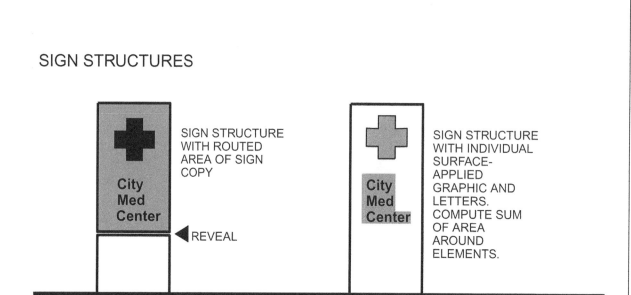

Pole-mounted and monument signs that are excessively tall in height or large in surface area can be a safety hazard if not constructed to resist the required wind and seismic loads. Even signs mounted to the roof or face of a building are subjected to these loads and must be designed to resist failure. According to Chapter 2 in the IBC, a sign is considered a "structure" and is therefore subject to a building permit.

Topic: Signs in Right-of-Way
Reference: IZC 1004.2
Category: Sign Regulations
Subject: General Provisions

Code Text: *No sign other than an official traffic sign or similar sign shall be erected within 2 feet (610 mm) of the lines of any street, or within any public way, unless specifically authorized by other ordinances or regulations of this jurisdiction or by specific authorization of the code official.*

Discussion and Commentary: In many instances, jurisdictions are held legally responsible for structures placed in a right-of-way, insofar as the right-of-way may be considered property of the jurisdiction. Signs are no different and, as such, must be set back from rights-of-way. Obstruction of vision is another area of concern if signs are placed in a right-of-way.

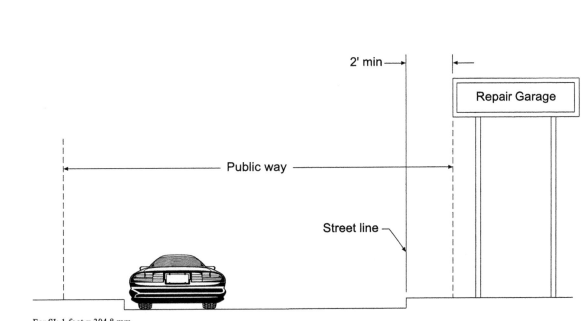

For SI: 1 foot = 304.8 mm.

Section 1004.3 prohibits signs from projecting over public walkways unless they meet certain criteria, including having a minimum clearance of 8 feet from grade level to the bottom of the sign. Signs projecting over vehicular access areas must be in conformance with the minimum clearances limitations set forth by the jurisdiction.

Topic: List of Exempt Signs **Category:** Sign Regulations
Reference: IZC 1005.1 **Subject:** Exempt Signs

Code Text: *The following signs shall be exempt from the provisions of this chapter. No signs shall be exempt from Section 1004.4.* See listing of seven types of signs that are exempt from all sign requirements other that those addressing traffic visibility.

Discussion and Commentary: With certain stipulations, seven general sign types are exempt from the requirements of the IZC. Such exempted signs include directional, warning or information signs authorized by a governmental body; flags of government or noncommercial institutions; religious symbols and seasonal decorations; and street address signs. Even though these signs may be exempt, they still must comply with the traffic visibility constraints cited in Section 1004.4.

Although specific types of signs may be exempt from the provisions of the IZC, they may require compliance with other codes if they are subject to wind, seismic or other structural load conditions, or if they contain electrical components.

Topic: Prohibited Devices and Locations **Category:** Sign Regulations
Reference: IZC 1006.1 **Subject:** Prohibited Signs

Code Text: *The following devices and locations shall be specifically prohibited:* See listing of seven types and locations of signs that are not permitted.

Discussion and Commentary: This section lists a number of general types of signs and devices that are not allowed by the IZC. Signs that interfere with traffic visibility or signals, signs encroaching on public rights-of-way, signs that flash or blink and can be mistaken for traffic signals, portable signs (unless temporary), and signs attached to vehicles or trailers are not permitted under most conditions. Vehicles and trailers used as static displays and balloons are also prohibited, as are streamers and pinwheels not part of a temporary promotion.

The provisions must be reviewed closely to determine if a particular sign is prohibited based on the stipulations set forth in the IZC. Some signs may be permitted if they do not specifically fall into these categories.

Study Session 11

Topic: Permits Required
Reference: IZC 1007.1

Category: Sign Regulations
Subject: Permits

Code Text: *Unless specifically exempted, a permit must be obtained from the code official for the erection and maintenance of all signs erected or maintained within this jurisdiction and in accordance with other ordinances of this jurisdiction. Exemptions from the necessity of securing a permit, however, shall not be construed to relieve the owner of the sign involved from responsibility for its erection and maintenance in a safe manner and in a manner in accordance with all the other provisions of this ordinance.*

Discussion and Commentary: Prior to the installation of a sign, all necessary permits must be obtained from the code official. A permit is mandated for all sign work unless such signs are specifically exempted by Section 1005.1. Even if a sign is classified as exempt, it still must comply with established safety provisions and maintained in compliance with all applicable provisions of the IZC.

Section 1007.2 specifies what construction documents must be submitted for a sign permit. These documents may also require structural calculations sealed by a registered design professional where required by the IBC.

Topic: Changes to Signs
Reference: IZC 1007.3
Category: Sign Regulations
Subject: Permits

Code Text: *No sign shall be structurally altered, enlarged or relocated except in conformity to the provisions herein, nor until a proper permit, if required, has been secured. The changing or maintenance of movable parts or components of an approved sign that is designed for such changes, or the changing of copy, business names, lettering, sign faces, colors, display and/or graphic matter, or the content of any sign shall not be deemed a structural alteration.*

Discussion and Commentary: The focus of the provisions addressing changes to existing signs is more on what is *not* considered a structural alteration than on what *is* considered a structural alteration. Unless an existing previously approved sign is structurally altered, enlarged or relocated, it typically does not require an additional permit.

Permit fees to erect, alter or relocate a sign shall be in accordance with the fee schedule adopted by the jurisdiction. Additional electrical permit fees may be appropriate in some instances.

Study Session 11

Topic: Specific Sign Requirements
Reference: IZC 1008.1 through 1008.3
Category: Sign Regulations
Subject: Specific Sign Requirements

Code Text: *Identification signs shall be in accordance with Sections 1008.1.1 through 1008.1.3. Temporary signs shall be in accordance with Sections 1008.2.1 through 1008.2.6. Signs of specific type shall be in accordance with Sections 1008.3.1 through 1008.3.7.*

Discussion and Commentary: Many specific types of signs are enumerated in Section 1008, along with the requirements for each. Those signs that are regulated include: wall-mounted and free-standing identification and directional signs; temporary signs such as real estate, event and political signs; and specific sign types, including awning, roof and window signs.

Two tables are included to allow the jurisdiction to specify the appropriate limitations as to the aggregate wall sign area and maximum percentage of building surface permitted for sign area for identification signs. In addition, a table addresses standards for the number, height and area of free-standing identification signs.

Topic: Master Sign Plan Required
Reference: IZC 1009.1
Category: Sign Regulations
Subject: Signs for Development Complexes

Code Text: *Landlord or single-owner controlled multiple-occupancy development complexes on parcels exceeding 8 acres (32 376 m^2) in size, such as shopping centers or planned industrial parks, shall submit to the code official a master sign plan prior to issuance of new sign permits. The master sign plan shall establish standards and criteria for all signs in the complex that require permits, and shall address, at a minimum, the following: 1) proposed sign locations, 2) materials, 3) type of illumination, 4) design of free-standing sign structures, 5) size, 6) quantity, and 7) uniform standards for nonbusiness signage, including directional and informational signs.*

Discussion and Commentary: In order for the code official to gain a general idea of what type of signs are being considered for a large development, as well as where the signs are intended to be located, the owner is required to submit an overall sign plan depicting a wide variety of information.

REQUIREMENTS FOR MASTER SIGN PLAN

1. PROPOSED SIGN LOCATIONS
2. MATERIALS
3. TYPE OF ILLUMINATION
4. DESIGN OF FREE-STANDING SIGN STRUCTURES
5. SIZE
6. QUANTITY
7. UNIFORM STANDARDS FOR NONBUSINESS SIGNAGE

Once approved, all signage within a multiple-occupancy development complex shall comply with the master sign plan. Any amendments must be signed and approved by the owner(s) within the complex before such amendment becomes effective.

Study Session 11

Study Session 11
IZC Chapter 10

1. Which of the following signs best describes a billboard?
   a. fascia
   b. banner
   c. marquee
   d. outdoor advertising

   Reference_____

2. An abandoned sign is defined as one that _____.
   a. is no longer in compliance with state laws
   b. is no longer in compliance with local ordinances
   c. has been abandoned for more than 6 consecutive months
   d. has ceased to be used, and the owner no longer intends to use it

   Reference_____

3. The extension of a building facade above the line of the structural roof is considered a(n) _____.
   a. parapet
   b. marquee
   c. on-premise sign
   d. wall or fascia sign

   Reference_____

4. The length of an exterior building wall oriented to the public way it faces is considered _____.
   a. a mansard
   b. frontage (building)
   c. frontage (property)
   d. an architectural projection

   Reference_____

5. Generally, a sign affixed to an exterior wall of a building that projects not more than 18 inches from the building wall is considered a(n) _____.
   a. menu board
   b. off-premise sign
   c. wall or fascia sign
   d. billboard

   Reference_____

6. Other than window signs, interior signs are _____.
   a. not covered by the IZC
   b. regulated only for size
   c. regulated only as to fire hazard
   d. required to conform as on-premise signs

   Reference_____

7. Examples of determining sign area include all but which of the following methods?
   a. the largest single face of a V sign
   b. the smallest geometric figure that comprises the sign face
   c. the graphic elements comprising the content or message of a sign
   d. the sum of the regular geometric figures that comprise the sign face

   Reference_____

8. Any sign to be erected shall conform to the *International Zoning Code* and the *International _____ Code*.
   a. *Fire*
   b. *Building*
   c. *Existing Building*
   d. *Property Maintenance*

   Reference_____

9. Signs projecting over public walkways must have a minimum clearance of _____ feet above the grade level, measured to the bottom of the sign.
   a. 8
   b. 9
   c. 10
   d. 12

   Reference_____

10. Animated signs are generally permitted only in _____ and _____ zones.

    a. agricultural, residential
    b. residential, industrial
    c. agricultural, commercial
    d. commercial, industrial

Reference_____

11. Nonconforming signs may be altered, provided _____.

    a. only the sign face is increased
    b. only electrical alterations are conducted
    c. only structural alterations are conducted
    d. the alteration will not increase the nonconformity of the sign

Reference_____

12. Which of the following is not considered an exempt sign?

    a. government flag
    b. small street address sign
    c. temporary pole sign
    d. court-authorized official notice

Reference_____

13. Which of the following is not considered a prohibited sign?

    a. flashing signs that appear to be traffic safety lights
    b. permanent streamers and balloons
    c. noncommercial flags displayed on flagpoles
    d. signs displayed on utility poles located in the public right-of-way

Reference_____

14. When required, the details of construction for obtaining a sign permit specifically include all of the following except _____.

    a. loads
    b. deflection
    c. stresses
    d. anchorage

Reference_____

15. Portable signs shall be displayed not more than _____ days in any calendar year.

    a. 120   b. 60

    c. 20   d. 10

    Reference_____

16. What is the maximum number of directional signs allowed for each street entrance on a lot?

    a. 1   b. 2

    c. 3   d. 4

    Reference_____

17. What is the maximum number of real estate signs allowed on a single residential lot?

    a. 1   b. 2

    c. 3   d. 4

    Reference_____

18. Real estate signs advertising the sale of lots shall be removed within _____ days following the sale of the last original lot in the subdivision.

    a. 2   b. 7

    c. 10   d. 30

    Reference_____

19. Development and construction signs shall be limited to no more than _____ sign(s) per single residential lot.

    a. 1   b. 4

    c. 6   d. 12

    Reference_____

20. Permit fees for signs shall be based upon the _____.
    a. size of the sign
    b. height of the sign
    c. valuation of the sign
    d. fee schedule adopted by the jurisdiction

    Reference_____

21. Generally, political signs must be removed within _____ following the election.
    a. 24 hours   b. one week
    c. 10 days   d. one month

    Reference_____

22. The aggregate area of all window signs shall not exceed _____ percent of the window area on which such signs are displayed.
    a. 10   b. 25
    c. 33   d. 50

    Reference_____

23. In general, the copy area of a canopy sign shall not exceed _____ percent of the face area of the canopy.
    a. 10   b. 25
    c. 33   d. 50

    Reference_____

24. Menu boards are limited in size to a maximum of _____ square feet.
    a. 6   b. 16
    c. 24   d. 50

    Reference_____

25. All multiple-occupancy development complexes exceeding _____ acres shall submit master sign plans.

    a. 5   b. 8

    c. 10   d. 18

Reference_____

Study Session

12

Legal Aspects of Code Administration, Chapters 3 and 4

Local Government Law and State Legislative Law

OBJECTIVE: To gain a basic understanding of state and local powers in regard to the adoption and administration of codes, including the limits of those powers through various rules and enabling legislation.

REFERENCE: Chapters 3 and 4, *Legal Aspects of Code Administration*

KEY POINTS:
- What are the different forms of local government?
- What are the components of Dillon's Rule?
- How does "enabling legislation" relate to Dillon's Rule?
- What is meant by "home rule?" Why is "home rule" generally an advantage to municipalities and, therefore, to building code enactment?
- What is the difference between "expressed power" and "implied power?"
- Why is enabling legislation important?
- What is "ultra vires" legislation? How does it apply to adoption of a building code?
- What is the appropriate process for local adoption of a building code?
- What type of state legislation enables local governments to enact building codes?
- What is the result of a state prescribing minimum code standards on local governments?
- What is the difference between a building code and a fire code?
- Why should the fire marshal and building official cooperate with each other?
- What is the purpose of zoning ordinances?
- What is a doctrine of preemption?
- What is a doctrine of sovereign immunity?
- What is declaratory relief?

Topic: Municipal Powers	Category: Local Governmental Law
Reference: *Legal Aspects,* Chapter 3	Subject: Dillon's Rule

Text: *One important rule governs all municipal law, and municipal attorneys must constantly refer to it in advising clients as to the extent of the power and authority of any local government. It is Dillon's Rule. It states that a municipal corporation has only those powers which are: (a) expressly granted to it by charter or other state legislation; (b) implied or necessarily incident to the express powers; and (c) essential and indispensable to the declared objects and purposes of the corporation. Almost every power and function of a municipal corporation must be traceable, directly or indirectly, to some state authorizing (enabling) legislation. If no authorizing legislation can be found, then the local government most likely lacks authority to undertake the operation.*

Discussion and Commentary: Dillon's Rule has been applied to municipal powers in many states. It is derived from a written decision by Judge John F. Dillon of Iowa in 1868 and is a cornerstone of American municipal law. It maintains that a political subdivision of a state is a creature of the state and thereby gets its powers from the state. It is used in interpreting state law when there is a question of whether or not a local government has a certain power.

If there is any reasonable doubt whether a power has been conferred on a local government, then the power has not been conferred. This is the rule of strict construction of local government powers.

Topic: Enabling Legislation	Category: Local Governmental Law
Reference: *Legal Aspects*, Chapter 3	Subject: Dillon's Rule

Text: *In the area of building code adoption, many states have held, notwithstanding the general application of Dillon's Rule, that there are certain inherent municipal powers, and no enabling legislation need exist in order to justify the enactment of such legislation. The adoption of a building code appears to be one of those inherent municipal powers. The courts have ruled that if the adoption, administration and enforcement of a building code is of such fundamental importance to the health and welfare of a community, it is not necessary for that community to have special and express legislation permitting it to regulate the construction of buildings in the area.*

Discussion and Commentary: Building codes are an important tool in controlling, regulating and ensuring that buildings and structures within a jurisdiction are constructed properly. Basic health, safety and the general public welfare are expected and relied upon by the jurisdiction's citizens. Without building codes, property values may decline, building-related incidents such as fires, collapse and deterioration may be more prevalent, and an increase in jurisdictional services such as police and fire personnel will be necessary.

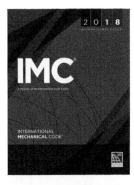

If a building code must be enacted in the absence of any express legislation, the opposing lawyer will undoubtedly argue that the legislation is *ultra vires*, which means that the local government entity has acted beyond the scope of its powers.

Topic: Home Rule	**Category:** Local Governmental Law
Reference: *Legal Aspects,* Chapter 3	**Subject:** Home Rule Municipalities

Text: *The home rule municipality is distinguished from other types of local government in that its charter is constitutionally derived from an authorization in a state's constitution. A state whose constitution contains a provision authorizing home rule municipalities allows the people of a city to establish their own charter by referendum. In other words, the state legislature enacts the charter and grants the powers to the local communities under which they must govern. In fact, one of the main reasons for the development of this type of municipality was the desire to stop the state legislative bodies from interfering with purely local affairs of which the state had limited knowledge.*

Discussion and Commentary: Even though a city may be considered a home rule municipality, this does not guarantee exemption from many state or federal mandates. If the state rules that some regulation is of statewide concern, such as driving under the influence and, in some cases, statewide construction codes, the municipality is bound to follow these regulations.

Generally, the home rule charter is seen as a grant of virtually unlimited powers to the municipality over local affairs. Essentially, this means that where there is no provision in the local home rule charter granting the authority to the municipality to enact a law in a certain area (e.g., building codes), the city may go ahead and enact legislation.

Topic: Adoption Process
Reference: *Legal Aspects,* Chapter 3
Category: Local Governmental Law
Subject: Local Adoption of a Building Code

Text: *The creation and enactment of a building code by a local governmental entity is an important legal step requiring caution and the advice of an attorney. While the selection or development of a building code is usually the task of a building official, responsibility for getting it legally operative must rest with a municipal attorney. There must be a close working relationship between the attorney and the building official in both areas in order to pass successfully an ordinance adopting a particular code. The provisions of enabling legislation must be followed precisely.*

Discussion and Commentary: Before a building code is adopted, it is merely a book with suggestions for constructing safe buildings, but once it is adopted, it becomes law in the jurisdiction. Therefore, the adopting ordinance must be prepared properly or it can be challenged in court. Some municipal attorneys do not understand all the ins and outs of a building code's technical aspects, but they are familiar with how the jurisdiction should adopt ordinances. The building official should comply fully with the adopting requirements established by the jurisdiction's legal counsel.

The building code allows, and often requires, the building official to make many decisions that are not always specifically addressed in the code. Although the code establishes criteria for these decisions, the building official should routinely check with the municipal attorney to verify that legal protocol is being followed.

Study Session 12

Topic: Enacting Building Codes **Category:** State Legislative Law
Reference: *Legal Aspects,* Chapter 4 **Subject:** Enabling Legislation

Text: *Many states have some form of legislation in place which enables local government to enact building codes. These statutes, which are prepared and enacted by a local, state or federal government, must be followed to the letter when establishing a local government code enforcement system. Most enabling legislation requires that buildings and other structures be divided into identifiable classes and that an official of some type be appointed to implement and enforce the provisions of the local ordinance. This official is generally known as the Building Official or by some similar title.*

Discussion and Commentary: Section 104 in the *International Building Code* establishes the duties and powers of the building official, but he or she should also work closely with the municipal attorney when adopting or amending codes. If the building official or any other Building Safety Department employee acts beyond his or her powers, it could result in serious legal ramifications for the jurisdiction.

Typically, an administrative board is set up to hear appeals of the building official's decisions. The board usually has three general powers: it is authorized to hear any appeal of a building official's decision, it has the authority to interpret the provisions of the code when the intent is assured, and it is empowered to consider new and innovative building techniques for use in its jurisdiction.

Topic: Code Application	**Category:** State Legislative Law
Reference: *Legal Aspects,* Chapter 4	**Subject:** State Building Codes

Text: *Rather than allow local governments to control construction, some states regulate it themselves. When states do this, there is no local building code department and no local control. A number of states now prescribe minimum code standards. In these states, the local government must meet a set of minimum standards in the code it adopts if it wishes to regulate building construction. Generally, these mandatory state building statutes do not apply to home rule municipalities.*

Discussion and Commentary: In addition to imposing a building code, some states also establish minimum qualifications for various Building Safety Department employees and require that code officials pass certification exams.

In some instances, states may impose a construction code that must be followed implicitly. If it establishes both minimum and maximum requirements, it is commonly referred to as a "mini-maxi code." In other cases, the state may only establish minimal requirements, but a jurisdiction can adopt more stringent regulations.

Study Session 12

Topic: Fire Code
Reference: *Legal Aspects,* Chapter 4

Category: State Legislative Law
Subject: Related Legislative Provisions

Text: *Although the fire and building codes often play against one another, they should actually complement each other. While the building code is designed to mandate the most current building construction techniques, the fire code (or fire prevention code) is designed to maintain the structure against the threat of fire during its existence. The building code is a construction code; the fire code is a maintenance code. To best enforce and administer all codes, it is necessary for the fire marshal's office and the building and code enforcement departments to cooperate.*

Discussion and Commentary: Many fire departments conduct annual or periodic inspections of existing buildings to ensure compliance with minimum safety requirements established in the fire code. Maximum occupancy loads, maintenance of required exits, types of hazardous materials present, availability of building access by fire apparatus, fire extinguisher locations, operation of fire sprinklers and alarms, unacceptable use of extension cords and overall general housekeeping are some of the areas that fire inspectors observe when they are conducting periodic inspections. On many occasions, the fire inspectors will need to work with the Building Safety Department to determine original building code requirements that were provided when the building was first completed.

By doing joint plan reviews and inspections where appropriate, the expertise of all parties is fully utilized. Furthermore, the property owner will not receive conflicting directions from two different agencies if there is cooperation from the beginning of a project.

Topic: Zoning Ordinances
Reference: *Legal Aspects,* Chapter 4
Category: State Legislative Law
Subject: Related Legislative Provisions

Text: *The underlying purpose of a zoning ordinance is to separate and regulate land uses which are not compatible with one another. It does very little good for a builder to get a building permit only to learn that the type of building he or she intends to build is not permitted under the zoning ordinance. To avoid this, building officials must have a close working relationship with the zoning officials in their jurisdictions.*

Discussion and Commentary: Generally, if a customer visits the Building Safety Department and asks about constructing an out-of-the-ordinary building, the customer should be referred to the Zoning Department to determine if the particular use would be allowed under the zoning ordinance. For example, a highly hazardous use may be permitted under the building code, with certain code restrictions, adjacent to a residential structure. However, the zoning ordinance may prohibit the hazardous use altogether in a residential zone.

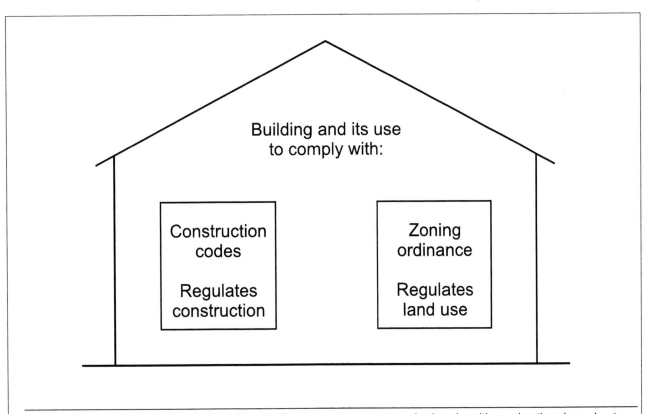

Building Safety Departments and Zoning Departments must work closely with each other in order to verify that only permitted uses are allowed in the established Zoning Districts.

Study Session 12

Topic: Precedence of Laws	**Category:** State Legislative Law
Reference: *Legal Aspects,* Chapter 4	**Subject:** Preemption

Text: *Preemption is a judicially created doctrine which says that a state may not pass a law that is inconsistent with federal law. If a state enacts such a law, the federal law will take precedence over the state law to the extent that there is conflict. Preemption allows the federal and state governments to regulate activities which would otherwise be subject to local control. The most obvious illustration of preemption arises in those states where the state has adopted a building code and prohibits the adoption of a code by its local governments.*

Discussion and Commentary: In an attempt to establish some degree of code uniformity, states will sometimes mandate that only certain codes or certain editions of codes be used throughout the state. While local amendments are often allowed (if they are more stringent than those of the state), in some states such amendments are prohibited.

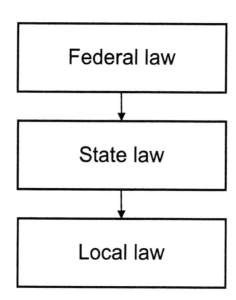

It is not necessary that a state building code specifically indicate that it intends to preempt the local municipality in the administration and enforcement of its own building code. Provided the state regulations are detailed and comprehensive, it will be determined by a court of law that the local government is not intended to have authority in that area.

Topic: Liability	**Category:** State Legislative Law
Reference: *Legal Aspects,* Chapter 4	**Subject:** Sovereign Immunity

Text: *In its broadest terms, sovereign immunity stipulates that the state may not be held liable for any wrongdoing which it or any of its agents may commit. This ancient doctrine originated in England where it was widely accepted that the King could do no wrong. In England, the King and all of his men were not held responsible for their actions. Sovereign immunity applies not only in the area of tort liability, but also in the field of regulation.*

Discussion and Commentary: It is not uncommon for the state authority to work with the local building official to meet many of the local code requirements as they apply to state-owned facilities, such as regulations addressing fire sprinklers and means of egress. However, by law, the state can generally bypass the local building department and construct the building according to their own established requirements. Exceptions to this fundamental rule include where the state has expressly waived the immunity from local regulation, where immunity is waived with respect to certain types of buildings, or where the state requests the assistance of the local building official of specific projects.

Some common state structures that generally have sovereign immunity are public schools, highway maintenance buildings, prisons, driver's license facilities and toll booths.

Study Session 12

Topic: Declaratory Relief
Reference: *Legal Aspects,* Chapter 4
Category: State Legislative Law
Subject: Sovereign Immunity

Text: *An experienced building official will usually know what types of state buildings are subject to local control. If the official is unsure, however, the best course is to sue the state for declaratory and injunctive relief. Declaratory relief is an interpretation by a court of law as to whether the state has immunity in this particular field. If the court holds that the state is not immune from local inspection, it could issue an injunction requiring the state to stop performing any work on the project until it has obtained a permit and is in compliance with all other code provisions.*

Discussion and Commentary: If a building is being constructed to perform its statutory function, such as a school building, then, in most instances, the building official will have no jurisdictional authority. If, however, the school district decides to build a house for its principal, this may not be considered a statutory function of a school, and the house may be subject to the local building codes. In this case, the building official should contact the municipal attorney and seek declaratory relief.

Even if a building is exempt from the local building codes, the state may still need to seek and pay for permits from the jurisdiction to obtain sewer and water hookups. In some instances, the local electrical utility will not energize the building until the local inspector has given written approval to do so.

Quiz

Study Session 12
Legal Aspects of Code Administration, Chapters 3 and 4

1. Which one of the following rules is typically referenced when determining if local government has certain powers?

    a. home rule

    b. Dillon's Rule

    c. the rule of equitable estoppel

    d. sovereign immunity rulings

    Reference _____

2. Generally, home rule makes it easier for a municipality to _____.

    a. enact local legislation

    b. enact state legislation

    c. override federal legislation

    d. receive federal grant monies

    Reference _____

3. In some instances, enabling legislation is not required to justify certain fundamentals such as adopting a(n) _____.

    a. city charter
    b. general plan
    c. building code
    d. annexation guideline

    Reference _____

4. If a municipality adopts a building code without enabling legislation, the courts may declare this as a(n) _____ action.

    a. statutory
    b. enabling
    c. *ultra vires*
    d. selective enforcement

    Reference _____

5. The building code is typically considered a construction code, whereas the fire code is often considered a _____ code.
   a. prescriptive
   b. specification
   c. maintenance
   d. performance

   Reference _____

6. Which doctrine stipulates that the state may not be held liable for any wrongdoing that it or any of its agents may commit?
   a. home rule
   b. public duty
   c. equitable estoppel
   d. sovereign immunity

   Reference _____

7. The general underlying purpose of a zoning ordinance is to _____.
   a. develop a general plan
   b. prohibit any land use variances
   c. separate and regulate land uses
   d. identify and regulate construction uses

   Reference _____

8. An interpretation by a court of law as to whether the state has immunity in a particular field is known as _____.
   a. home rule
   b. declaratory relief
   c. enabling legislation
   d. subdivision

   Reference _____

9. Generally, a _____ is viewed as a corporation established by the state legislature for the good of those inhabitants that live in a prescribed area.
   a. county
   b. jurisdiction
   c. municipality
   d. local authority

   Reference _____

10. A power which has been "set forth and declared exactly" is known as _____ power.
    a. implied
    b. enabled
    c. expressed
    d. essential and indispensable

    Reference _____

11. Which of the following would not be considered a type of municipality?
    a. city
    b. county
    c. borough
    d. township

    Reference _____

12. _____ powers arise from those powers expressly granted but that may not be specifically authorized.
    a. Implied
    b. Enabled
    c. Expressed
    d. Essential and indispensable

    Reference _____

13. Responsibility for getting a building code legally operative by a local government usually rests with the _____.
    a. city clerk
    b. building official
    c. board of appeals
    d. municipal attorney

    Reference _____

14. A _____ must frequently be published in the local newspaper when a building code is being proposed for adoption.
    a. legal notice
    b. public hearing
    c. notice of intent
    d. brief news article

    Reference _____

15. Generally, the _____ charter is seen as a grant of virtually unlimited powers to the municipality over local affairs.

    a. enabling
    b. home rule
    c. public duty
    d. sovereign duty

    Reference _____

16. Typically, a specified number of copies of the building code must be officially on file in the _____ for access by the public.

    a. clerk's office
    b. building department
    c. attorney general's office
    d. city/county attorney's office

    Reference _____

17. Certain legal procedures must be followed when adopting a building code, as any omission may result in _____.

    a. voidance of the entire building code
    b. refunds for certain building permits
    c. additional record keeping for permits
    d. requiring all applicants to appear before the board of appeals

    Reference _____

18. In many cases, if the state adopts a building code it will not apply to _____ municipalities.

    a. charter
    b. home rule
    c. public duty
    d. largely populated

    Reference _____

19. State-regulated storm water management was initiated by the states' desire to participate in the National _____ Program.

    a. Flood Insurance
    b. Flood Prevention
    c. Historical Buildings Register
    d. Community Development Block Grant

    Reference _____

20. State buildings require local permits and inspections if the state has waived its right of _____ immunity.

   a. implied
   b. enabled
   c. sovereign
   d. public duty

   Reference _____

21. If a state adopts a state building code and prohibits the local municipality from adopting its own building code, this is known as _____.

   a. preemption
   b. implied immunity
   c. equitable estoppel
   d. sovereign immunity

   Reference _____

22. Existing structures are primarily the concern of the fire department and the _____ department.

   a. zoning
   b. public works
   c. building safety
   d. code enforcement

   Reference _____

23. Rather than publishing the entire code in the local newspaper during the adoption process, the code itself is typically filed with the municipal/county clerk for the purpose of _____.

   a. public notice
   b. notice of intent
   c. public reference
   d. adoption by reference

   Reference _____

24. A county form of government is usually considered a(n) _____.

   a. charter entity
   b. extension of the state
   c. home rule entity
   d. equal to any municipality

   Reference _____

25. Something that is _____ no longer has legal force or binding effect.

   a. restricted
   b. discretionary
   c. preempted
   d. null and void

   Reference _____

Study Session 12

Study Session

13

Legal Aspects of Code Administration, Chapters 6 through 8
Administration and Enforcement, Administrative Law and Constitutional Law

OBJECTIVE: To gain a basic understanding of the concepts that relate to the enforcement and administration of the building code, including the handling of complaints; powers and rules of procedures for building code boards of appeal; and various ways in which federal constitutional law impacts the day-to-day operation of a building department.

REFERENCE: Chapters 6 through 8, *Legal Aspects of Code Administration*

KEY POINTS:
- What is the most important step in the administration and enforcement of building codes?
- What procedures are necessary for the issuance of a building permit? What information should be provided by the applicant?
- For what reasons may a building permit be revoked? What legal concerns are associated with revocation of a permit?
- What is the doctrine of equitable estoppel?
- How can a disclaimer on a permit application avoid liability?
- Why are the plans examination and inspection functions potential sources of liability?
- What is a discretionary act? A ministerial act? With what activities are such acts associated?
- When should civil prosecution be used by building departments?
- What is a civil complaint? What six pieces of information are typically required for a civil complaint?
- What are the three types of injunctive relief?
- What steps should be taken when seeking a temporary restraining order or injunction?
- What are the general guidelines for handling complaints?
- What type of evidence should be gathered for testimony in a court case?
- When should the building department adopt administrative guidelines?

KEY POINTS (Cont'd):

- What is the Board of Building Code of Appeals (BBCA) and what qualifications are necessary of its members? What powers are granted to a BBCA?
- What are the three main avenues of appeal? Where does the burden of proof lie?
- What are the general criteria related to search and seizure issues? How does the Camara ruling affect building department procedures?
- What action is necessary to be considered "consent"?
- What is the "plain view doctrine"? What are its limitations?
- What special considerations for access to private property are held for emergency situations? For abandoned buildings?
- When is a search warrant required? What information is necessary for obtaining a warrant?
- What is "substantive due process"? How should it be applied?
- Can code provisions be applied retroactively?
- How is the 14th Amendment to the Constitution applicable to code enforcement? What two concepts address equal protection?
- When does discriminatory enforcement occur?

Topic: Legal Documents	Category: Administration and Enforcement
Reference: *Legal Aspects,* Chapter 6	Subject: Permit Issuance

Text: *The issuance of the building permit is the most important step in the enforcement and administration of building codes. The application for the building permit and the permit itself are the two most important documents a building code official has to determine what the builder or contractor is doing on the job site. It is crucial that the building permit be issued in a prescribed fashion and that all the necessary steps be taken to ensure that the permit is issued properly.*

Discussion and Commentary: Section 105 of the *International Building Code* establishes criteria for permit issuance, expiration, and suspension or revocation. The building official, as well as the entire Building Safety Department staff, should be intimately familiar with this section so that all permits are legally processed according to the code. Failure to comply with these requirements could leave the jurisdiction vulnerable to undesirable legal action.

Because permit technicians receive the majority of inquiries regarding permit requirements, it is important for them to become familiar with what projects require permits and what needs to be accomplished in order to receive a permit.

Topic: Legal Documents
Reference: *Legal Aspects,* Chapter 6

Category: Administration and Enforcement
Subject: Permit Revocation

Text: *Once an application is approved and a permit is granted and construction has begun on a building site, it becomes difficult to revoke the issued permit. This is true even if a mistake exists on the permit itself. This does not mean that a building official cannot revoke a building permit. If a permit is mistakenly issued, and it is obvious that the issuance was a mistake, the building department will be able to revoke the permit without much trouble if, for example, it is obvious that allowing the permit to stand would pose tremendous danger to the safety of the general public. The courts will likely use a common sense approach to determine whether or not a permit should be revoked.*

Discussion and Commentary: Section 105.6 of the *International Building Code* establishes when a permit can be suspended or revoked. However, many times other legal criteria will be presented by the applicant that may penalize the jurisdiction for issuing the permit erroneously, especially if the applicant acted in good faith and relied on the jurisdiction's expertise.

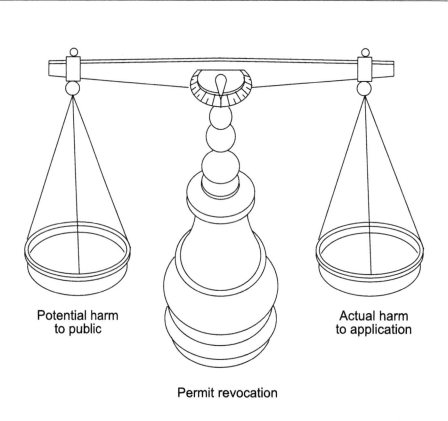

Permit revocation

It is often difficult to determine whether a code violation is serious enough to warrant revocation of a mistakenly issued permit. Because the entire building code relates to safety and construction, any violation of a provision has the potential to result in considerable harm to members of the public.

Topic: Theories
Reference: *Legal Aspects,* Chapter 6

Category: Administration and Enforcement
Subject: Permit Revocation

Text: *The doctrine of equitable estoppel is a doctrine by which the municipality may be precluded by its actions, or by its failure to act, from asserting a right which it otherwise would have had. If another party has justifiably relied upon the action or lack of action of the municipality, and this reliance has changed his or her position so that he or she would suffer injury if the municipality is allowed to repudiate its action, then the court will not allow the municipality to do so under the principle of equitable estoppel.*

Discussion and Commentary: The best defense to legal action taken against the jurisdiction is to make sure that all aspects of the permit application have been thoroughly reviewed by all appropriate departments before issuing the permit. The permit technician should also be certain to obtain all of the necessary information, including a complete description on the application of what the project will entail. Failure to understand the scope of the application can lead to negative legal consequences.

Some courts permit the revocation of the permit, but at the expense of the building official. The courts typically feel that while revocation may be necessary for the protection of the public, the burden of the mistake should fall on the person who negligently issued the permit rather than to the builder or developer. Although this theory is not widely accepted, building officials should check with their municipal attorney.

Topic: Disclaimers
Reference: *Legal Aspects,* Chapter 6
Category: Administration and Enforcement
Subject: Permit Revocation

Text: *In an attempt to avoid liability, the building department can print a disclaimer on the building permit and application to help prevent misunderstandings. This disclaimer can state that the applicant warrants the truthfulness of the information in the application, and that if any of the information provided is incorrect, the building permit may be revoked. Furthermore, the application and permit can provide that if the permit is issued wrongfully, whether based on misinformation or an improper application of the code, the building permit may be revoked.*

Discussion and Commentary: The small print at the end of a permit application can save time and money for the jurisdiction if it spells out the limits of the permit once it is issued. Many municipalities are extremely busy, and occasionally a permit is issued in error or without the final signature from a required department. The sooner a mistake is discovered, the better the chance of revoking the permit.

UNDER PENALTY OF INTENTIONAL MISREPRESENTATION AND / OR PERJURY, I DECLARE that I have examined and / or made this application and it is true and correct to the best of my knowledge and belief. I agree to construct said improvement in compliance with all provisions of the Ordinances of the City of _____. I realize that the information that I have stated hereon forms a basis for the issuance of the Building Permit herein applied for and approval of any plans in connection therewith shall not be construed to permit any construction upon said premises or use thereof in violation of any provision of the _____ City Code or any other ordinance or to excuse the owner or his successors from complying therewith. **WHERE NO WORK HAS BEEN STARTED WITHIN 180 DAYS AFTER THE ISSUANCE OF A PERMIT OR WHEN MORE THAN 180 DAYS LAPSES BETWEEN APPROVAL OF REQUIRED INSPECTIONS, SUCH PERMIT SHALL BE VOID.**
I hereby certify that I am the OWNER at this address or that, for the purposes of obtaining this approval, I am acting on behalf of the owner. All contract work on this project will be done by a contractor holding a valid privilege tax license and contractor's license issued by the State of _____ and the City of _____.

Although a disclaimer may not prevent the application of the doctrine of equitable estoppel, it may help the court resolve the issue in the building official's favor. It should be noted, however, that a disclaimer cannot entirely overrule judge-made law regarding the revocation of permits.

Topic: Potential Liability	**Category:** Administration and Enforcement
Reference: *Legal Aspects,* Chapter 6	**Subject:** Plans Examination

Text: *One of the most frightening areas of potential liability in the enforcement of the building code is the examination of building plans by members of the building code department. To perform the function of plans examiner, the building code department must have a qualified expert in the area. It is sometimes difficult to find well-qualified people to assume these responsibilities. The division of plans examination within a building code department must be thorough in everything it does. A small mistake could mean the loss of many lives and the imposition of legal liability.*

Discussion and Commentary: It is rare for even a seasoned plans examiner to identify every possible code violation on a set of plans, but these oversights must be kept to a minimum through the use of comprehensive checklists, education, available reference books, time management and reduction of interruptions during plan review. Very few, if any, plans examiners are experts in all fields of construction, but they should know their limitations and consult experts when they reach a point of unfamiliarity.

Notes and records should be kept of the plans examiner's impressions as the examination is conducted. Those notes and records should be maintained in the master file of the particular project in question. A standard plan review form should be used for every plan review.

Topic: Civil Complaints
Reference: *Legal Aspects,* Chapter 6
Category: Administration and Enforcement
Subject: Civil Prosecutions

Text: *Once a violation has been found, some action must be taken to enforce the code. Ordinarily, if the structure has been completed, the summary procedures of the revocation of a permit or issuance of a stop work order are not available. Once construction has been completed, prosecution in the city courts becomes the final method of enforcement. Normally, with a civil complaint, the notice of violation may be served either through the mail or physically delivered to the alleged offender.*

Discussion and Commentary: Section 114 of the *International Building Code* spells out how code violations should be handled, including delivery and prosecution. As with other legal issues, the building official should work closely with the municipal attorney to be assured that due process is followed exactly; otherwise, the case may be dismissed.

THE SIX ELEMENTS OF A CIVIL COMPLAINT:

1. NAME OF THE PERSON OR ENTITY TO BE CHARGED
2. DESIGNATING THE CHARGE
3. BODY OF THE CHARGE
4. DATE AND TIME OF THE OFFENSE
5. SIGNATURE OF THE COMPLAINING WITNESS
6. NOTARY OR AFFIDAVIT

Although service of a notice of violation is common practice, occasionally a jurisdiction will require that an alleged offender be arrested under an arrest warrant.

Topic: Types of Injunction	**Category:** Administration and Enforcement
Reference: *Legal Aspects,* Chapter 6	**Subject:** Injunctive Relief

Text: *An injunction is sought by the building official. The remedy is, in essence, an order of the court which requires that the defendant cease and desist from all conduct which amounts to a violation of the building code. In almost every jurisdiction in the United States today, injunctive relief is broken into three types: a temporary restraining order (TRO), a temporary or preliminary injunction, and a permanent injunction.*

Discussion and Commentary: It is always hoped that total cooperation from an alleged code offender can be obtained without formal legal remedies but this is, unfortunately, not always the case. The building official should be very familiar with Sections 114, 115 and 116 of the *International Building Code* and should, again, work closely with the municipal attorney.

TEMPORARY RESTRAINING ORDER (TRO): Issued by the court without notice to the other party and without the other party being heard.

TEMPORARY INJUNCTION: A judicial order issued pending a full hearing by the court after notice is given to the opposing party and after a brief hearing.

PERMANENT INJUNCTION: A judicial order that is issued after the court has heard all the evidence in the case.

Injunctive relief is a judicial order prohibiting specified conduct. Such an act is the use of judicial authority to handle a problem and is not a judgment for money.

Study Session 13

Topic: Guidelines
Reference: *Legal Aspects*, Chapter 6
Category: Administration and Enforcement
Subject: Handling Complaints

Text: *A significant portion of time is spent by building code departments responding to complaints regarding parcels of property. Some general guidelines relating to handling those complaints may be useful. First of all, the person who receives the complaint should obtain as much information as possible. The name of the complainant, his or her address, phone number, the date that he or she viewed the alleged violation, and the nature of the alleged violation are all important. The department should establish a standard procedure for handling of the complaint once it is received and reduced to writing.*

Discussion and Commentary: Many jurisdictions will accept and respond to anonymous complaints. There are pros and cons to this type of procedure. Among the benefits, citizens are more apt to notify the building department of a violation if they know their name will not be needed. Many citizens do not want their neighbors to know that they filed a complaint for fear of reprisal. On the other hand, anonymous complaints can be falsely filed and used to harass neighbors because the complainant knows that he or she will remain under the cloak of anonymity.

As soon as a complaint is received, it should be routed to the proper inspector. Within a few days an inspection should be made, a report completed and the appropriate action taken.

Topic: Written Procedures	**Category:** Administration and Enforcement
Reference: *Legal Aspects*, Chapter 6	**Subject:** Administrative Guidelines

Text: *Every building code department will find that as more and more applications are made under the building code, the department will make certain decisions which are not expressly resolved by the code. Any written set of rules simply cannot cover every single situation which could possibly come up during the construction of buildings. The department should adopt written administrative guidelines to cover those areas not already covered by the code. These may relate to the manner in which inspections are made, the manner in which citizens' complaints are to be handled, and the order of authority within the department. In each of these cases, the general rule should be reduced to a written form.*

Discussion and Commentary: Standard Operating Procedures (SOPs) provide a common tool used for developing written procedures within Building Safety Departments. They should establish, at a minimum, the purpose, reasoning and justification behind the policy, the required implementation date, the details of the procedure to be followed, and a notice that the policy may be updated or abolished in the future if it is found to be inadequate or unnecessary. A simple memo from the building official may suffice until a formal SOP is established.

CITY OF _____ BUILDING SAFETY DIVISION
STANDARD OPERATING PROCEDURE XX-01

Required Zoning Setbacks
The purpose of this Standard Operating Procedure (SOP) is to promote uniformity and consistency among the Building Safety Division staff and other related departments involving the approval of required front, side and rear yard setback requirements.

Effective immediately, when conducting an initial inspection on a property to determine proper zoning setbacks, the structure must be in accordance with the approved site plan, which must be on site. If it is determined that the structure has deviated from the approved site plan, it is permissible to approve the location if it is no greater than six (6) inches from the originally approved point. However, in no case shall the required setbacks be encroached upon.

If it is discovered that the structure has deviated greater than six (6) inches from the approved location or if the structure is discovered to encroach upon the required setback, the project is to be disapproved and the builder is to be notified to revise the site plan and resubmit it to Building Safety for review. Building Safety will forward the revised plan to Planning and Zoning. A revision fee of $--- will be charged for the review. Planning and Zoning has committed to a quick turn around of approving revised site plans.

Written or administrative guidelines facilitate uniform administration of the code. If a decision on a prior situation has been established in writing, the same decision can be easily made in future applications of the rule.

Topic: Authority of the Board
Reference: *Legal Aspects,* Chapter 7

Category: Administrative Law
Subject: Board of Building Code Appeals

Text: *The IBC includes a section dealing with the Board of Building Code Appeals. The board of appeals shall be appointed by the governing body and shall hold office at its pleasure. The board shall adopt rules of procedures for conducting its business.*

Discussion and Commentary: The *International Building Code* provides three different avenues of appeal to the board. An appeal is allowed: 1) if the true intent of the code or the legally adopted rules have been incorrectly interpreted; 2) if the provisions do not fully apply; or 3) if an equal or better method, material or design is being proposed. The IBC also indicates that "the board shall have no authority to waive requirements of this code." In other words, if the code specifies a requirement that cannot be interpreted in any other way, an appeal would not be permitted. For example, if the code specifically requires all buildings to have a fire sprinkler system, this would not be a code requirement that could be appealed, insofar as there is no evidence supporting any other interpretation.

Section 113 and Appendix B of the IBC set forth additional criteria for the establishment, authority and functions of a board of appeals.

Topic: Appeals Procedures	**Category:** Administrative Law
Reference: *Legal Aspects*, Chapter 7	**Subject:** Board of Building Code Appeals

Text: *Certain standard procedures should be followed by boards of building code appeals. These include establishing rules of procedure; holding open public meetings; forming a quorum; giving an appellant notice; presenting proof; granting remedies; ensuring the legality of rulings; rehearing a case; and handing down orders.*

Discussion and Commentary: It is important that meetings of the board of appeals be conducted in an open and impartial manner. The meetings must be available to members of the public at large to allow for their observation and/or participation. Whereas the attendees at most board meetings are limited to interested parties, there should be an opportunity for anyone to sit in on the hearing.

Standardized procedures may help to prevent serious damage to particular cases that may appear in front of a court after an adverse decision by the board. Most of the necessary procedures are rather simple to put into effect, and they make it very easy for the board's attorney to defend the board's decision.

Topic: Burden of Proof
Reference: *Legal Aspects,* Chapter 7

Category: Administrative Law
Subject: Board of Building Code Appeals

Text: *Burden of proof refers to who must prove the issue in controversy and how much proof must be presented to an administrative tribunal or to a court of law in order to be awarded the sought-after relief. In any case before the board of appeals, the burden of proof rests with the appellant. The appellant must show that he or she is entitled to the relief requested.*

Discussion and Commentary: If there is a disagreement in the application of a provision in the building code, with the building official interpreting the code in one manner and the appellant interpreting it differently, the appellant must submit convincing reasoning or documentation to prevail. The decision could also be based on the use of a better material or method than that which is stated in the code, or it might concern an appellant needing additional time to achieve code compliance due to extenuating circumstances. In any case, it is up to the appellant to convince the board that his or her request should be granted.

Before the appellant presents proof, the building official should explain to the board why the appeal was brought, why the building department rejected the initial application and the exact scope of the relief being requested by the appellant. This presentation will prepare the board for the case in front of them.

Topic: Discriminatory Enforcement	**Category:** Constitutional Law
Reference: *Legal Aspects,* Chapter 8	**Subject:** Equal Protection Clause

Text: *Discriminatory enforcement does not look at the facial validity of the law, but rather how the law is applied. When an individual who is found in violation of a building code raises the defense of discriminatory enforcement, he or she is claiming to be impermissibly singled out for enforcement. The best way to avoid this kind of problem is to establish written policies for the department. In so doing, everyone in the office will know which provisions to enforce and the approved method of enforcement. The policies should be followed scrupulously.*

Discussion and Commentary: The building codes department must be careful to always apply the codes evenhandedly. If a provision is applied in an interpretative manner for one applicant, it should be applied in the same manner for all others who have a similar condition. The building official is granted great authority, but with such power comes a responsibility to enforce the law in a fair and nondiscriminatory manner.

Legal challenges based on discriminatory enforcement are rarely upheld, but it is important to remember that although most of these charges are dismissed, safeguards and written policies should be established. This will save the municipality from spending much time and money defending itself against these charges.

Study Session 13

Study Session 13

Legal Aspects of Code Administration, Chapters 6 through 8

1. What is typically considered the most important step in the enforcement and administration of building codes?

    a. inspection of the work

    b. issuance of a stop work order

    c. issuance of the building permit

    d. obtaining a signature on the permit application

    Reference _____

2. The doctrine by which a municipality may be precluded by its actions, or inactions, from asserting a right which it otherwise would have had is known as _____.

    a. implied power
    b. public duty
    c. equitable estoppel
    d. sovereign immunity

    Reference _____

3. The board of appeals shall be appointed by the _____.

    a. building official
    b. governing body
    c. city/county clerk
    d. city/county attorney

    Reference _____

4. In any appeal to the Board of Building Code Appeal, the burden of proof rests with the _____.

    a. appellant
    b. building official
    c. city/county attorney
    d. board of appeals chairperson

    Reference _____

5. To obtain a search warrant to conduct a property inspection, the building official must first have _____.

   a. probable cause
   b. a reasonable suspicion
   c. issued a permit for the property
   d. written complaints from adjacent properties

   Reference _____

6. The requirement that any and all legislation enacted by a government must bear some rational relationship to a legitimate governmental function is known as _____.

   a. constitutional
   b. equal protection
   c. equitable estoppel
   d. substantive due process

   Reference _____

7. If a person raises claims that he or she was impermissibly singled out for code enforcement, that individual will usually raise the defense of _____.

   a. due process
   b. equal protection
   c. discretionary authority
   d. discriminatory enforcement

   Reference _____

8. An order issued by a court requiring a municipality to perform the functions they were responsible to perform is known as a(n) _____.

   a. injunction
   b. search order
   c. writ of mandamus
   d. temporary injunction

   Reference _____

9. An act performed under the authority, policies and procedures of a supervisor, such as a building official, is known as a _____ act.

   a. voluntary
   b. ministerial
   c. discretionary
   d. mandatory

   Reference _____

10. Which of the following is not one of the six elements involved in preparing a typical complaint?

    a. maximum allowable fine

    b. description of the violation

    c. date and time of the offense

    d. signature of the complaining witness

    Reference _____

11. A judicial order that is issued after the court has heard all of the evidence in the case is known as a _____.

    a. search warrant   b. formal complaint

    c. temporary injunction   d. permanent injunction

    Reference _____

12. Which of the following is not a type of injunctive relief?

    a. technical injunction   b. temporary injunction

    c. permanent injunction   d. temporary restraining order

    Reference _____

13. An administrative decision that was made without reliance on either the law or the facts would typically be considered _____.

    a. ministerial   b. unfounded

    c. unconstitutional   d. arbitrary or capricious

    Reference _____

14. Every order or decision by the building board of appeals must be _____.

    a. in writing

    b. agreed upon by all parties

    c. forwarded to the municipal court

    d. agreed upon by the building official

    Reference _____

15. A violation observed while the building official is at a location where he or she is legally entitled to be is admissible because of the _____ doctrine.
    a. plain view
    b. public duty
    c. equal protection
    d. sovereign immunity

    Reference_____

16. Courts will typically uphold retroactive portions of the building code if the building official can show that the building is _____.
    a. in disrepair
    b. an extreme eyesore
    c. hazardous
    d. detrimental to surrounding property values

    Reference_____

17. Generally, when checking for violations at one address, the building official should also check for similar violations in the vicinity to avoid the claim of _____ enforcement.
    a. selective
    b. discretionary
    c. discriminatory
    d. arbitrary and capricious

    Reference_____

18. The first thing a person who receives a complaint should do is obtain _____.
    a. the date of the complaint
    b. the name of the complainant
    c. the nature of the alleged violation
    d. as much information as possible

    Reference_____

19. Because it is the most difficult to demonstrate, the key element in convincing a judge to issue a temporary restraining order or temporary injunction is _____.
    a. public interest
    b. relative harm to other party
    c. probable cause of violation
    d. immediate irreparable harm

    Reference_____

20. Written rules established by a building department that address applications not expressly resolved by the code are typically known as _____.

    a. statutes   b. ordinances

    c. administrative guidelines   d. federal or state directives

Reference_____

21. A hearsay statement is permissible in court when it is _____.

    a. stated under oat

    b. acceptable to the presiding judge

    c. an admission of a party involved

    d. presented by the prosecution

Reference_____

22. The Board of Building Code Appeals usually derives its power from the _____.

    a. building code   b. city council/county board

    c. city/county attorney's office   d. department of building safety

Reference_____

23. The building official may enter a property without violating the Constitution when he/she _____.

    a. shows proper identification

    b. obtains the owner's consent

    c. enters during reasonable business hours

    d. has issued a legitimate permit for the project

Reference_____

24. When preparing a civil complaint, the first decision that must be made is _____.

    a. who is to be charged

    b. when did the violation occur

    c. where did the violation occur

    d. what is the maximum penalty or fine

Reference_____

25. One of the most common areas of potential liability in the department of building safety is _____.

    a. records retention   b. plans examination

    c. policy administration   d. administrative guidelines

Reference_____

Legal Aspects of Code Administration, Chapters 9 through 12
Related Property Law Concepts, Liability for Intentional Wrongdoing, Negligent Wrongdoing and Civil Rights Actions

OBJECTIVE: To gain a basic understanding of fundamental property law concepts, intentional torts and absolute immunity, civil rights and the elements composing a claim of negligence, as well as the possible defenses and immunities that a building official might raise in response to a charge of negligence.

REFERENCE: Chapters 9 through 12, *Legal Aspects of Code Administration*

KEY POINTS:
- What is the purpose of a zoning ordinance? How does a "comprehensive zoning plan" differ from a "zoning plan"?
- What is considered a "conditional use"? Why is a conditional use designation necessary?
- What is a "nonconforming use"? For what purpose is a "special use permit" normally utilized?
- What is the rationale behind restrictive covenants and homeowners' associations?
- Why is a building official generally not able to enforce restrictive covenants?
- Is there a difference between a public right-of-way and a public easement?
- Who has the power of eminent domain?
- What is a party wall and where is it usually erected?
- What is the purpose of subdivision regulations?
- What is a P.U.D. or a P.A.D.?
- What is the difference between an intentional tort and negligence?
- What is considered "malicious prosecution"? What are the four elements of the legal theory addressing malicious prosecution?
- Why is absolute immunity important to public officials?
- What four elements must be proved in order to show negligence?
- Why is the public duty doctrine critical in a negligence claim?
- What is breach of duty?

KEY POINTS (Cont'd):
- What is the distinction between misfeasance, malfeasance and nonfeasance?
- When does damage or injury occur?
- What civil rights legislation is particularly applicable to building code officials?
- What two elements must be proven to establish a cause of action related to the Civil Rights Act of 1871? What are the important aspects of the Act?

Topic: Restrictive Covenant
Reference: *Legal Aspects,* Chapter 9

Category: Property Law Concepts
Subject: Covenants

Text: *A covenant is an agreement or promise between two or more people to either do something or to refrain from doing something. Restrictive covenants in the area of property law consist of a provision in the deed to the property in question which limits the use of the property and prohibits certain uses. In addition, the builders may create a homeowners' association. A homeowner's association is a legally recognized entity, sometimes a not-for-profit corporation, made up of all the owners of all the lots, who act together for the common interest pursuant to a declaration of covenants. The declaration of covenants sets forth all the restrictive covenants to be enforced on all the lots and the homeowners' association makes sure all members follow the restrictions.*

Discussion and Commentary: Many times a homeowners' association will ask or demand that the building official enforce the requirements of that particular association. However, unless the jurisdiction has adopted those particular rules, the building official does not have the authority to enforce them or to even delay the issuance of a permit until the association's regulations are in compliance. Section 105.3.1 of the IBC requires the building official to issue the permit when it complies with the laws and ordinances of that jurisdiction.

International Building Code

105.3.1 Action on application. The building official shall examine or cause to be examined applications for permits and amendments thereto within a reasonable time after filing. If the application or the construction documents do not conform to the requirements of pertinent laws, the building official shall reject such application in writing, stating the reasons therefor. If the building official is satisfied that the proposed work conforms to the requirements of this code and laws and ordinances applicable thereto, the building official shall issue a permit therefor as soon as practicable.

Where a restrictive covenant is more restrictive than the building code, the building official may only enforce the building code provisions. He or she shall not go further to enforce any restrictive covenant. Of course, if the building code is more restrictive than the rules of the covenant, the building code shall prevail.

Topic: Public Easement
Reference: *Legal Aspects,* Chapter 9
Category: Property Law Concepts
Subject: Easements

Text: *An easement is a grant of an interest in land entitling a person to use land possessed by another. This simply means that while the owner of an easement across another person's property does not have a financial interest in possessing it, he does have an interest in using it for some particular purpose. One of the most common types of easement is a public right-of-way, or public easement. A highway is, in the majority of cases, an easement so that the public may travel.*

Discussion and Commentary: Many easements on private property are used for above-ground or underground utilities such as sewer, water, storm, gas, electric, telephone, cable, etc. Although the property owner is in possession of this easement, the utility companies are authorized to access the easement in order to install, maintain or add to their systems. In most communities, buildings or structures cannot be built on an easement because they may interfere with access to the utility systems. However, some minor, easily removable structures, such as fences, above-ground pools and playground equipment, may be allowed.

In most well-developed jurisdictions, a lot is considered buildable only if it is accessible directly from a public right-of-way.

Topic: Eminent Domain
Reference: *Legal Aspect,* Chapter 9

Category: Property Law Concepts
Subject: Easements

Text: *A state or municipality can require that a private property owner relinquish some or all of his or her rights in the land so that the public may use it under its power of eminent domain as long as it compensates the owner for it. Federal, state and local governments have the power of eminent domain, which means they have the power to take title of property for public use upon payment of just compensation. The government's use of its power to obtain property in this way is also known as condemnation of the specified land. However, if the government does not compensate the owner, the use of the land will be considered a "taking" and held to be a violation of the Fifth Amendment.*

Discussion and Commentary: The Fifth Amendment of the United States Constitution provides that private property may not be taken for a public use without payment of just compensation, and the government is required to pay the fair market value of the property it acquires by eminent domain. Many times, real estate appraisers are utilized to establish property values, but if the owner and the government cannot agree on the fair market value, a jury will ultimately decide.

As an example, California's Eminent Domain Law generally has defined fair market value as

"The fair market value of the property taken is the highest price on the date of valuation that would be agreed to by the seller, being willing to sell but under no particular or urgent necessity for doing, nor obliged to sell, and a buyer, being ready, willing and able to buy but under no particular necessity for so doing, each dealing with the other with full knowledge of all the uses and purposes for which the property is reasonably adaptable and available."

On occasion, an owner will voluntarily transfer land for use by the public. This is known as a dedication. For example, a developer may dedicate a street to the municipality for use by the general public. For the dedication to be valid, the governmental authority must accept the donation of the property.

Topic: Party Walls
Reference: *Legal Aspects*, Chapter 9

Category: Property Law Concepts
Subject: Common Property Rights

Text: *There are some property rights that are shared by one or more owners and/or occupants. These are called common property rights. A party wall is one type of common property right. It is a wall erected on an interior lot line as a common support to a structure on both sides, under different ownerships, for the benefit of both in supporting the structure. It also functions as a fire wall between the two buildings, for example, a tenant of a commercial property in a strip mall sharing a party wall with his or her neighboring tenant.*

Discussion and Commentary: Section 706.1.1 of the *International Building Code* also addresses party walls and how they are to be constructed. Negatively altering a party wall may have legal consequences if damage to the adjacent property occurs because of a fire, insofar as the IBC requires a party wall to be constructed like a fire wall and without any openings.

International Building Code

706.1.1 Party Walls. Any wall located on a lot line between adjacent buildings, which is used or adapted for joint service between the two buildings, shall be constructed as a fire wall in accordance with Section 706. Party walls shall be constructed without openings and shall create separate buildings.

Party walls are also common in residential subdivisions containing townhomes and/or condominiums. The party wall is located on a lot line that may be shown on a plat of survey or described in a legal document.

Topic: Land Development
Reference: *Legal Aspects,* Chapter 9

Category: Property Law Concepts
Subject: Subdivision Regulations

Text: *Subdivision regulations were developed primarily during the 1920s and 1930s as a means of controlling the future development and expansion of urban and municipal properties. Long-range urban planners began to discover during this time that the manner in which available open space was developed by private construction firms was crucial to the way the city developed overall. They realized that some control over this development pattern had to be exerted by the municipality in order to prevent unbridled growth and haphazard design. Subdivision regulations lay out conditions for approval of a subdivision plan.*

Discussion and Commentary: A planned unit development (PUD) or planned area development (PAD) is a specialized type of subdivision that describes a large-scale real estate development project. The document that establishes a PUD or PAD is very complicated because it is so comprehensive, dealing with covenants, conditions and restrictions that regulate the use of common areas, assessments, voting rights, architectural regulations and other matters. For example, two-story homes may not be allowed to back up to major streets, or two homes may not be allowed to have the same front facade if they are adjacent to each other.

The building official and permit technician must be aware of the existence of the various regulations relating to PUDs and PADs because building permits are frequently issued for the lots very soon after the planning commission approves the plat. By checking the regulations or plat before issuing permits, the building official can ensure that all proper conditions are in compliance.

Study Session 14

Topic: Causing Injury
Reference: *Legal Aspects,* Chapter 10

Category: Liability for Intentional Wrongdoing
Subject: Intentional Torts

Text: *Tortious or wrongful conduct can be either intentional or negligent. Intentional torts, as the name implies, involve conduct that the actor intended to occur. Negligence, on the other hand, involves conduct that was not intended to cause harm or injury, but nonetheless did so, and also breached some duty of care imposed by the law. A person may be liable for an injury if he or she does not act with the same level of care a reasonable person would use under similar circumstances. In some situations, it is not very easy to determine whether certain conduct is intentional or negligent. To some extent, all actions are intentional. The relevant question focuses on whether the results were intended.*

Discussion and Commentary: Any injury to one person caused by another is called a tort. As a part of civil law, tort law is not intended to prove criminal liability; rather, it is designed to help victims win compensation (damages) for their lost wages, pain and suffering, medical bills and other related costs. If someone knows his or her actions will cause harm but follows through with them anyway, he or she is committing an intentional tort.

Intentional Tort — Wrongful conduct that was intended.

Negligence — Involves conduct that was not intended to cause harm or injury but which, nonetheless, did so and that also breached some duty of care imposed by the law

---

It is important to distinguish between intentional and negligent tortious conduct because many state liability statutes, indemnification legislation and insurance policies cover only negligent tort and not intentional wrongdoing.

Topic: Protection from Malicious Prosecution   **Category:** Liability for Intentional Wrongdoing
Reference: *Legal Aspects,* Chapter 10   **Subject:** Absolute Immunity

Text: *In at least the state of California, public officials, including building officials, are absolutely immune from malicious prosecution cases. This protects virtually any official from a malicious prosecution suit as long as the underlying prosecution was within the scope of his or her employment. The policy underlying this act is to protect public officials from tort liability so that they may more ably discharge their duties to the public without fear of lawsuits.*

Discussion and Commentary: Even if a building code official lives in a state that provides absolute immunity from malicious prosecution suits, it is always better to refrain from acting in a malicious or arbitrary manner. No one wants to be named in any suit, even if they may ultimately be cleared.

Absolute Immunity	A policy of protecting public officials from tort liability. A high-level executive officer cannot be held liable for his or her discretionary acts or missions.
Malicious Prosecution	Concerns the wrongful institution of criminal proceedings by one private citizen against another, resulting in damages.

It is imperative that building code officials check with their municipal attorney to determine if state law provides for absolute immunity.

Study Session 14

Topic: Summary
Reference: *Legal Aspects,* Chapter 11

Category: Negligent Wrongdoing
Subject: Elements of Negligence

Text: *To prevail on a claim of negligence, a plaintiff must satisfy four elements. The defendant, possibly a building official or permit technician, must have: 1) owed a duty to another to act according to a certain standard; 2) failed to act in accord with that standard, and therefore; 3) breached that duty; 4) thereby causing, in the eyes of the law, an injury or damage to the other. The plaintiff must prove each and every element of a negligence claim by a preponderance of the evidence.*

Discussion and Commentary: Sometimes a building official may owe a duty to someone but fail to act properly, resulting in a breach of the duty owed. Even though most of the elements for prevailing on a claim of negligence seem apparent, there may have been no injury or damages caused. In this case, negligence most likely could not be proven. Even though the building official may be legally exempt from prosecution, it still may not be the best way to maintain a long-term career in the code industry. The jurisdiction's personnel manual, as well as the local press, may have a different view of what is considered negligence.

Elements of Negligence

1. Defendant owed a duty to another to act according to a certain standard.
2. Defendant failed to act according to that standard, and therefore
3. Defendant breached that duty, thereby
4. Defendant caused, in the eyes of the law, an injury or damage to the other party.

Knowing, understanding and following the established procedures of the Building Safety Department is the best approach to remaining free of a claim of negligence.

Topic: The Public Duty Doctrine	**Category:** Negligent Wrongdoing
Reference: *Legal Aspects,* Chapter 11	**Subject:** Elements of Negligence

Text: *The first and second elements of negligence* (owed a duty to another to act according to a certain standard and failing to do so) *afford the greatest protection to public officials, including building officials. A duty, in negligence cases, may be defined as an obligation to conform to a particular standard of conduct toward another. Most of these obligations are to act with the same care as a reasonably prudent person would under the same or similar circumstances. In most cases involving building codes, however, the question is not the level of care owed, but to whom the duty is owed.*

Discussion and Commentary: The *public duty doctrine* is a court-created provision that makes it difficult to successfully sue a public official for negligence. Under this doctrine, many courts have held that the public official has a duty to the public in general, but not to specific individuals. However, if it can be shown that individuals make up the general public, then there could be a possibility that a breach of duty has occurred.

Duty	An obligation, to which the law will give recognition and effect, to conform to a particular standard of conduct toward another.
Public Duty Doctrine	A doctrine that provides that a plaintiff who alleges inadequate performance of a governmental activity has the burden to show that the municipality owed a specific duty to the plaintiff and not simply to the general public.

There are some states that do not adhere to the public duty doctrine. It is very important to consult with the municipal attorney to determine whether or not the state is a public duty state. Because the case law is ever changing, this should be checked every few years to make sure that the law has not been changed.

Topic: Breach of Duty	Category: Negligent Wrongdoing
Reference: *Legal Aspects*, Chapter 11	Subject: Elements of Negligence

Text: *Breach of duty is the third element of a negligence cause of action. It is the neglect or failure to fulfill in a just and proper manner the duties of an office. The duty owed by the building code official must in some manner be violated. If the duty is satisfied, no liability will ensue. There are essentially two ways in which a duty can be breached: by action or inaction. For example, failing to make a required inspection would be considered inaction, which breaches a duty of care. Alternatively, an inaccurate inspection would be considered an active breach of duty.*

Discussion and Commentary: In proper legal terms, breach of duty can result through misfeasance, nonfeasance and malfeasance. Misfeasance is the improper performance of some act that a person may lawfully do. Nonfeasance is the nonperformance of some act that a person is obligated or has the responsibility to perform. Malfeasance is the doing of an act that a person ought not to do at all. Conducting a poor inspection could be considered misfeasance. Not conducting a required inspection could be considered nonfeasance. Accepting a gratuity for allowing a code violation could be considered malfeasance.

Misfeasance — The improper performance of some act that a person may lawfully do.

Nonfeasance — The nonperformance of some act that a person is obligated or has the responsibility to perform.

Malfeasance — The performance of some act that a person ought not do at all.

Modern courts have largely abandoned the distinction between misfeasance, malfeasance and nonfeasance. Courts are finding governments and their employees liable for omissions as well as acts.

Topic: Damages or Injury
Reference: *Legal Aspects,* Chapter 11

Category: Negligent Wrongdoing
Subject: Elements of Negligence

Text: *The fourth element of a cause of action for negligence is injury or damage. For plaintiffs to prevail on a claim of negligence, they must have suffered some injury as a result of a duty owed specifically to them. This element is satisfied by personal injury or property damage. Although a plaintiff might claim that he or she is suffering from emotional distress as a result of the building official's negligence, the plaintiff will not prevail without showing that the emotional distress was adequately severe to require medical attention.*

Discussion and Commentary: Regardless of the situation, no building code official wants to be named in a claim of negligence. Legally he or she may escape prosecution, but his or her reputation may suffer. Understanding and following department protocol is one of the best ways to eliminate or reduce legal liability.

SOME EXAMPLES OF INJURY OR DAMAGE:

- Emotional distress
- Pain and suffering (such as grief, fright, anxiety, humiliation, and depression)
- Permanent disability
- Mental impairment
- Earning capacity impairment
- Medical bills
- Interest due from money withheld
- Property damage
- Loss of wages
- Loss of profits

If an inspector performs an inspection improperly, or not at all, and this act did not cause the party to whom the duty was owed a legally recognized injury, by law there will be no legal liability.

Study Session 14

Topic: Accessibility
Reference: *Legal Aspects,* Chapter 12

Category: Civil Rights Actions
Subject: Americans with Disabilities Act

Text: *In 1990, Congress continued its intervention in both the private and public sectors on behalf of disabled persons with its wide-ranging Americans with Disabilities Act (ADA). This act covers employment discrimination, public transportation, public accommodations and telecommunications. It sets the design criteria for public accommodations and commercial facilities so that a disabled person can mainstream more comfortably. Included are hotels, restaurants, offices, stores and all residential facilities where operations will affect commerce.*

Discussion and Commentary: Whereas the Fair Housing Act is applicable to multi-family residential uses, Title III of the Americans with Disabilities Act addresses commercial applications. The ADA is a civil rights law and is enforced by the Department of Justice. Generally, with few exceptions, all new buildings must comply with the ADA requirements. Buildings that are being remodeled must also comply to a certain extent unless they can show financial hardship. Governmental buildings, such as city halls, are regulated under Title II of the act and must be in full compliance.

ADA Regulation for Title II:

Prohibits discrimination on the basis of disability in all services, programs and activities provided to the public by state and local governments, except public transportation services.

ADA Regulation for Title III:

Prohibits discrimination on the basis of disability in "places of public accommodation" (businesses and nonprofit agencies that serve the public) and "commercial facilities" (other businesses). The regulation includes minimum standards for ensuring accessibility when designing and constructing a new facility or altering an existing facility.

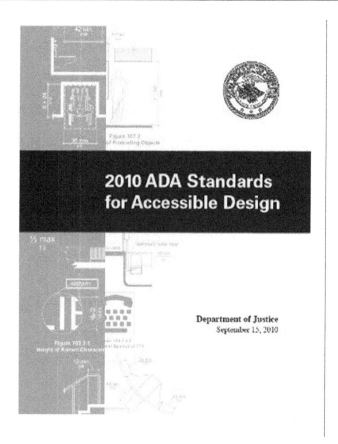

Generally, the building official is authorized to enforce the code adopted by the state or local jurisdiction and is not responsible for interpreting or enforcing any federal regulations such as ADA. However, a few states have referenced the ADA Accessibility Guidelines (ADAAG) as a state law, thus making the local building official responsible for enforcement.

Quiz

Study Session 14
Legal Aspects of Code Administration, Chapters 9 through 12

1. A local law is known as a(n) _____.

    a. statute   b. ordinance

    c. restrictive covenant   d. encumbrance

    Reference _____

2. A(n) _____ is a claim or encumbrance on a property to secure a debt or obligation.

    a. lien   b. title

    c. warranty   d. attachment

    Reference _____

3. Conduct that was not intended to cause harm or injury, but nonetheless did so, and also breached some duty of care imposed by the law is known as _____.

    a. negligence   b. tort liability

    c. intentional tort d. malicious prosecution

    Reference _____

4. The building official and the municipality can each be sued because _____.

    a. both entities enforce municipal ordinances
    b. they are two separate and distinct legal entities
    c. the building official is employed by the municipality
    d. the building official's liability is set forth by the building code

    Reference _____

Study Session 14

5. A doctrine that provides that a plaintiff who alleges inadequate performance of a governmental activity has the burden to show that the municipality owed a specific duty to the plaintiff and not simply to the general public is known as the _____ doctrine.

   a. home rule
   b. public duty
   c. sovereign immunity
   d. malicious prosecution

   Reference _____

6. The nonperformance of some act that the building official is obligated or has a responsibility to perform is known as _____.

   a. civil liability
   b. tort liability
   c. malfeasance
   d. nonfeasance

   Reference _____

7. The type of immunity usually applied to building safety personnel is _____ immunity.

   a. limited
   b. absolute
   c. qualified
   d. sovereign

   Reference _____

8. Procedural due process means that parties whose rights are to be affected are entitled to be heard, and therefore must be _____.

   a. notified
   b. considered
   c. implicated
   d. entitled

   Reference _____

9. The federal requirement that sets the design criteria for public accommodation and commercial facilities so that a disabled person can mainstream more comfortably is known as the _____.

   a. FHA
   b. ADA
   c. HUD
   d. USDA

   Reference _____

10. The requirement that mandates general access design standards for new housing with four or more units is known as the _____.

    a. FHA
    b. ADA
    c. HUD
    d. USDA

    Reference _____

11. A wall erected on an interior lot line as a common support to a structure on both sides, under different ownerships, for the benefit of both in supporting the structure is known as a _____.

    a. party wall
    b. curtain wall
    c. bearing wall
    d. partition wall

    Reference _____

12. A warranty deed ensures the buyer that the property is _____.

    a. sold "as is"
    b. free from liens and encumbrances
    c. guaranteed not to be in a flood plain
    d. in full compliance with all local codes

    Reference _____

13. The act of occupying a space that belongs to someone else is considered a(n) _____.

    a. variance
    b. encroachment
    c. permissive use
    d. adverse possession

    Reference _____

14. Which of the following is not another term for a special use?

    a. Conditional use
    b. Exceptional use
    c. Special exception
    d. Nonconforming use

    Reference _____

15. A specialized type of subdivision that describes a large-scale real estate development project is known as a(n) _____.
    a. comprehensive plan
    b. urban renewal project
    c. conditional subdivision
    d. planned unit development

    Reference _____

16. _____ takes place when a community puts into place a plan to revitalize depressed areas in that community.
    a. Urban renewal
    b. Conditional planning
    c. Comprehensive planning
    d. A planned unit development

    Reference _____

17. Intentionally entering land which is under the possession of another is known as _____.
    a. trespassing
    b. right of entry
    c. encroachment
    d. licensure

    Reference _____

18. The Americans with Disabilities Act (ADA) was adopted by Congress in _____.
    a. 1983
    b. 1988
    c. 1990
    d. 1992

    Reference _____

19. The Fair Housing Act (FHA) was adopted by Congress in _____.
    a. 1968
    b. 1983
    c. 1988
    d. 1990

    Reference _____

20. Building officials may purchase _____ insurance to protect themselves in the event an error was made which may give rise to liability.
    a. indemnification
    b. full indemnification
    c. errors and omissions
    d. variable indemnification

    Reference_____

21. One of the four elements necessary for a successful malicious prosecution lawsuit against a building official is _____.
    a. absence of probable cause
    b. negligence
    c. malfeasance
    d. abuse of process

    Reference_____

22. A state or municipality can require that a private property owner relinquish some or all of his or her property for public use under its power of _____.
    a. public domain
    b. eminent domain
    c. sovereign immunity
    d. inverse condemnation

    Reference_____

23. *Caveat venditor* means _____.
    a. let the seller beware
    b. let the buyer beware
    c. the King can do no wrong
    d. a man's home is his castle

    Reference_____

24. Acquiring title to property by possessing it for a specified period of time under specific circumstances is known as _____.
    a. eminent domain
    b. inverse possession
    c. adverse possession
    d. inverse condemnation

    Reference_____

25. Personal property differs from real property in that it is _____.

    a. temporary

    b. a part of the land

    c. permanently affixed

    d. tangible and moveable

Reference_____

Answer Keys

Study Session 1
Basic Code Enforcement, Chapter 1

1. d   Sec. 1.2.1
2. a   Sec. 1.3
3. c   Sec. 1.3.1
4. b   Sec. 1.4
5. c   Sec. 1.7.2
6. d   Secs. 1.9.1, 1.9.3
7. a   Sec. 1.6
8. c   Sec. 1.12
9. b   Sec. 1.3.2
10. d   Secs. 1.5, 1.7
11. a   Sec. 1.6
12. b   Sec. 1.8
13. d   Sec. 1.2.2
14. b   Sec. 1.6
15. a   Sec. 1.8
16. b   Sec. 1.10
17. c   Sec. 1.7.1
18. b   Sec. 1.7.4
19. a   Sec. 1.7.4
20. c   Sec. 1.11.1
21. d   Sec. 1.12.1
22. d   Sec. 1.12.7
23. a   Sec. 1.12.3
24. a   Sec. 1.7.5
25. c   Secs. 1.9.1, 1.9.3

Study Session 2
Basic Code Enforcement, Chapters 2 through 4

1. c   Sec. 2.4
2. d   Sec. 2.5
3. d   Sec. 2.2
4. c   Sec. 2.5.2
5. b   Sec. 2.5.2 and Table 2-2
6. b   Sec. 4.5.6
7. b   Sec. 2.4.4, Item 4
8. b   Sec. 3.1
9. c   Sec. 3.3 and Table 3-1
10. b   Sec. 3.7
11. b   Sec. 3.8.2
12. a   Sec. 3.8.1
13. a   Sec. 3.8.2
14. d   Sec. 3.9.5
15. b   Sec. 3.6
16. a   Sec. 3.6
17. c   Sec. 3.7.1
18. c   Sec. 3.8.1
19. a   Secs. 4.1, 4.5.1
20. d   Sec. 4.3
21. d   Sec. 4.2
22. c   Sec. 4.7.2
23. d   Sec. 4.7.2
24. a   Sec. 4.6
25. d   Sec. 4.3

Study Session 3
Basic Code Enforcement, Chapters 5 through 7

1.	c	Sec. 5.2
2.	d	Sec. 5.2
3.	a	Sec. 5.3
4.	c	Figure 5-5
5.	b	Figure 5-5
6.	c	Sec. 5.4.1
7.	a	Sec. 5.4.3
8.	d	Sec. 5.4.6
9.	a	Sec. 5.5
10.	b	Sec. 5.5
11.	d	Sec. 5.6.2 and Figure 5-19
12.	a	Sec. 5.6.1, 6.1.1
13.	a	Sec. 5.6.5
14.	a	Sec. 5.7.2
15.	b	Sec. 6.1.1
16.	b	Sec. 6.1.2
17.	d	Sec. 6.2.2
18.	a	Sec. 7.2
19.	a	Sec. 7.3.1
20.	c	Sec. 7.3.3, Step 4
21.	d	Sec. 7.3.4, Step 5.5
22.	a	Sec. 7.3.5
23.	c	Sec. 7.4.2
24.	d	Sec. 7.4.4
25.	c	Sec. 7.5

Study Session 4
2018 IBC Sections 101 through 104

1. d   Sec. 101.3
2. d   Sec. 101.2
3. a   Sec. 101.4
4. b   Sec. 102.1
5. c   Sec. 103.1
6. d   Sec. 102.1
7. d   Sec. 102.4
8. b   Sec. 102.4.2
9. d   Sec. 104.7
10. c   Sec. 104.7
11. c   Sec. 101.2.1
12. a   Sec. 104.10
13. c   Sec. 104.1
14. c   Sec. 104.4
15. a   Sec. 103.3
16. c   Sec. 104.5
17. b   Sec. 104.8
18. b   Sec. 104.6
19. d   Sec. 104.6
20. b   Sec. 104.8.1
21. c   Sec. 104.9.1
22. a   Sec. 104.11.2
23. b   Sec. 104.11.1
24. c   Sec. 102.6
25. a   Sec. 104.10.1
26. b   Sec. 104.2.1
27. d   Sec. 102.6.1
28. c   Sec. 102.2
29. a   Sec. 104.2.1
30. d   Sec. 102.6.2

Study Session 5
2018 IBC Sections 105 and 107

1. c Sec. 105.3.2
2. b Sec. 105.1.1
3. c Sec. 105.5
4. b Sec. 105.2, #B1
5. d Sec. 105.1.2
6. b Sec. 202
7. b Sec. 105.3.2
8. b Sec. 105.2, #B1
9. a Sec. 105.2, Electrical
10. c Sec. 105.3
11. a Sec. 105.6
12. d Sec. 107.2.6
13. c Sec. 105.3.1
14. d Sec. 107.4
15. b Sec. 107.3.4.1
16. c Sec. 105.2.1
17. d Sec. 107.3.1
18. d Sec. 107.3.4
19. c Sec. 105.2
20. a Sec. 104.2, 105.1, 107, 110.1
21. c Sec. 107.1, Exception
22. c Sec. 107.2.2
23. b Sec. 105.7
24. d Sec. 105.2, #B9
25. c Sec. 107.5

Study Session 6
2018 IBC Sections 108 through 116

1. d   Sec. 110.5
2. c   Sec. 111.4
3. b   Sec. 110.3
4. c   Sec. 112.3
5. c   Sec. 110.3.11.1
6. a   Sec. 110.3.8
7. c   Sec. 110.3.5
8. b   Sec. 109.3
9. d   Sec. 108.2, 3103.1.1
10. c   Sec. 13.1
11. c   Sec. 111.2
12. c   Sec. 111.4
13. a   Sec. 110.3.4
14. c   Sec. 110.1
15. a   Sec. 110.4
16. b   Sec. 115.2
17. b   Sec. 113.2
18. c   Sec. 2135 C $89 = $190,015
    450 X $51 = $22,950
    Valuation = $ 212,965 (round up to $213,000)
    First $100,000 @ $1,408
    Remaining $113,000 @ $8/1000 = $904
    $1,408 + $904 = $2,312
19. c.   5673 X $92 = $521,916
    620 X $65 = $40,300
    Valuation = $562,216 (round up to $563,000)
    First $500,000 @ $4,579
    Remaining $63,000 @ $7/1000 = $441
    $4,579 + $441 = $5,020
20. d   Sec. 116.1

Study Session 7
2018 IBC Chapter 3 and Sections 508 and 509

1.	b	Sec. 302.1
2.	a	Sec. 302.1
3.	a	Table 509
4.	d	Sec. 311.3
5.	d	Sec. 312.1
6.	d	Sec. 308.3
7.	a	Sec. 303.2
8.	c	Sec. 303.4
9.	a	Table 508.4
10.	c	Sec. 305.1
11.	c	Sec. 310.4
12.	d	Secs. 308.2, 308.3
13.	d	Sec. 307.6
14.	d	Sec. 312.1
15.	d	Secs. 310.2, 310.3
16.	d	Sec. 309.1
17.	d	Sec. 312.1
18.	c	Sec. 303.1.1
19.	a	Secs. 508.2.3, 508.2.4
20.	b	Sec. 305.2
21.	d	Sec. 311.2
22.	b	Sec. 303.5
23.	a	Sec. 307.3
24.	d	Sec. 302.1
25.	c	Sec. 310.4

Study Session 8
2018 IBC Chapters 6 and 12

1.   d   Sec. 602.2
2.   d   Sec. 602.3
3.   d   Sec. 602.4.4, Table 2304.11
4.   d   Sec. 602.5
5.   a   Table 601
6.   b   Sec. 1207.1
7.   c   Sec. 1207.3
8.   c   Sec. 1208.2
9.   b   Sec. 1204.2
10.   b   Sec. 1202.5.1
11.   c   Sec. 202
12.   d   Sec. 202
13.   b   Sec. 202
14.   d   Sec. 202
15.   b   Sec. 1207.2
16.   d   Sec. 1207.4, #1
17.   b   Sec. 1203.1
18.   c   Sec. 1209.2.2
19.   c   Sec. 1209.2.3
20.   a   Sec. 1209.3.2
21.   a   Sec. 1206.2
22.   d   Sec. 1204.3
23.   d   Sec. 1208.2
24.   b   Sec. 1208.1
25.   a   Sec. 1202.1

Study Session 9

2018 IZC Chapters 1 and 3 through 7

1.	b	Sec. 101.3
2.	c	Sec. 110.2
3.	b	Sec. 101.3
4.	a	Sec. 102.1
5.	a	Sec. 104.6
6.	c	Sec. 104.7
7.	c	Sec. 103.7.1
8.	c	Sec. 106.3
9.	a	Sec. 106.8
10.	b	Sec. 107.4
11.	d	Sec. 108.2.2
12.	c	Sec. 202
13.	a	Sec. 202
14.	b	Sec. 202
15.	a	Table 602.1
16.	d	Sec. 304.1
17.	a	Sec. 501.1
18.	b	Sec. 401.1
19.	b	Sec. 401.1
20.	d	Table 502.1
21.	c	Table 602.1
22.	b	Table 502.1
23.	c	Table 502.1
24.	d	Sec. 701.1
25.	b	Sec. 501.1

Study Session 10
2018 IZC Chapters 8, 9, 11, 12 and 13

1.	b	Table 801.2.1
2.	c	Sec. 801.2.2, Table 801.2.1
3.	b	Sec. 801.2.4
4.	a	Sec. 801.3.1, Exception 2
5.	d	Sec. 801.4.1
6.	a	Table 802.1
7.	b	Sec. 803.2
8.	a	Sec. 804.3
9.	c	Sec. 805.1
10.	d	Sec. 806.1
11.	b	Sec. 901.2, #3
12.	d	Sec. 902.2, #4
13.	c	Sec. 1102.1
14.	d	Sec. 1102.2
15.	c	Sec. 1103.3
16.	a	Sec. 1202.1
17.	d	Sec. 1203.2
18.	a	Sec. 1206.1
19.	c	Sec. 1207.1
20.	a	Sec. 1205.1
21.	d	Sec. 1301.1
22.	d	Sec. 1302.6
23.	d	Sec. 1302.4.1
24.	b	Sec. 1301.2
25.	b	Sec. 1304.1

Study Session 11
2018 IZC Chapter 10

1. d Sec. 1002
2. d Sec. 1002
3. a Sec. 1002
4. b Sec. 1002
5. c Sec. 1002
6. a Sec. 1002
7. c Sec. 1002
8. b Sec. 1004.1
9. a Sec. 1004.3
10. d Sec. 1004.6
11. d Sec. 1004.9, #1
12. c Sec. 1005.1
13. c Secs. 1006.1 and 1002, "Sign"
14. b Sec. 1007.2
15. c Sec. 1008.2.5
16. b Sec. 1008.1.3
17. a Sec. 1008.2.1, #1
18. c Sec. 1008.2.1, #2
19. a Sec. 1008.2.2, #1
20. d Sec. 1007.4
21. c Sec. 1008.2.6, #2
22. b Sec. 1008.3.6, #1
23. b Sec. 1008.3.1, #1
24. d Sec. 1008.3.7
25. b Sec. 1009.1

Study Session 12
Legal Aspects of Code Administration, Chapters 3 and 4

1.	b	Chapter 3, Dillon's Rule
2.	a	Chapter 3, Home Rule
3.	c	Chapter 3, Enabling Legislation
4.	c	Chapter 3, Ultra Vires Legislation
5.	c	Chapter 4, The Fire Code
6.	d	Chapter 4, Sovereign Immunity
7.	c	Chapter 4, Zoning Ordinances
8.	b	Chapter 4, Sovereign Immunity
9.	c	Chapter 3, Municipalities
10.	c	Chapter 3, Expressed Power
11.	b	Chapter 3, Municipalities
12.	a	Chapter 3, Implied Power
13.	d	Chapter 3, Local Adoption of a Building Code
14.	c	Chapter 3, Local Adoption of a Building Code
15.	b	Chapter 3, Home Rule Municipalities
16.	a	Chapter 3, Local Adoption of a Building Code
17.	a	Chapter 3, Local Adoption of a Building Code
18.	b	Chapter 4, State Building Codes
19.	a	Chapter 4, Storm Water Management
20.	c	Chapter 4, Sovereign Immunity
21.	a	Chapter 4, Preemption
22.	d	Chapter 4, The Fire Code
23.	c	Chapter 3, Local Adoption of a Building Code
24.	b	Chapter 3, Counties
25.	d	Chapter 3, Ultra Vires Legislation

Study Session 13
Legal Aspects of Code Administration, Chapters 6 through 8

1.	c	Chapter 6, Permit Issuance
2.	c	Chapter 6, Theories
3.	b	Chapter 7, Creation of the Board of Building Code Appeals
4.	a	Chapter 7, Burden and Presentation of Proof
5.	a	Chapter 8, Warrants
6.	d	Chapter 8, Substantive Due Process
7.	d	Chapter 8, Discriminatory Enforcement
8.	c	Chapter 6, Disclaimers
9.	b	Chapter 6, Inspections
10.	a	Chapter 6, Civil Prosecutions
11.	d	Chapter 6, Types of Injunctive Relief
12.	a	Chapter 6, Types of Injunctive Relief
13.	d	Chapter 7, Administrative Discretion
14.	a	Chapter 7, Orders
15.	a	Chapter 8, The Plain View Doctrine
16.	c	Chapter 8, Retroactive Code Provisions
17.	c	Chapter 8, Discriminatory Enforcement
18.	d	Chapter 6, Handling Complaints
19.	d	Chapter 6, Seeking a Temporary Restraining Order or Injunction
20.	c	Chapter 6, Administrative Guidelines
21.	c	Chapter 6, Evidence
22.	a	Chapter 7, Introduction
23.	b	Chapter 8, Consent
24.	a	Chapter 6, Civil Prosecutions
25.	b	Chapter 6, Plans Examination

Study Session 14
Legal Aspects of Code Administration, Chapters 9 through 12

1.	b	Chapter 9, Zoning Ordinances
2.	a	Chapter 9, Ownership Transfer
3.	a	Chapter 10, Intentional Torts
4.	b	Chapter 10, Distinction between Governmental and Official Liability
5.	b	Chapter 11, The Public Duty Doctrine
6.	d	Chapter 11, Breach of Duty
7.	c	Chapter 11, Immunities
8.	a	Chapter 12, Deprivation of federal Constitutional or Statutory Rights
9.	b	Chapter 12, The Americans with Disabilities Act
10.	a	Chapter 12, The Fair Housing Act
11.	a	Chapter 9, Common Property Rights
12.	b	Chapter 9, Ownership Transfer
13.	b	Chapter 9, Easements
14.	d	Chapter 9, Zoning Ordinances
15.	d	Chapter 9, Subdivision Regulations
16.	a	Chapter 9, Subdivision Regulations
17.	a	Chapter 10, Trespass
18.	c	Chapter 12, The Americans with Disabilities Act
19.	a	Chapter 12, The Fair Housing Act
20.	c	Chapter 11, Indemnification and Insurance
21.	a	Chapter 10, Malicious Prosecution
22.	b	Chapter 9, Easements
23.	a	Chapter 9, Ownership Transfer
24.	c	Chapter 9, Easements
25.	d	Chapter 9, Ownership Transfer

In addition to the referenced text locations, many of these answers also appear in the Index of Terms.

Invest in Your Future
Join the ICC community and get connected now

No other building code association offers more I-Code® resources and training to help you achieve your career goals than the International Code Council® (ICC®)

Exclusive member benefits include:
- **Free I-Code Book** – New Members receive a free I-Code book or download.
- **Free Code Opinions** – Access to expert code opinions and tech assistance.
- **Earn CEUs** – Get involved in the code development process, and earn valuable CEUs for your time.
- **Exclusive access** – To 'Member News' articles in the Building Safety Journal.
- **Member Discounts** – Enjoy substantial member discounts on I-code resources, training and other products.
- **Career Center** – Post resumes and search for new job opportunities in the building industry.
- **Corporate and Governmental Members:** Your staff can receive free benefits too.*

Join now to get connected. There's an ICC Membership category that's right for you.

Visit **www.iccsafe.org/mem1** or please call **888-ICC-SAFE** (422-7233) x33804.

*Some restrictions apply. Speak with an ICC Member Services Representative for details.

Overwhelmed with a backlog of Plan Reviews?

The I-Code experts at ICC's Plan Review Services *can help you reduce your plan review backlog, even in the busiest construction season.* With more than 200 years of combined experience with applications of the codes, no plan review is too complex or too large for our experienced team of I-Code professionals.

With expertise in ALL the International Codes® (I-Codes®), we can perform complete plans reviews or a specific aspect of a plan.

Either way, you'll receive the most detailed and precise plan reviews in the industry!

Codes Reviewed

- ICC International Codes
- State and local amendments based on the I-Codes (except Performance Code)

Disciplines Reviewed

- Building (structural & nonstructural)
- Electrical
- Mechanical
- Plumbing
- Fire Protection Systems (includes sprinklers)
- Energy Conservation
- Accessibility

To learn how ICC's I-Code experts can help you reduce your plan review backlog, call 888-422-7233, x5577. Or visit www.iccsafe.org/PLR5

People Helping People Build a Safer World®

GET IMMEDIATE DOWNLOADS OF THE STANDARDS YOU NEED

Browse hundreds of industry standards adopted by reference. Available to you 24/7!

Count on ICC for standards from a variety of publishers, including:

AISC	CSA	HUD
APA	DOC	ICC
APSP	DOJ	ISO
ASHRAE	DOL	NSF
ASTM	DOTn	SMACNA
AWC	FEMA	USC
CPSC		

DOWNLOAD YOUR STANDARDS TODAY!
shop.iccsafe.org

18-15754

ASSESSMENT center

The ICC Assessment Center (formerly known as ICC Certification & Testing) provides nationally recognized credentials that demonstrate a confirmed commitment to protect public health, safety, and welfare. Raise the professionalism of your department and further your career by pursuing an ICC Certification.

ICC Certifications offer:

- Nationwide recognition
- Increased earning potential
- Career advancement
- Superior knowledge
- Validation of your expertise
- Personal and professional satisfaction

Exams are developed and maintained to the highest standards, which includes continuous peer review by national committees of experienced, practicing professionals. ICC is continually evolving exam offerings, testing options, and technology to ensure that all building and fire safety officials have access to the tools and resources needed to advance in today's fast-paced and rapidly-changing world.

Enhancing Exam Options

Effective July 2018, the Assessment Center enhanced and streamlined exam options and now offers only computer based testing (CBT) at a test site and PRONTO. We no longer offer paper/pencil exams.

Proctored Remote Online Testing Option (PRONTO)

Taking your next ICC certification exam is more convenient, more comfortable and more efficient than ever before with PRONTO.

PRONTO provides a convenient testing experience that is accessible 24 hours a day, 7 days a week, 365 days a year. Required hardware/software is minimal – you will need a webcam and microphone, as well as a reasonably recent operating system.

Whether testing in your office or in the comfort of your home, your ICC exam will continue to maintain its credibility while offering more convenience, allowing you to focus on achieving your professional goals. The Assessment Center continues to add exams to the PRONTO exam catalog regularly.

Checkout all the ICC Assessment Center has to offer at iccsafe.org/certification